A NEW SPECIES
OF TROUBLE

Also by KAI ERIKSON

WAYWARD PURITANS:
A STUDY IN THE SOCIOLOGY OF DEVIANCE

EVERYTHING IN ITS PATH:
DESTRUCTION OF COMMUNITY
IN THE BUFFALO CREEK FLOOD
* * *
IN SEARCH OF COMMON GROUND:
CONVERSATIONS WITH ERIK H. ERIKSON
AND HUEY NEWTON *(editor)*

Encounters *(editor)*

THE NATURE OF WORK *(editor, with Steven Peter Vallas)*

A NEW SPECIES OF TROUBLE

The Human Experience of Modern Disasters

KAI ERIKSON

W · W · NORTON & COMPANY
New York   London

Chapter 4 appeared in different form in the Harvard Business Review. Copyright © 1989 by the President and Fellows of Harvard College. Portions of Chapter 6 appeared in *The Nation*. Copyright © 1985 The Nation magazine/The Nation company.

First published as a Norton paperback 1995

The text of this book is composed in Galliard
with the display set in Galliard
Composition by Crane Typesetting Service, Inc.
Manufacturing by The Haddon Craftsmen, Inc.
Book design by Jacques Chazaud

Library of Congress Cataloging-in-Publication Data
Erikson, Kai T.
A new species of trouble : explorations in disaster, trauma, and
community / Kai Erikson.
p.   cm.
Includes index.
1 . Disasters—Social aspects—United States—Case studies.
2. Disaster victims—United States—Psychology—Case studies.
I. Title.
HV555.U6E75   1994
363.3'48'0973—dc20   93-24721

ISBN 0-393-31319-0

W. W. Norton & Company, Inc., 500 Fifth Avenue, New York, N.Y. 10110
W. W. Norton & Company Ltd., 10 Coptic Street, London WC1A 1PU

2 3 4 5 6 7 8 9 0

John Hersey died as this volume
was being readied for publication.
I dedicate it to his memory
both because I count the gift of his friendship
as one of the treasures of my life
and because he was among the first
to write about the human aspect of
what he knew to be a new form of horror.

Contents

A NEW SPECIES
OF TROUBLE

Prologue

Over the past twenty years, research errands of one kind or another have taken me to a number of communities still stunned by the effects of a recent disaster. These include a valley in West Virginia known as Buffalo Creek, devastated by a fearsome flood; an Ojibwa Indian reserve in Canada called Grassy Narrows, plagued by contamination of the waterways along which members of the band had lived for centuries; a town in South Florida named Immokalee, where three hundred migrant farm workers were robbed of the only money most of them had ever saved; a group of houses in Colorado known as East Swallow, threatened by vapors from silent pools of gasoline that had gathered in the ground below; and the neighborhoods surrounding Three Mile Island.

In one respect, at least, these events were altogether different. A flood. An act of larceny. A toxic poisoning. A gasoline spill. A nuclear accident. My assignment in each of those cases was to learn enough about the people who thought they had been damaged by the blow to appear on their behalf in a court of law, so each was a separate research effort, and each resulted in a separate research report.

In another respect, though, it was clear from the beginning that those scenes of trouble had much in common. I was asked to visit them in the first place, obviously, because the persons who issued the invitations thought they could see resemblances there. And just as obviously, I was drawn to them because they touched a corresponding set of curiosities and preoccupations in me. Moreover, common themes seemed to come into focus as I moved from one place to another, so that those separate happenings (and the separate stories told of them) began to fuse into a more inclusive whole. One of the excitements of sociological work in general is to watch general patterns—dim and shapeless at first—emerge from a wash of seemingly unconnected details, and that, as I will report in a moment, was part of what happened here.

I should begin, though, by tracing at least a part of the intellectual itinerary that brought me to the communities I will be discussing.

For me, the journey began in the mountains of West Virginia. I went to Buffalo Creek for the first time in the winter of 1973, one year after a terrifying wall of black water and debris ground its way down a narrow valley, killing 125 persons and leaving homeless 4,000 of the 5,000 who lived there. My involvement (as was to be the case elsewhere) was wholly fortuitous. I had been invited there originally to confer with a law firm about to file suit on behalf of 650 survivors, but I found myself spending large stretches of the next year and a half there. It was, as I later noted in a book I wrote about the flood, a singular act of presumption, since

I knew almost nothing about the anatomy of disaster, the ways of Appalachia, or anything else that could qualify me as an expert. But I was very moved by what I saw and heard on that first visit, and looking back on it now more than twenty years later, I remember being drawn to the place as if by a compulsion. During my first hours in the valley I went to a large gathering in the gymnasium of the local school where a group of lawyers and their assistants were collecting information from the people who had just become their clients. I wrote at the time:

> Tables had been spaced at intervals across a gymnasium floor and the room was filled with people awaiting their turn, lined along the walls on benches or standing around in quiet family clusters. The whole scene looked as if it had been painted in shades of gray. The children neither laughed nor played. The adults acted as if they were surrounded by a sheath of heavy air through which they could move and respond only at the cost of a deliberate effort. Everything seemed muted and dulled. I felt for a moment as though I was in the company of people so wounded in spirit that they almost constituted a different culture, as though the language we shared in common was simply not sufficient to overcome the enormous gap in experience that separated us. I got over that feeling before long, but the sense of being in the presence of deep and numbing pain remained an important part of the emotional climate in which this study was done.

My impressions of that day were to become a more sharply etched sample of feelings I was to have many times again, for that was the look of trauma.

Another note from that first day:

> I was driving down Buffalo Creek late that night when the storm that had been threatening all day finally broke with mountain vengeance. I pulled over to the side of the road near one of the several trailer camps on the creek and stayed

there as half the lights in the camp flashed on, children began to cry, and small groups of men trudged out into the darkness to begin a wet vigil over the stream. Something of the mood of that camp reached across the creek to where I was parked, and I had to fight off a compelling urge to drive away, to escape. I had been in the hollow for only twelve hours.

That, too, was the look of trauma.

Grassy Narrows is the home of a band of several hundred Ojibwa Indians in northwestern Ontario. One flies to Winnipeg, drives east on the highway to Kenora, then turns north and travels fifty miles along a logging road—dirt and gravel in the warmer seasons, covered by thick crust of ice in winter. The people of Grassy Narrows were trying to recover from a series of misfortunes when I visited there in 1979, the most recent of them (and in some ways the cruelest) being the discovery that the local waterways, on which they had depended for food, livelihood, and a sense of natural coherence for all the history they knew, had been contaminated by methylmercury. I was invited because the young but remarkably wise chief had happened across a copy of the book I had written on the West Virginia flood—talk about contingency!—and concluded that his people were living through times very like those experienced by the people of Buffalo Creek. I visited Grassy Narrows with Christopher Vecsey, a historian of the Ojibwa, and spent a week or so with Hiro Miyamatsu and the wondrous Anastasia Shkilnyk, talking to residents, looking around, and helping the band design research efforts as part of legal actions then under way.

Among many memories one stands out. Late one night Chris and Hiro and I, burdened by the miseries we had been contemplating all day, ran for half a mile or so across the frozen lake with a thin moon shining and the temperature at forty degrees below zero—three lumbering creatures, wedged into heavy boots, wrapped in layers against the cold, and flapping like loose bundles of cloth in the dark. The scene plays in my mind as if I had been a witness onshore, and I wonder if any of our hosts saw then what I see now.

Immokalee is many miles and a whole world removed from the forests of Canada. It is the home of thousands of migrant farmhands who work the fields of South Florida during the winter growing season and then ride the warm weather north as summer moves up into the Carolinas, the mid-Atlantic states, and then upstate New York. Three hundred farm workers, two hundred of them recent arrivals from Haiti, were stunned to learn in the winter of 1983 that the money they had banked in a local convenience store was simply missing—stolen, they soon learned, by the store manager. The savings were modest by most standards, but they had special meaning to these poorest of people, and the loss they experienced was a blow of truly traumatic proportions. I entered that scene at least in part because the law firm I had worked with in Buffalo Creek offered its services to the local legal assistance attorney who had brought suit on behalf of the farm workers—another turn of fortune's wheel.

East Swallow, to fill out the roster, is a gathering of modest dwellings in Fort Collins, Colorado, where residents learned that thousands of gallons of gasoline had leaked from "incontinent" tanks and had worked their way along underground passages into the spaces below their houses. The fumes issuing from those hidden recesses were so sharp at times that they almost stung, and the worry they induced— these were highly toxic vapors after all—were still sharper. I went there for the first time in the summer of 1986 at the invitation of an attorney who knew something of the other research errands I had run, and I have included a report of the event in the pages to follow because it is a different kind of community in distress.

I first visited Three Mile Island in the early 1980s, but I did not write the report on which Chapter 4 is based until other of the explorations described here had taken place. It reflects the learnings from a number of different research experiences, then, and it can be read as something of a summary as well as the account of a particular happening.

Not long after the now-famous emergency in 1979 the Nuclear Regulatory Commission required new power plants to submit workable evacuation plans as a condition for receiving licenses to go on-line. Most of those plans, in my view, were not only inadequate but dangerously so. They appeared to have been devised by traffic engineers who simply did not let human habits or human feelings enter their calculations at all. The plans envisioned long streams of traffic flowing away from the site of an emergency with courtly efficiency—no one moving against the tide in an effort to locate missing children, no one leaving a post to look to the safety of scattered family members, no one disrupting that neat choreography with a display of human emotion. I thought this scenario would not work for a moment, and I was asked to testify to that effect not only before hearings at Three Mile Island but at the Shoreham plant on Long Island, the Diablo Canyon plant in San Luis Obispo, California, and the Indian Point plant north of New York City.

At each of those hearings the power companies had retained their own sociologists to testify about the adequacy of their evacuation plans, and the debate that ensued offered an interesting comment on the logics of sociology itself. My colleagues were arguing that disasters are so well known a class of event—the social science shelves, after all, are full of studies of earthquakes, hurricanes, tidal waves, and the like—that we need but look at what happened in those other cases to know what will happen in this one. I thought their argument was obdurately wrong (nothing is better calculated to sharpen one's feelings of righteousness than an adversarial hearing!), but my reason for bringing the matter up again now so long after the fact is that the kind of reasoning they were using is so familiar in sociological circles that it almost ranks as an intellectual reflex. If one knows how a class of events works, then one can predict with fair accuracy that any given member of that class—any specimen of that genus—will act in the same way. So if the data show that volunteer fire fighters can normally be counted on to report to their posts and motorists can normally be counted on to drive calmly away when a levee breaks or a gas tank explodes, then one has reason to assume that the same will happen when a reactor core melts. The flaw in that logic, I thought, is that nuclear accidents are simply not made of the same stuff as levee breaks and gas tank explosions. They belong to a different species of trouble. That remains my contention, and the argument found in Chapter 4, published elsewhere, appears in various forms throughout the book.

I went back to Three Mile Island after the original hearing to assist in a legal action brought by local residents who feared that they had been injured by radiation from the failed reactor, and the quotations appearing in Chapter 4 are from interviews undertaken by Esther Berezofsky for that purpose.

I have been using the expression "research errand" to refer to my explorations into the field rather than the more familiar (and far more comfortable) "study" because, with one exception, the time I spent in each of the places I talk about was relatively short. Both the pace and the size of the studies

I undertook were scaled to the needs of a legal action rather than to the less hurried rhythms of academic research. The exception was Buffalo Creek. The court calendar in that instance was crowded enough to slow things down for many months, and my own calendar was clear enough for me to devote a year and a half to that project.

"Errands," though, would be just the right word for most of the other ventures. My usual procedure was to visit the site for one longer stay or (more commonly) for a number of shorter ones and then to arrange for more extensive research to be done by an associate. When the time came to write a report, I would have quite a number of interviews to draw on and a good store of other data to provide a context for them. I conducted all my own interviews on Buffalo Creek (I also relied heavily on legal depositions), and I conducted a scattering of the other interviews cited here. But most of the voices you will hear in what follows are responses to questions I asked someone else to pose. All this was accompanied by a good deal of reading, of course, as will be clear from the inevitable endnotes, so even when visits to the field totaled no more than a matter of days, the research investment can be measured in months.

The chapters to follow can be read as a group of brief studies—line drawings rather than detailed portraits—that fuse into a few more general points. This may not be the way sociological research is usually done, but it is the way lives work out sometimes.

Several themes that appear and reappear in the accounts to follow emerged gradually as I moved from one to the other of the communities I will be describing here. I noted those themes in the reports I issued at the time, of course, but I did not always appreciate their broader significance until I had encountered them more than once and could thus move with them from the plane of the singular to the plane of the general.

In particular: Soon after the black wall of water and debris ground its way down Buffalo Creek, attorneys for the coal company involved called the disaster "an act of God." When asked what that meant, a spokesperson explained helpfully that the dam was simply "incapable of holding the water God poured into it." However people elsewhere may look upon that act of theological reasoning, the residents of Buffalo Creek understood it to be blasphemy. They knew that one does not blame God lightly for the wrongdoings of humankind, even if the phrase does have another meaning in legal language, and they knew, too, that the phrase itself reflected a degree of indifference bordering on contempt. On both of those counts they reacted with fury.

I thought then that the sharpness of the reaction had a lot to do with cultural particulars: the immediacy of Appalachian spirituality, the paternalism of Appalachian coal camps, the communality of Appalachian society. I would suggest now, though, that the people of the valley were drawing on local languages and sensibilities to express feelings that are far more general, for people elsewhere seem to respect a profound difference between those disasters that can be understood as the work of nature and those that need to be understood as the work of humankind. And that has proved to be a prevailing pattern elsewhere, not only in the places I discuss in the following chapters but in the expanding literature on communities in crisis.

Or again: People living within range of the damaged reactor at Three Mile Island were among the first in this country to suspect that they might have been exposed to dangerous levels of radiation, although we have since learned that quite a number of people living near nuclear facilities like those at Hanford (Washington), Rocky Flats (Colorado), and Fernald (Ohio), as well as others living downwind from Nevada's Nuclear Test Site, may have been endangered without knowing so. I was impressed at Three Mile Island by how sensitive people are to radiation and how much they fear its effects, but I assumed, as many others have before and since, that those levels of dread are peculiar to radiation and evoked only by it. I soon came to think, though, that the larger family of troubles in which radiation is so prominent a member includes toxic poisons of many different kinds, especially the invisible ones that seem to work their way stealthily into the tissues of the human body and the textures of human life. The people of Grassy Narrows and East Swallow share a good deal in common with those of Three Mile Island, as I hope the chapters to follow will suggest. And in the same way the disasters at Love Canal and Bhopal belong in the same class as the one at Chernobyl—not because the *size* of the problems they created were at all comparable but because the *nature* of the problems they created were so. This point, again, is one of the main burdens of Chapter 4 and a recurring theme throughout the book.

A final example: It has occurred to me often that the kinds of trauma one finds in the wake of acute shocks like the Buffalo Creek flood are very like those resulting from longer-term, more chronic conditions. I had raised the matter without carrying it very far in my book on Buffalo Creek. As I tried to bring that report to a close, I asked what would happen if:

> instead of classifying a condition as *trauma* because it was induced by a disaster, we would classify an event as *disaster* if it had the property of bringing about traumatic reactions. According to the terms of this rule, any event or condition that could be shown to produce trauma on a large scale would have earned a place on the current roster of "disasters."
>
> Were we to do this, either as a parlor game or as a serious intellectual exercise . . . we would be required to include events that have the capacity to induce trauma but that do not have the quality of suddenness or explosiveness normally associated with the term. For example, people who are shifted from one location to another as the result of war or

some other emergency often seem to be traumatized afterward, and this is certainly the case for many of those who are evacuated from urban areas on the grounds that their old neighborhoods are scheduled for renewal. . . . Our list might also have to include such slow-developing but nonetheless devastating events as plague, famine, spoilage of natural resources, and a whole galaxy of other miseries.

And if we carried the logic of that notion to its natural conclusion:

[We would be] edging toward the notion that *chronic conditions* as well as *acute events* can induce trauma, and this, too, belongs in our calculations. A chronic disaster is one that gathers force slowly and insidiously, creeping around one's defenses rather than smashing through them. People are unable to mobilize their normal defenses against the threat, sometimes because they have elected consciously or unconsciously to ignore it, sometimes because they have been misinformed about it, and sometimes because they cannot do anything to avoid it in any case. It has long been recognized, for example, that living in conditions of chronic poverty is often traumatizing, and if one looks carefully at the faces as well as the clinic records of people who live in institutions or hang out in the vacant corners of skid row or enlist in the migrant labor force or eke out a living in the urban slums, one can scarcely avoid seeing the familiar symptoms of trauma—a numbness of spirit, a susceptibility to anxiety and rage and depression, a sense of helplessness, an inability to concentrate, a loss of various motor skills, a heightened apprehension about the physical and social environment, a preoccupation with death, a retreat into dependency, and a general loss of ego functions. One can find those symptoms wherever people feel left out of things, abandoned, separated from the life around them. From that point of view, being too poor to participate in the promise of the culture or too old to take a meaningful place in the structure of the community can be counted as a kind of disaster.

These were the kinds of reflection one sometimes engages in as one brings a long manuscript to a close, but I am not sure that I really meant them as anything more than casual observations in passing. My experience since, however, has led me to think that chronic conditions and acute events can leave much the same human residue and that the line separating the chronic from the acute becomes ever more blurred when one looks carefully at that residue. In one sense, at least, trauma can be defined as the psychological process by which an acute shock becomes a chronic condition, a way of keeping dead moments alive (about which I will have more to say in the concluding section of the book). But the main points to be made now are that many modern catastrophes are both chronic and acute in character, however one tells stories about them, and that the human consequences of homelessness and poverty and abuse are very like those of emergencies of a more immediate kind. The Ojibwa of Grassy Narrows offer an interesting case in point since they have experienced both the emotional erosions that come from exposure to chronic conditions and the pains that result from sharper blows to the spirit. The chapter on homelessness, with which I end the first part of the book, pursues those same themes, as does the essay on trauma that brings the volume to a close.

These, then, as I suggest in the Epilogue, are the signifying characteristics of this new species of trouble. They are seen as having produced by human hands, they involve some form of toxic contaminant, and they blur the line we have been in the habit of drawing between the acute and the chronic.

Chapters 6 and 7 move us afield, in both space and time. The first is a look backward at the past we created by the bombings of Hiroshima and Nagasaki in 1945, and the second is a look ahead at the future we may be creating by our current plans to entomb high-level nuclear wastes in rock formations deep under Yucca Mountain, Nevada.

* * *

Let me end this introduction by describing one moment that seems to me now to have been decisive in my resolve to gather these pieces together in a book.

The fate of the migrant workers from Immokalee whose savings had been stolen was debated in the Collier County Courthouse in Naples, Florida, in 1988. My task in those proceedings was to testify about the "consequential damages" experienced by the migrants beyond the dollar value of their loss—the traumatic shock and pain they had endured as a result. I had presented my testimony in writing before the trial even opened, as often happens in cases like this one, so my day in court was given over almost wholly to cross-examination. That is a procedure designed to keep one on edge, of course, and the attorney assigned the job did it all too well. I was aware during the whole of my time on the stand of a state trooper who was serving as bailiff— a large, unblinking man who stared at me from the back of the room with a look that I took to be one of pure malice. When I was finally dismissed from the witness stand at the end of a long and draining day, I was asked to sit in the recently vacated jury box for a few moments while the attorneys gathered at the bench to discuss one or another point of law. The trooper came across the courtroom and sat next to me, huge and grave. "I know exactly what you mean," he said quietly, and when I turned to him in alarm and astonishment, he added: "I was in Vietnam."

This book owes a great deal to that trooper and that moment.

PART ONE

1

The Ojibwa
of Grassy Narrows*

G rassy Narrows is a gathering of sixty or seventy frame dwellings at the end of a logging road in northwestern Ontario. It has the look of a village, since the houses are drawn into a loose cluster. But it has none of the feel of a

---

*An earlier (and far shorter) version of what appears here took the form of a report to the Grassy Narrows Band Council written in 1979 by Christopher Vecsey and me in the hope that it might prove useful in mediation efforts then under way. That draft drew heavily on the observations of Hiroyuki Miyamatsu and Anastasia Shkilnyk and on the teachings of John Beaver, Andy Keewatin, Pat Loon, Isaac Pahpassay, Tom Payash, and, especially, Simon Fobister, then chief of the Grassy Narrows Band. Shkilnyk later published an extraordinary book on Grassy Narrows, *A Poison Stronger Than Love: The Destruction of an Ojibwa Community* (Yale University Press, 1985), for which I wrote a foreword and from which I have borrowed ever since with an abandon she will not only understand but approve. Additionally, passages from this chapter appeared in Christopher Vecsey and Robert W. Venables, eds., *American Indian Environments: Ecological Issues in Native American History* (Syracuse University Press, 1980). What follows are my conclusions in my words, so I have signed my name to it, but it is a mutual effort all the same.

village: It has no center, no pattern, no pathways cut by the flows of time, no sense of organic wholeness. It is the home of a small band of Ojibwa Indians—maybe four hundred in all—whose ancestors are reckoned to have lived in the general vicinity for centuries.

I

It was evident to everyone by the middle of the 1970s that something was very wrong with the people of Grassy Narrows. Even when measured against the levels of squalor and suffering found in many Indian communities throughout North America, the tenor of everyday life in that small gathering of homes had moved to the very edge of what we generally mean by "human." Anastasia Shkilnyk first came to Grassy Narrows in 1976 and remembered later:

> I could never escape the feeling that I had been parachuted into a void—a drab and lifeless place in which the vital spark of life had gone out. It wasn't just the poverty of the place, the isolation, or even the lack of a decent bed that depressed me. I had seen worse material deprivation when I was working in squatter settlements around Santiago, Chile. And I had been in worse physical surroundings while working in war-devastated Ismailia on the project for the reconstruction of the Suez Canal. What struck me most about Grassy Narrows was the numbness in the human spirit. There was an indifference, a listlessness, a passivity that I could neither understand nor do anything about. I had never seen such hopelessness anywhere in the Third World.[1]

Grassy Narrows, clearly, was a deeply troubled community. Death from old age had become a rarity there; infants died from neglect and outright abuse; older children killed one another and themselves with apparent abandon.

It is hard to know how to take the measure of that kind of misery, but here is a calculation done with the help of a pair of Mennonite missionaries who have spent a number of years at Grassy Narrows and know the place intimately. They are the experts in such matters. They have done most of the burying, after all, and they hear most of the local reports, so they know better than all the coroners in Canada how death comes to Grassy Narrows:

In the four-year span from 1974 to 1978 thirty-five persons died at the reserve.[2] Only *four* of them died as human beings are supposed to: of old age, illness, or common accident. They averaged seventy-five years of age. *Six* died of alcohol poisoning or heart failure brought on by excessive drinking. They averaged fifty years of age. *Six* died of alcohol-related accidents like drownings, fires, and exposure to the elements, and *nine* died of alcohol-induced stabbings, beatings, gunshot wounds, and intentional drownings. They averaged thirty-five years of age. *Five* persons, at an average age of twenty-two, committed suicide, and *four* died in infancy, two of them as a result of alcohol abuse. A grisly count. Twenty-three of those deaths were the direct consequence of alcohol, and if you add the five suicides, all of them alcohol-related, the number grows to twenty-eight. That leaves seven persons, two who died of natural causes in infancy, four who died in the way adults are meant to, and one fifty-two-year-old whose death not even the missionaries could explain. Those astonishing figures mean that 80 percent of the deaths at Grassy Narrows could be attributed directly or indirectly to alcohol abuse during the period in question and took place at an average age of thirty-three.

Drinking in Indian society often takes the form of extended binges or sprees in which people gather together, pool resources, and drink with concentrated fury until they run out of money or become unconscious. The impulse to binge drinking may run deep, since hunting and gathering people the world over celebrate moments of particular plenty—successful hunts, bountiful harvests—with feasting. Any comparison here has to be made with caution, but the kinds of spree that convulse Grassy Narrows, beginning as they do when checks arrive at the band office, are like an inversion, almost a mockery, of that old pattern. It can be an immensely expensive recreation, too, even if one does not count the costs to human health or human dignity. In the case of Grassy Narrows, for example, the supply of liquor needed to keep a three-or four-day binge going has to be replenished again and again by runs to the nearest store, fifty miles away, and each such run even in those days cost something like $90 by taxi and $120 by plane. These are, after all, the north woods.

There is nothing unfamiliar in any of this. Hugh Brody, writing of a far less troubled community in northern British Columbia, saw Indians drink "with an abandon that may astonish and frighten a stranger":

> Suddenly there is deep trouble. Often rage. There is wreckage. Perhaps it is accumulated bitterness, the ghosts of generations of Indians frustrated by the apparently inescapable advance of the white man's frontiers who lurch, and stagger, inchoate and seemingly imponderable, into the present.[3]

And it has been going on for a long time. One hundred and fifty years before Brody visited British Columbia, a missionary among the Ojibwa, himself of Indian origin, spoke of the misery alcohol can bring to native villages:

> I have often seen such scenes of degradation as would sicken the soul of a good man; such as husbands beating their wives, and dragging them by the hair of their head; children screaming with fright, the older ones running off with guns, tomahawks, spears, knives, and other deadly weapons, which they concealed in the woods to prevent the commission of murder by their enraged parents; yet, notwithstanding this precaution, death was not infrequently the result.[4]

This was 1825 or so, but similar scenes had been recorded throughout the preceding two hundred years, ever since white Europeans came to the eastern shores of Canada in the early seventeenth century.[5] So spree drinking is hardly new, but the sheer ferocity with which it is pursued at Grassy Narrows, according to experienced observers of such things, gives it a unique cast.

A drinking spree hits Grassy Narrows "like a tornado," says Shkilnyk, who has weathered several of them. Infants become dehydrated, and children go without food because no one takes care of them; women are beaten with mindless brutality; girls as young as ten or twelve are raped by gangs of boys not much older. And as we already know, people die. Missionaries and coroners and sociologists tend to be orderly people. They like to know how people met their ends, especially when, as in cases like this one, the horror is so hard to come to terms with. But the standard categories seem to blur when one tries to give these deaths a logical term to know them by. If someone falls senseless into a snowdrift and freezes to death, should we call it exposure? If someone else bleeds to death because a knife blade nicked an artery in a moment of glazed confusion, should we call it homicide? If yet a third person, stupefied and beyond caring, lies down in the path of an approaching train, should we call it suicide? The usual words do not seem to work well enough, and in the end all one can say is that these deaths were brought on by a kind of abuse that follows from anger, despair, and profound demoralization.

A rough survey was conducted on alcohol use among the adults of Grassy Narrows.[6] Fully two-thirds of the people polled counted themselves as either *heavy* drinkers (32 percent) or *very heavy* drinkers (34 percent) when given four alternatives to choose among. That's 66 percent of the adult population generally. But the proportion reaches 70 percent for persons in their twenties and a staggering 80 percent for those in their thirties—the very years, of course, in which adults are supposed to be raising children. No matter what allowance we decide to make for the imprecision of the questions asked in that rough survey or for cultural differences in the meaning of "self-reporting," these are amazing findings. And so are the other fragments one can extract from that hard landscape.

Item: The superintendent of a special detachment of the Ontario Provincial Police assigned to Grassy Narrows wrote to the band chief in April 1978: "Our personnel feel that gas sniffing is common to *most* children on the reserve."[7] Now gas sniffing is extremely dangerous to the central nervous system, especially in childhood, and it was not at all uncommon in the Grassy Narrows of those times to encounter children as young as six with visible neurological impairments. "Wipeouts" they are called. Whether it makes sounder clinical sense to count them as the victims of gas poisoning or of fetal alcohol syndrome, their fate is, for all practical purposes, sealed. A schoolteacher reports of one six-year-old:

> Alicia started sniffing gas when she was three years old. She's burnt now, and the brain damage is permanent. In class, she can't concentrate, and she's lost her retention ability. She has lost her sense of balance. She sways all over the place and topples over in her chair. She falls down sixty times a day, like a Raggedy-Ann doll. She has constant bruises on her arms and legs just from falling down on the floor all the time. . . . Alicia is just like Pamela, whose father gave her gas so that she would sleep with him. She did, and now she's burnt too and always in trouble with the guys. All the boys gang-rape her because they know she's a wipe-out. It's going to be exactly the same for Alicia and for many other girls like her.

Item: In 1976 officers of the Ontario Provincial Police, posted just outside the reserve, were called upon 673 times to investigate some disturbance. In 1977 the number was

698. Investigations of that kind occur only when someone actually calls for help or when the sounds of commotion reach beyond the outer edges of the reserve, so it is no more than a partial index to the volume of trouble. But even so, it amounts to more than ten alarms for every household.

Item: In one period of eleven months between 1977 and 1978 thirty-one persons made convincing enough suicide attempts to have their names recorded by the Ontario Provincial Police, twenty-six of them between the ages of eleven and nineteen. Three of those attempts were (in our odd way of phrasing it) "successful." The real number of those who tried with one or another degree of urgency, we may presume, was a good deal larger, and even that total would not include the ones who courted death so recklessly that the outcome almost has to be listed as an act of self-destruction. We are speaking here of a population of around four hundred persons. If the number of those who actually made an attempt to take their own lives was larger by half than the number of those who came to the attention of the provincial police (a reasonable assumption), and if the number of teenagers in Grassy Narrows was somewhere near the national mean (another reasonable assumption), then a fearsome proportion of Grassy Narrow's young people made some effort to kill themselves in that one year alone.

In the midst of all this mayhem, moreover, the elders of the band exercised few, if any, sanctions—not when young girls were raped, not when infants were neglected, not when houses were vandalized or even burned to the ground, not when adults were mauled with fists—because, as one man of sixty-eight, himself so viciously beaten that he had to be hospitalized, said: "The kids, they had been drinking, and when a person is drinking, he is not himself." The Ojibwa have always held that one's behavior while "under the influence of" drink has to be blamed on alcohol rather than on the person. It is without agency, without motive. Too, the Ojibwa have been known by visitors as far back as the seventeenth century and by anthropologists in more recent times for their reluctance to discipline children (in ways familiar to white visitors, anyway), so the pattern may be an old one.[8] In some ways, at least, it is an easy view to sympathize with. How can one hold children responsible for behavior that issues from a numbed stupor and from conditions of life that are often beyond bearing? But whatever that casual attitude meant in older times, there are now messages in it for young people that are hard to mistake and harder yet to reverse. The first is that there are no rules. And the second is that no one really cares about anyone. The elder who was so prepared to overlook the savagery of his young neighbors, moreover, was probably wrong. The kids may not have been acting responsibly or knowingly within the meaning of either Canadian or Ojibwa law when they attacked, but they *were* being themselves. This was an explosion of fury and anguish, of cruelty and self-hatred—a feeling that they and their kind simply do not matter.

When one pieces all these different fragments together, one has the portrait of a deeply damaged community. Grassy Narrows in the 1970s seemed to have moved off the scale we normally use to measure the amount of human wreckage found in urban slums or any other of the world's troubled neighborhoods. It was almost a new kind of social space, occupied by a special strain of human being.

"We are now a people with a broken culture," said Simon Fobister, the chief of the Grassy Narrows Band, to a government delegation visiting the reserve in December 1978.[9] That is so appealing an expression—natural, artless, the kind of thing that thoughtful old Indian chiefs are asked to say in Hollywood films—that one is apt to underrate its wisdom. But it is hard to think of a term in the technical vocabulary of the social sciences that fits the data better. The Ojibwa people have been counting on their native culture for hundreds of years to tune their moral and conceptual reflexes, to organize and give rhythm to their everyday lives, to give shape to things. That old mold was simply broken, and the result was a kind of bewilderment and disorientation that the usual sociological concepts—anomie, estrangement, alienation—are not rich enough to capture or reflect.

But why? What had happened here? I would like to offer two answers to that question, each of them requiring a step farther back in time.

II

I was invited to Grassy Narrows in the winter of 1979, when the temperature never reached above forty degrees below zero and the world was frozen as hard as obsidian, because the people of the reserve had recently experienced a disaster of major proportions.

Authorities discovered in early 1970 that twenty thousand pounds of highly toxic mercury had been working its way down the Wabigoon River from a paper and pulp plant eighty miles upstream from Grassy Narrows. A three-hundred-mile stretch of the English and Wabigoon river system—along the edges of which the Ojibwa had lived for all the history they knew—had been contaminated, and indications were that it would remain so for half a century or more. The deposits of mercury had been building up for the better part of a decade, moreover, meaning that the people of the reserve may have been exposed to the poison without their knowing anything of its dangers over quite a period of time.

Methylmercury, as it happens, is a particularly mean chemical. Like many forms of toxicity, it cannot be smelled or tasted or seen, and it is very difficult to locate in human tissues by any clinical test short of autopsy. Moreover, it makes its way with a kind of cold and efficient malice straight to those parts of the body where it can do the most harm. It is drawn to the vital organs, in particular to the brain, and it has a special attraction for the unborn, migrating with deadly accuracy and purpose to the placenta and then to the fetus when in the body of a pregnant woman. In Minamata, Japan, for example, where mercury poisoning on a large scale first came to public attention, children in utero at the time of exposure frequently had larger concentrations of mercury in their bloodstreams than did their mothers.

In addition, mercury poisoning has its own sly camouflage. Its clinical symptoms include numbness of the mouth and of the extremities, impaired vision and hearing and speech, clumsiness in walking and handling objects, depression and apathy, memory loss, tremors, and, in some, explosive shifts in mood. Now if you were asked where one might find a group of persons with slurred speech and difficulty in focusing, with a lumbering gait and uncertain coordination, with a glazed and numbed look about them interrupted at times by volatile outbursts of temper, what might you suggest? Those who know such precincts, at any rate, would almost surely nominate shelters for the homeless, wards for the mentally ill, centers for those who abuse alcohol and drugs, and, in general, asylums for the miserable. It is almost as if mercury poison mimics and ridicules the suffering of the already damaged.

To make matters worse, the very fear that mercury generates can act to simulate the real thing. I do not simply mean that apprehension about this or that symptom of mercury poisoning can help provoke its appearance, as is certainly true enough, but that dread itself has among its behavioral by-products the kind of disequilibrium, depression, memory loss, and volatility that mercury is known for.

And there were reasons indeed for fear. Fish from the local waters were dangerously contaminated, and everyone on the reserve had consumed large quantities of it. Samples of blood and hair had been taken periodically in Grassy Narrows, a procedure that tests for the presence of mercury in the body without being able to specify where it is located or what it is doing, and quite a number of people had elevations high enough to qualify them as "at risk." The full weight of science, then—white man's science—had delivered the uncertain diagnosis that there were many reasons for alarm but no clear indications that the poison had yet done serious harm to human tissue. As of this writing, no one really knows for sure how much (if any) harm was done by the invasion of mercury, so Grassy Narrows is no Minamata. But among the many troubles then haunting Grassy Narrows was a corrosive fear that had to be ranked as a health hazard in itself. That was one of the problems at Three Mile Island and at Love Canal, too, and at all those places where toxic poisons are known to have been released in potentially dangerous quantities but where the instruments of science cannot really measure the size of the problem. An expert can only say: If I find elevated body loadings of mercury in your blood, I cannot tell you what that says about your health or that of your offspring. And if I find no traces of mercury in your system, I nonetheless can offer you no reassurances that you have been spared.

The clinical effects of the mercury spill, then, were inconclusive, but the economic effects were as blunt as a hammer blow. For all practical purposes, the people of Grassy Narrows lost their river system when the fish in it were declared unsafe for human consumption. They lost a major source of protein, of course, but they also lost their two most important sources of income: commercial fishing, on which working families had been depending for years, and hiring out to local lodges as guides for sports fishing or as maintenance and kitchen staff. The closing of the rivers ended the last significant source of outside employment for the Indians of Grassy Narrows, and as we shall see later, it virtually ended the last economic activity relying on old native skills.

The people of the reserve also lost confidence in what had traditionally been one of the kindest and most reliable elements in their surround—the living waters. To begin with, methyl mercury leaves no detectable mark or odor or taste on the fish exposed to it, nor do the fish act differently or die more quickly as a result. That, clearly, was bewildering to a people who had long counted on their own highly developed senses to know good food from bad. And the notion that the waters themselves could become poisoned and still not betray that secret to the shrewdest of human perceptions was more frightening yet. When I visited Grassy Narrows and was trying to earn at least a wary measure of respect, I went to the local school and asked a classroomful of children to draw pictures of the lake for me. They thought it a peculiar project, given that the lake was then submerged under fifteen feet of ice, but they did what they could to humor me. The lake they produced, almost without exception, was drawn in black crayon, and I thought I was in the presence of an extraordinary set of data when the menacing dark shapes appearing in that already black water were revealed as sharks. Two thousand miles from the nearest ocean! Sharks! What better evidence of a nature turned menacing? Alas, it turned out that the Band Council had recently shown the movie *Jaws* to the children of the reserve, and that, of course, places a severe limit on what I dare claim for those drawings. Still, it may make sense to suppose that those sharks arrived in Grassy Narrows just in time to give substance and contour to what was otherwise a shapeless dread.

The mercury came from a paper mill in the beginning, but it had been absorbed into the natural world by the time it reached Grassy Narrows. So the environment itself had been darkened and contaminated and had become less reliable. An elder tried to explain: "We call it 'pijibowin.' This is the Ojibwa word for poison. You can't see it or smell it, you can't taste it or feel it, but you know it's there. You know it can hurt you, make your limbs go numb, make your spirit sick. But I don't understand it. I don't understand how the land can turn against us."[10] So the problem was not only a medical one and an economic one but a psychological or even spiritual one, for the apprehensions and uncertainties that followed the discovery of mercury poisoned the mind in a way that clinical tests could not even begin to trace. This poison is a pervasive fear that the world of nature and the world of human beings can no longer be relied on in the old way. The fish are full of poison, the waters are contaminated, the land itself, as we shall see in a moment, is diseased, and the social world is in disarray.

III

It seemed clear to many of those who visited Grassy Narrows in the late 1970s, though, that—as bad as the mercury crisis had been—the sorrows visiting the reserve traced back beyond the coming of *pijibowin*, even beyond the memories of the oldest of those with whom we talked. Mercury was not the only or maybe even the most virulent disaster to have reached that scene of distress.

It is difficult to draw statistical information from places like these, but the scattered data then available on such indices of social disruption as the prevailing rates of alcoholism, suicide, child neglect, hospitalization, drug overdose, violent death, and so on showed two things clearly: first, that native communities in the Kenora district ranked way above the regional average on those grim scales and, second, that Grassy Narrows and Whitedog, the two reserves affected by mercury poisoning, ranked way above that already high Indian average.[11] The ravages of *pijibowin*, then, put Grassy Narrows (and Whitedog) into a special category, but at the same time, ravages of another kind had done enormous damage to those communities beforehand. These data do not lend themselves to an easy arithmetic when one tries to assign weights to the two sources of trouble, but that does not matter for our present purposes.

In fact, a number of different shock waves had pounded the people of Grassy Narrows before the mercury crisis of the middle 1970s, each one of them, in its own manner, a result of contact with white people and white ways. If we could measure each of these shocks on a kind of Richter scale, they would surely prove to have varied considerably in size and intensity. But we are concerned here with the influence of all that pounding on the people exposed to it, and that requires a different kind of calculus. The most modest of quakes can be devastating when the ground underneath has already been shaken loose and the timbers above weakened by earlier convulsions, so we need to be asking here how those blows reinforced one another, how their effects accumulated over time. *Pijibowin* crept into the lives of a people who were already as vulnerable to misfortune as can easily be imagined.

When the first European fur traders moved into the region around Grassy Narrows in the early eighteenth century, the Ojibwa people had been living there for years. Both their economic and their spiritual existence depended on a close communion with the environmental envelope in which they lived. Their totemic names, their myths and legends, their ceremonies, their religious views all reflected their unity with the natural world. The ways of nature were their ways; the rhythms of nature were their rhythms. They did not regard themselves as living *off* the land so much as absorbed into it, nourished by it, a part of it.[12]

An old Ojibwa band can best be understood as a confederacy of small, mobile, clan-based family groups of somewhere between twelve and thirty who trap and hunt together when on the move and settle in together during their summer encampment. Each band has a chief and a tribal council whose job it is to adjudicate disputes among the various family groups, to distribute surpluses so that no one is in need, and, especially, to speak for the band in matters involving other native groups or the provincial and federal governments. The basic cells of Ojibwa life, then, were families, but the larger confederacy was important, too. Marriage within the band, although not required by custom, was nonetheless so common that everyone in Grassy Narrows was related to everyone else, and thus the occasions when the family groups gathered for work or for celebration were vital and sustaining. They were also rather infrequent and—there is no paradox in this—all the stronger for being so.

People in the old days were scattered among the islands and peninsulas of the English and Wabigoon river system by clans, a cluster of two or more log cabins in a common clearing a quarter of a mile or so from the nearest clan neighbor. These groupings—the Loons, Fobisters, Assins, Hyacinthes, Fishers, Keewatins, Ashopenaces, Necanapenaces, Beavers, Taypaywaykejicks, Lands, Kokopenaces—formed a wide, irregular circle around the island on which the Hudson's Bay trading post had been built in 1911. Everyone lived near the shore since the warm waters of summer and the ice of winter were the village thoroughfares.

Looking at Ojibwa life through lenses shaped in quite another tradition, one might easily assume that the spaces separating family encampments and the times separating their meeting were a pattern imposed by circumstance—the economy of a hunting and gathering life, say, or the topography of a subarctic wilderness. And those things are of course true. But it is wrong to assume, as many people did, that the pattern would disappear as soon as the circumstances changed, like something released from a constraining mold. It had a force of its own. It was the natural configuration of Ojibwa territoriality, the architecture of Ojibwa society. And it was far more important to the Ojibwa sense of fitness and coherence than anyone knew. Older members of the band remember how it was then:

> On the old reserve, every family had its own place, and the people lived far from each other. The old reserve was a

beautiful place. You could see for miles. We were not crowded there. Your neighbor was about half a mile away. . . . In those days we didn't live bunched up in one place all year round. I think we were happier the old way. There was no hunger, and sickness was cured by the medicine man.

On the old reserve, every family [clan] lived together. We weren't all mixed together like we are today. . . . It was traditional for all the clans to live separately from each other. That's the way we have always lived. It was much better that way.

We don't live like the white man. That's not our way. The white man lives close together, but we don't. We like to live far apart, in families. On the old reserve, you knew your place. Everybody respected your place. Nobody would build right next to your place. . . . It was your place, [with] your force around it. . . . As soon as they started to bunch us up, the problems started—the drinking, the violence.

The Ojibwa year was marked by times of dispersal and times of convergence. As winter began, each family group moved out into the bush along traplines that had been fixed by tradition to gather the furs of beaver, muskrat, mink, otter, lynx, and fox, returning briefly at Christmas to celebrate and resupply. When the ice broke up in the spring, they returned to their summer encampments at the old reserve. There they hunted, fished, planted gardens, sometimes hired out as guides, and formed into larger parties to gather berries and to harvest wild rice. When the snows came again and the circle of the working year closed, each family returned by snowshoe and dogsled—or, as modern times reached northwestern Ontario, by snowmobile or even airplane—to their distant traplines.

The family groups retained their integrity both by the activities that occupied them at their center and by the margins of space that set them apart and insulated them. The work of the extended family was in every way a communal endeavor. People recognized clear divisions of labor, as one would expect, but everyone was engaged in the same general pursuit, and everyone had an essential part to play. That was also true when the time came to tend gardens, to catch fish, or to gather rice and berries and herbs. A pair of old-timers, both of them women, recalled:

> I was born on a trapline, and I grew up in the bush. Trapping was our way of life. Trapping kept the family together, because everyone had something to do. The men had to lay traps and check them. The women skinned the animals, did the cooking and looked after the kids. The old people taught the kids manners—how to behave—and told them stories from a long time ago. The kids had work to do, and if they were old enough, they had to set snares for rabbits and chop wood. [CBC*]

> On the trapline, I used to work hard, very hard. It's not easy to skin animals and stretch skins properly. If you don't do it right, the price of fur will not be good. I had to take care of my family, to cook and look after the children, cut wood, set snares, and fetch water. We were on the trapline all winter long. In the spring, it was time to plant gardens. Later in the summer we went looking for berries. We dried them for the winter. Many women looked after the fishing nets while the men were guiding in the tourist camps. On the old reserve, the women had to make food for the winter—they dried and smoked fish and meat. In the fall, we tanned hides and made some clothing. When wild rice season started, men and women worked together in canoes, and then finished the rice in the Indian way. [CBC]

For a long time life in the old reserve remained relatively isolated, even as the modern world began to press in on it

---

*See note 10, on p. 244.

from all sides. People moved out to the edges of their terrain from time to time to bring berries and rice and fish to market, and they left it altogether to hire out as guides or to take on whatever other wage work presented itself. So there were points of contact with the white world. But no roads yet reached Grassy Narrows, and the people of the reserve were more or less contained within ancestral lands, participating in the larger economy of Canada by drawing on old native skills and old native lores. For a moment, at least, the differing rhythms of a nineteenth-century Ojibwa band and a twentieth-century industrial nation formed a kind of counterpoint.

IV

But the shock waves of which I spoke a few pages ago were already under way, weakening the cultural fiber of Ojibwa life in ways that would one day matter.

First, the influenza epidemic that spread across North America in 1918 and 1919 killed a large portion of the people of Grassy Narrows. A shock of that size, naturally, would leave a lasting mark on any human society, but the damage done to this one seems to have had a dimension all its own. The population eventually recovered. (By one estimate, at least, Grassy Narrows numbered 178 people in 1917, just before the epidemic, and 242 in 1949, thirty years later.[13]) But the epidemic created a spiritual crisis from which the people of the reserve were slow to recover. The problem was that traditional healers proved powerless to cure or even to explain that alien disease—some elders call it "the German Curse" to this day—which placed an enormous strain on the Ojibwa system of belief, and the arrival on the scene of white medical personnel helped corrode that faith even further. Christopher Vecsey asked an old chief: "What happened to the Indian doctors when this flu epi-

demic came through?" He responded: "They were just buf-
faloed. They didn't know what to do. Some of them even
blamed themselves. They didn't know anything."[14] There is
a deep irony in all this, for at the very moment modern
medicine was being called upon to control the strains of a
virus infecting the Ojibwa people, another and more subtle
kind of disease was infecting the tissues of Ojibwa culture
itself, and the name of that malady was doubt.

Second, the Canadian government had been charged by
a treaty signed in 1873 to provide education to the Ojibwa
people, and it elected to meet that obligation by building
residential schools, many of them run by missionaries, at
some distance from the reserves themselves. Whatever their
intent, the effect of these schools was to separate children
from their families for long stretches of time and to help
strip them of their language, their native skills, their religion,
and their very identity as Indians. Old men in Grassy Narrows still speak of their schooling with a sharp bitterness.
They remember it not only as an assault on themselves as
persons but as an assault on their traditional way of life as
well, and even now, years later, they tell of the confusion
they felt in returning to the reserve after a compulsory season
or two in school—estranged from the Ojibwa religion but
not accepted into the faith of the missionaries, lacking the
immense skills of their ancestors but not introduced to useful new trades, and, in many other ways, strangers to both
cultures at once.

Third, the introduction of Western medicine and Western
education into Ojibwa culture had an indirect impact on the
integrity of native religion. Those who find comfort in the
thought are welcome to assume that white personnel in
charge of the public health programs and the Indian schools
did not really intend a bad result, but in the 1930s and 1940s
missionaries who did intend exactly that result enlisted the
Royal Canadian Mounted Police in discouraging Ojibwa
religious activities, raiding ceremonies, disrupting services,

and, in doing so, forcing what was left of the old faith underground. Some religions thrive under persecution, gathering strength from the power of the opposition they attract, but the Ojibwa faith, already weakened by spasms of doubt, can truly be said to have collapsed. The people of Grassy Narrows lost a great deal more in that collapse than a handful of native precepts that did not accord well with official Christianity. They began to lose some of the security that came from knowing themselves a balanced part of the ecology of nature, and they lost some of the spiritual insulation, as it were, that had been one of their major sources of protection from disaster and disruption.

The hope of the missionaries, of course, and of most of the well-meaning persons who joined them in their efforts to convert the Ojibwa people was that the Indians would embrace Christianity as a new system of meaning and explanation. But even though most Ojibwa have converted formally, this fond hope has not been realized—in part because the people of Grassy Narrows, like Indians everywhere on this continent, feel that they have been rejected by those very Christians who want to bring them into a fellowship of faith and in part because Christianity, for whatever reason, has not provided them with a world view consonant with the realities of their existence. Spiritually, then, they are caught between a past that no longer provides them with a sense of their place in the order of things and a future that must be faced without the kind of promise that a shared faith can offer. Meantime, the old religion has been receding into memory, a private preoccupation of the aging rather than an integrative force for the young. The theme is an old one in Ojibwa lore, even though it has taken on a special urgency in modern times. A white settler, writing in the first decade or two of the nineteenth century, tells a story that, in one version or another, resurfaces frequently in travelers' accounts:

In connection with this subject, he told us the anecdote of the baptized Indian, who, after death, went to the gate of the white man's heaven, and demanded admittance; but the man who kept watch at the gate told him no redskins could be allowed to enter there. "Go," said he, "for to the west there are the villages and the hunting grounds of those of your own people who have been on the earth before you." So he departed thence, but when he came to the villages where the dead of his own people resided, the chief refused him admittance. "You have been ashamed of us while you lived. You have chosen to worship the white man's God. Go now to his village and let him provide for you." Thus he was rejected by both parties.[15]

V

In 1963 the Canadian Department of Indian Affairs began to move the people of Grassy Narrows from their scattered holdings along the English and Wabigoon rivers to a site five miles to the south and east where a logging road had just been cut through the bush to Kenora. By gathering together in this more concentrated spot, the theory went, residents would have access to electricity, schools, plumbing, medical attention, police, social services, and, not incidentally, the Hudson's Bay Company trading post, which had moved from its island in the middle of the old reserve to the head of the recently opened road. It was hoped by white authorities that those five miles were a measure of the distance between the timeless world of a hunting and gathering people and the world of a modern industrial society. As often happens in shifts like this, however, no one really knew—not even the Ojibwa most intimately affected—how long a stretch that five miles would turn out to be.

Houses in the new reserve were rough and spare. Only a

few had the promised piped-in water; fewer yet had running toilets. They looked as if they had come off an assembly line—neatly the same, neatly spaced, arrayed in symmetries like a military post or low-cost subdivision. This may be an appropriate geometry for places where the land is flat, the roads straight, and a kind of quadrate orderliness admired, but it makes very little sense in this wilderness clearing where nature is a thing of rises and curves. And it is wholly alien to the native sense of patterning.

Almost overnight the clan groupings lost a good part of their old coherence. They had been held together by the pull of mutual activities and mutual responsibilities, as I noted a few pages ago, but the vigor of those ties depended at least in part on the feelings that come from sharing a contained group space. Those feelings disappeared all at once. No thought at all seems to have been given to clan membership in the assignment of housing, either by the Department of Indian Affairs or by the leadership of the band, and as a result, people were distributed across the new reserve almost wholly at random. The department should have known better. Whether the Grassy Narrows Band Council should have known better may be another matter, for it often happens in human affairs that the most important cultural designs are the ones a people finds it hardest to see and to find words for. No matter how blame is assigned, however, the sense of spacing that once invited interclan collaboration now invited a good deal of interclan tension, and to that extent Grassy Narrows had become a tight concentration not only of persons but also of troubles. "You look at a map of the old reserve. We were stretched out along the bay by clans. When we were moved here, we were packed in. That was bad. But what was more bad was that the clans were pushed together. There was no sense of clan area. It isn't so much that we were pushed together as that our clans were mixed up. It's too late now. The damage is done."[16]

Space is so compact in the new reserve that traditional ways of relating no longer work. Every people, every culture have their own sense of how much distance should be reserved between neighbors, how wide a margin is necessary to protect the privacy of a family or household. And when that sense of spacing is violated, the result is that neighborliness itself can break down. People who find themselves too pressed together by a change in location can become more distant both emotionally and spiritually—for hostilities and aggressions that were once insulated by a cushion of space now fill the narrow gaps like charges of electricity. "On the old reserve, your closest neighbor was maybe a quarter mile away. What we don't have now is space. When you're all bunched up like we are now, problems start. We're too crowded, too close [CBC]."

Almost overnight, too, work became an individual occupation rather than a family pursuit, and that shift in the emotional center of gravity was an extremely telling one. Trapping and traditional forms of hunting began to disappear with the move to the new reserve, and it was not long, as we have seen, before fishing—the last of the native skills that the new living arrangement could accommodate—was brought to an abrupt stop. Fishing, like hunting, can be a way of life as well as a livelihood, a source of cultural coherence as well as a source of subsistence, and both were family ventures in the sense that they involved the coordinated effort of everyone in the clan group. The move from trapping to fishing, then, involved but a short distance culturally. Peter J. Usher and his colleagues note:

The household being the basic unit of production, all members had a role to play in the fishery, which became a central means of transmitting knowledge, skills, and values about the Indian way of life and living on the land. . . . We refer here not simply to fishing skills, but also to the traditional systems of tenure and resource management, in which the knowledge and judgement of the elders play an important role.[17]

Income lost from the closing of the waterways, as it happens, was in large part replaced by a variety of subsidies, transfer payments, wages from government programs, and one-time cash awards—$8.5 million in the form of compensation for damages and $4 million in the form of funds for reconstruction. But, as Usher et al. add, "there was no replacement for the cultural, social, and institutional functions of the fishery."[18] Or the traplines before it. Or, for that matter, the way of life of the bush generally. It was the end of a social form as well as the end of an industry.

Conditions of life in the new reserve, then, sooner or later brought an end to most of the livelihoods that family groups engaged in together, so "work," when it was available at all, increasingly called on separate individuals to leave the household for a day or a week or even a season and then to return with an envelope of money for their trouble.

Grassy Narrows had become a cash economy. There may not have been much cash to go around by most modern criteria, but this was nonetheless a strange new method of organizing the distribution of goods for a hunting and gathering people.

"Disposable income" the economists often call it. They do not mean thereby to place it in the same class as disposable diapers or paper cups, but in this case, anyway, that might be the right grouping—because the people of Grassy Narrows were not familiar enough with the peculiarities of cash to see it as much else. In the old reserve they might salvage an uneaten morsel of food for days or store a piece of leather thong for years against future want, but in the new reserve they were not sure what to make of momentary surpluses of cash—even if the reserve *did* have banks (as it did not), and even if there really *was* enough money to think in terms of savings (as there was not). So cash is disposed of, both in the sense that people spend it quickly, sometimes fiercely, and in the sense that virtually all of it drains right back out of the reserve to the Hudson's Bay Company and to white merchants in Kenora. The Ojibwa borrow it for a moment to buy groceries and gadgets and alcohol, but it then passes on, an indirect grant from the government of Canada to the most comfortable people in northwestern Ontario

"Cash," moreover, like wage work itself, has an intensely private feel to it. An entire family group may share the meat from a successful day of hunting or the rice from a successful day of harvesting because it was a collective activity to begin with. But a pay envelope or a welfare check is simply not like that. One may share it—indeed, one is expected to— but it has been made out to a person, and in that respect, too, the center of gravity shifts from the extended family to the individual household and from the individual household to the individual person. (The social organization of drinking poses an ironic and horrifying exception to that shift since it may now be the most communal activity in which people engage. But that is another story for another time.)

Almost overnight, finally, the Ojibwa of Grassy Narrows changed not only their diet but their whole way of relating to nature. "I cannot think of any other people in the world," said a highly placed physician in the Canadian Department of Health and Welfare, "which has had, in such a short period of time, such a complete change in their nutritional habits as the northern Ontario Indians [CBC]." In the old reserve, people hunted for moose, deer, beaver, muskrat, and a variety of fowl; they fished for pickerel, trout, whitefish, pike; they gathered blueberries, raspberries, strawberries, rice; and they grew turnips, onions, potatoes, squash, pumpkins, and corn in their own summer gardens. These foods were eaten fresh or preserved in half a dozen native ways for leaner times, and it scarcely needs to be said that this was sufficient. A grocery list for a day's shopping at

Hudson's Bay might include flour, lard, baking powder, salt, sugar, tea, and raisins, but as for the rest, the bush was source enough.

By those standards, though, the new reserve was dead space. Gardens were not replanted, in part because the soil proved flinty and unyielding. Hunting became more and more difficult, too. Creatures of the forest, of course, remain dispersed even when hunters elect to concentrate, and in any event they avoid settled places when they can. So it does not take long to thin out the neighboring woods. The same is true for gathering. When people set out from the same fixed spot day after day, their range, like that of tethered animals, is considerably reduced, and the spaces within their reach are soon picked clean. And fishing, of course, which not only survived the relocation but expanded as a result of it, was soon lost.

Thus the producer of food is converted all at once into a consumer. One brings groceries home now rather than grouse and pickerel and rice—odorless parcels of food pressed into cellophane wrappings, waxed cartons, plastic containers, tin cans. And so much of it is junk—white bread, carbonated beverages, processed rice, candies, pastries— that it is not uncommon to see these once-sturdy people, but a generation removed from the bush, with decayed teeth and suffering from obesity, anemia, and a variety of other ailments. It's an old and familiar story. One can learn from a parent how to prepare bannock or cook muskrat, the habits of generations providing all the nutritional lore one needs, but how does one pick sensibly from those endless rows of packaged goods when one first encounters them?

Schools, people were soon to learn, are the natural enemy of the hunting and gathering life since the very instant children are committed to a winter of classroom instruction their parents are committed to the sedentary patterns of the village. That may seem obvious a generation later, but it was not how the people of Grassy Narrows reckoned at the time. Canadian authorities probably had a number of reasons for wanting to draw people into that compressed space, but one of them, clearly, was to anchor them, to make them stand still. One old Indian agent, writing in 1885 about the establishment of missionary schools, hoped that "the Indian would be gradually and permanently advanced to the scale of civil society" and that "his migratory habits, and fondness for roaming, would be cured, and an interesting class of our fellowmen rescued from degradation."[19] One hundred years have passed since then, and we still have not yet learned to ask: Why is that a good thing? It makes a certain sense to argue that traplines interfere with schooling and that schooling is the main ticket of admission to the benefits of modern Canada. Right or wrong, that is at least logical. But the urgency with which white neighbors approach these reforms often seems to emerge from a different set of motives. It was clear one hundred years ago and it seems equally clear now that migratory people who live off the land and have no more than a passing regard for the idea of private property can so offend the sense of order of stationary villagers that they are provoked to acts of stern and willful charity.

The irony here is that Ojibwa children rarely stay in school long enough to find out if education really does open doors into the promise of modern Canada. By that time, though, their parents are fixed into what the physician quoted a moment ago called "those hideous little houses," where their native inclinations and skills are without focus and where they slide into a kind of dependency that comes all the more easily—the chemistries of human life often act this way—because it is the exact contrary of life in the old reserve.

The most important point I want to make may be the hardest to find adequate English words for. The traditional Ojibwa were in motion a good part of the year, looping out from established base camps and traveling along more or less established traplines and hunting routes. Most of their white neighbors viewed that land as an inert surface across which travelers had to make their way, but the Ojibwa, knowing it so much better, always regarded it as living matter with intentions and humors of its own. The people of the old reserve buried their dead in the ground, but the souls of those ancestors combined with the spirits of rivers and trees and all the other things of nature to fill the natural world with motion and personality. It was obvious that people had to remain in harmony with all those transcendental forces, and it was just as obvious that the moods of a place had to be understood and its powers consulted before it was safe to take up residence there.

The elders of Grassy Narrows are unanimous in their feeling that this elementary precaution was never taken and that the new reserve was built on malignant ground.

The old Indians believed there were certain areas that were not good for people to live on. In the Indian religion, everything has a spirit and all life comes from the Great Spirit. Animals, trees, rivers—even rocks and stones—they have life, just like a man has. There is what you call a life force in all living things. . . . That is why there are some places that are better than others to settle. Places where the life force is strong, places where man and nature come together spiritually. When it came to the move, our old people had ways of knowing about the land on the new reserve. They said the new reserve was a bad place spiritually. They said the land was too poor to grow anything, it was too close to the road, and the hunting would not be good. They said the new reserve would not support life. They tried to warn the people not to move. But we had no choice. [CBC]

In the Indian religion, there is good land and land that is bad. . . . So there is no such thing as empty space. All space is filled with spirits, but one cannot see them. Land over which troubled spirits travel is not good for people to live on. . . . This land where we are now—this spot—is unfit for people to live on because it is already owned by a bad spirit. Maybe that is why there is so much trouble here.

On the old reserve, they used to gather at the rock formation—"Little Boy Lying Down," they called it. From there they sent an echo across the space. They could tell by the strength of the echo if the land was good. Good echoes meant that the land would give people strength, that they could live well and survive there, that the land would support them. Another way to tell whether the land was good to live on was by the light that comes off the land. The old people used to be able to see this light. The place where the new reserve is—it is not a good place. It is not a place for life.

Diagnoses like these understandably have a way of becoming wiser with hindsight. We have no sure way of learning how insistent those "old people" who "had ways of knowing about the land" really were at the time of the move, but even if the diseased condition of the new space became more evident to them with the passing of time, the sense of having settled on troubled land remains acute.

The spirits of the dead, it is often said, are a good deal more agitated when the persons whose bodies they once occupied came to a violent end. They hover restlessly as if too many things remain unsettled before they can be induced to begin their journey to the land of the dead. If that is so, even in part, the new reserve must be electric with silent stirrings and unseen tumults.

I noted earlier that the failure of Ojibwa medicine to stem the white man's epidemic, the German Curse, resulted in serious doubts not only about the competence of native healers but about the sovereignty of the whole cosmology on which native medicine rests. That seemed to be part of the prevailing mood of Grassy Narrows when I visited: a loss of confidence in tradition, a loss of the sureties that a culture is supposed to confer, a loss of the sense of the wholeness of things. Of all the losses the people of Grassy

Narrows have had to endure, this may be the worst. Too many of them live without context, without meaning.

> Can we go back to the trapline as a family? To keep our culture? I don't think so. I would be afraid now to leave my wife and kids in a small log cabin on the trapline while I went out for two or three days. They may take sick, and what do I do? Before, you see, our people were much stronger. They were eating a different kind of food—not cans, but fresh wild meat, fish, wild rice. And besides that, every family had someone who knew about medicine, who could heal with bark or roots or herbs and other things, who had the power to help. So the trapping families made their own medicine and took care of themselves. They didn't need your doctors and nurses. And now? We are weaker physically from eating your kind of food and not having as much wild meat. So I'd be afraid of leaving my family in the bush. Your kind of first aid wouldn't help us in the bush. One more thing. When we lived as families on the old reserve, we had our spiritual elders. Every family had a spiritual person, someone who solved all kinds of problems, who helped persons trap better and be more successful in hunting. For other things there were other medicine men who had even greater power and could help in other ways. Now this religion is missing from the new reserve. There is no knowledge to give to the next generation. There are no more medicine men. Now we have nothing. Not the old. Not the new.

And they are pressed together in ways that make breathing hard for a people with their cultural reflexes.

The most miserable people on record, if Colin Trumbull's account can be relied on, may very well be the Ik of northern Uganda, a nomadic hunting and gathering people who, like the Ojibwa of Grassy Narrows, had been excluded from their traditional hunting grounds and required to settle into permanent compounds. Trumbull wrote:

The Ik, like all hunters, must have been as much a part of their natural world as the mountains and winds and rains and the very game they hunted and wild fruits they gathered. Wherever they went there was beauty, for, as Didigwari [once God of the Ik] had told them, there would always be enough. But when they were imprisoned in one tiny corner, the world became something cruel and hostile, and in their lives cruelty took the place of love.[20]

The story of Grassy Narrows deserves to be told for its own sake, of course, because it tells us a great deal about the nature of culture and of human misery. But the story can be told as a kind of parable, too, for it is a more sharply accented version—a magnified portrayal—of a process that has occurred among native peoples the world over. Virtually all Indians in Canada and the United States, certainly all the hunters among them, have been ripped loose from a cultural fabric in which things made sense, having little idea, as can be said for the members of any society, how deeply they relied on that fabric for meaning and security and a sense of self. The people of Grassy Narrows went through that process in one brief season, and the price they paid can be seen as a grotesque exaggeration of a kind of pain the world has had more than its just share of.

And the future? Anastasia Shkilnyk left Grassy Narrows discouraged about prospects for the years to come, and her account of life on the reserve during the late 1970s certainly provides data enough for so dark a forecast. Yet there may be reasons to take heart. A report like this one has to be written in the present tense, but it nonetheless describes a time now past. Observers who have been there since— Usher prominent among them—think they see "positive signs" and a measure of new "confidence" in a community that nonetheless remains, by any standard, in poor social repair. We must hope so.

2

The Haitians of Immokalee

You don't take poor people's money. . . .
It's bad when people take things from anybody.
But when peoples are poor, you just don't do that.
You just don't do that.

When you're in Haiti, you have your garden.
Here, your money is your garden.

I

The town of Immokalee lies in South Florida at the edge
of the Everglades. It is surrounded by rangeland with
clumps of slash pine and palmetto bushes, and the soil un-
derfoot, most of it drained swampland, is wet and fertile.
The principal business of the area, understandably, is agri-
culture: peppers, tomatoes, squash, and cucumbers; oranges, lemons, grapefruit, and melons.

Estimates of Immokalee's population vary from a low of
8,000 to a high of 25,000. When census takers went
through town for the 1980 census, they counted 13,700
inhabitants. But people drift in and out of Immokalee so
easily that any figure is like trying to measure the height of
a shifting body of water as the tides go in and out. For most
purposes, Immokalee can be said to have a population of

10,000 during the summer months and 20,000 or more in the middle of winter. That same ebb and flow can be found in other parts of Florida, of course, as tourists move south with the sun, but the variation in Immokalee's population is created wholly by seasonal farm workers.

The commercial area of Immokalee is a scatter of buildings laid out along two main streets: a row of convenience stores, fast-food restaurants, drive-ins, assorted small shops, used car lots, farm machinery outlets, feedstores, cafés, a sprinkling of churches, and the like. It seems hurriedly assembled, as befits a boomtown (the census of 1950 listed a population of fewer than a thousand), and it does not appear to have weathered even Florida's gentle climate very well. The most affluent of Immokalee's neighborhoods are very pleasant indeed, but much of the town is made up of housing that ranges from the spare to the decrepit.

The poorest part of Immokalee, known as South Immokalee on census charts but as El Centro by many locals, "resembles a densely-populated, inner city ghetto far more than a small rural town," in the opinion of two seasoned observers of such scenes.[1] It is lower and flatter and more spread out than most urban centers. There are no tenements. The spaces between are wider. But it has the feel of a ghetto all the same, with its rank housing and bail bondsmen and dark, seedy bars.

Immokalee is host to a number of people who call themselves winos, attracted to the area by warm winters, the opportunity for sporadic farm work, and the easy ways of the town. Those with three dollars to spare can bed down at Ernie's Flop House, where the lights seem never to go out, and those who do not command such a sum curl into whatever recess they can find outside. They all fit into the civic culture of Immokalee. One veteran of Ernie's explains in a deposition: "I was collecting unemployment at the time. See, I had come to Immokalee and I was a real alcoholic. As a result, I didn't have a place to live or anything. I was living out, just made me a little hut or something like that, like most of the guys do when they just get started. Then I came over here. Back then it was two dollars a night."

Immokalee is known as a hard, brawling frontier town. I could see no more than the surface of things in my own cautious wanderings, of course, but I was impressed by the grittiness of the streets during the day and by the sense of menace that seemed to hover over them at night. People made half senseless by alcohol and drugs are a commonplace, as are homeless people circling vaguely for a place to lie down, and although I am not aware of having seen it, drug deals seem to be frequent and blatant. Prostitutes, looking hard and efficient, make the rounds. Experienced locals have guessed that fifteen of them work the streets of Immokalee all year around (one of the busiest and most prominent of those being a Cuban man of thirty-one in drag), and a complement of others—a different kind of migrant worker!—moves to town during the picking season. Ten of the fifteen are thought to be HIV-positive, and it is easy to credit the report that venereal diseases generally are very common. Men outnumber women in Immokalee by a significant margin, especially among farm workers, and it is a young population, averaging a shade under twenty-five years of age.

At the heart of El Centro is a huge parking lot, an acre or more of pavement, where crew leaders in recycled school buses meet the gangs of workers they will drive to the fields at dawn and bring back again at day's end. At five of a winter morning, an hour and a half before the first appearance of light, one can see thin streams of people making their way toward the center of Immokalee, some of them having walked two or three miles before they begin their grueling day in the fields. By five-thirty hundreds of men and women are milling around the loading dock. Visitors dropped by parachute into the middle of that scene would be hard put to guess where in the world they were, and if they were to study the accents and costumes and postures of the crowd gathering in the early darkness for clues, they would only become more confused. It would seem obvious to them that they were in the third world, and the predominance of various forms of Spanish over Creole and English and native dialects of half a dozen different sorts would certainly suggest the Western Hemisphere. But unless one had the presence of mind to look at a license plate or a nearby sign, the scene spread out before one would be so full of contrasting sights and sounds that one would not know how to center it or to frame it.

It is still dark at six. A new bus drives slowly into the parking area to join the twelve or fifteen already parked there. The crowd seems to move slightly as if there had been a minor shift in the prevailing center of gravity. A few people, presumably acting on some quiet prearrangement, get on the bus; a handful of others cluster near it, not clamoring for attention or making any overt inquiries, so far as I can tell, but looking available. Another bus drifts in, and again there is an almost imperceptible ripple of movement toward it. By six-fifteen or so half the buses are still in their docks, some of them largely filled and others only partly so. But by now streams of people are beginning to move off into the early mists of morning, knowing already, by signals I have no inkling of, that there will be no work for them that day. To me, a total stranger, the scene has an odd choreography. There are logics to its shifts and flows, clearly, but even though I have the advantage of knowing what business is being transacted, I still have no idea how the thing is done.

By seven the sun is well into the sky and a couple of buses are still in the parking lot, together with a few scatterings of people carrying lunches in small white garbage bags. But the day clearly has begun.

II

At the edge of the parking lot is a grocery store once known as Fred's or Fred's Barn. It is open when the first migrant arrives at five, and it is still open when the last one returns in the late afternoon. "The work day is over in Immokalee," said a 1981 story in the *Miami Herald*:

> Buses rumble across the asphalt parking lot of Fred's, "The Home of Friendly Service," a barn-shaped shell of corrugated metal. . . . Inside Fred's, migrants fill shopping carts with beans and rice, tortillas, flour, hot sauce and cases of beer. The cashiers seldom look up. They can tell from the color of the hands whether to say the price in Spanish or in English. Before the last bus comes in at 4:00 P.M., the first bottle of rotgut makes the rounds, the first drunken field worker pitches face forward onto Fred's parking lot. . . . Across the street from Fred's, at Ernie's Flop House, some migrants have paid two dollars a night to sleep. Inside, a young Indian and two older Mexicans sit on a battered brown couch, staring at a black-and-white TV. The picture dissolves into horizontal lines. No one moves to fix it. As a full moon rises, the older men at Ernie's lie down on narrow cots spread beneath a yellow light bulb. Outside, you can hear them hacking into the night. And out beyond the camps, beyond the pool halls and juke joints and flop houses, beyond Fred's and Ernie's, lie the silent green fields. Another day awaits. . . .[2]

That may be too exuberant a description by half. But it offers a good introduction to Fred's Barn because one can so easily sense from it how migrant farmhands, most of them having no knowledge of American ways, might come to think of the parking lot as something like a village square and of Fred's as something like a civic institution. This is the real center of the migrant's world. No one mistakes it for a government installation or anything even remotely like that, but for people who know little more than the rhythms of the peasant village a scene like that has its own logic. It is institutional. It is governed by rules. It has order. It can be trusted.

Fred's Barn was then—and its successor is still now—a convenience store, offering coffee and sandwiches and an array of groceries. In Fred's day, though, it also had a teller's window. Farmhands are normally paid in cash at the end of each working day, and one of the services Fred Edenfield had offered for years was to keep whatever cash the migrants thought of as surplus—bills of low denomination, usually— in the store safe. As Fred pointed out later, "We did this as an accommodation for them because they didn't feel safe in keeping it. Some of them didn't have a place they could lock it up in their house at night, and that's the way it was started, and that's the way it continued. We was doing them a service at no charge to them and at no profit to us."[3] That's fair. The practice had begun in 1947, when Fred operated a smaller grocery in another part of Immokalee. "These farm workers at that time called it 'getaway money,' " Fred re- membered later. "In other words, they would bring you five dollars at the end of the day or ten dollars or something like that. You'd just write it down, and then when the season was over they'd come in there and get it so they had money to go to South Carolina or wherever they were going. That's the way it started—'getaway money.' "[4]

That was when migrant workers in South Florida were for the most part single and from the United States. But the arrangement continued long after the American workers had been displaced by Mexicans, Jamaicans, Haitians, and Central Americans from half a dozen different regions. It was indeed a convenience. The convenience to Fred and his partners was substantial, since the practice drew customers and created goodwill. The convenience to the customers, however, was greater yet. In the first place, they did not trust others—or, often, themselves—with the money. In the second place, few of them spoke English well enough to go to a local bank, and even if they could have found someone to translate their words faithfully, they would not have understood the measured phrases in which business is transacted in such places. What do they know of credit? Of interest? Of penalties for low balances? And in the third place, the bank is a long way off when you have no transportation and when you spend virtually all the hours of daylight in the fields.

On June 2, 1983, rumors began to circulate throughout South Immokalee that something had gone very wrong at Fred's Barn. A nervous crowd of people, the majority of them Haitian, began to collect, beginning a short-lived run on what everyone called the bank. Police officers summoned to the scene thought they could sense a "riot situation" in all that swarming, so they closed the store and impounded its records. The rumors turned out to have a grim substance. The store owed nearly $400,000 to its various depositors, but it had a cash balance of no more than $1,500. Fred's filed a petition for bankruptcy eight days later, and the manager of the store, William Gerald Crawford, called Gerald, was arrested and charged with grand larceny. The assets of the store were liquidated by order of the court and distributed to depositors, but even so, some $275,000 had disappeared from the lives of as poor a gathering of people as could be imagined. In November Crawford was found guilty of grand theft and sentenced to thirty months in the state prison.

In order to make sense of what follows, you will need to know that Fred's was operated by a corporation known as Edenfield and Crawford. In 1965, when the store first opened, the trustees of the corporation were Fred Edenfield, president and chairman of the board of directors, his wife, Mae, his daughter, Charlotte, and her husband, Gerald

Crawford. In 1975 Gerald took over the day-to-day management of the store, and the corporation, still called Edenfield and Crawford, was reorganized with Gerald as president, Charlotte as vice-president, and Fred, who retained a controlling interest in the business, as secretary-treasurer. This detail is important for our purposes only because Fred—a person of very considerable resources, by all accounts—took the view that he was no longer in active control of the business by the time of the default and therefore had no responsibility for the store's debts. That would be a matter of legal debate later, but the people of South Immokalee come from peasant lands where words have meaning, stand for things, are anchored somewhere in reality. Everyone called Fred's the bank, and by every standard other than fine shadings of law—about which migrant workers know almost nothing—that is what it was. How could anyone claim otherwise? And it was Fred's. Fred's Barn. The Barn of Fred. What else could such words mean?

Immokalee old-timers had no doubt where the responsibility lay. A black American woman said: "I always known it as Fred's, and I always believed—you know, people trusted their money there. . . . And they really thought that it was going to be safe and trusting. They really thought that would have, you know, a safe place for their money."* A Hispanic man added: "I knew Fred. . . . I trusted Fred for thirty years and deposited part of each check when I cashed it. . . . I thought it was as safe as the bank." And the newcomers, large number of them Haitian, were working on the same assumption. "All the Haitians were putting money in there," said one gloomily. "I didn't know that Fred was a thief!"†

---

*Unless otherwise indicated, quotations are from interviews.

†With very few exceptions, the interviews with Haitian farm workers were done with the help of interpreters, so the words transcribed are a translation.

III

The men and women who drift into Immokalee each year to work the winter harvest are part of a relatively new occupation, as history measures such things at least. The first migrant farm workers in America probably were white hoboes who traveled from farm to farm in California in the latter half of the nineteenth century along what came to be known as the dirty plate route, named thus because the going rate for a day's work was reputed to have been a serving of food on an already used plate. They were followed by tens of thousands of Chinese coolies who became jobless when the Union Pacific line was completed in 1869 and then by a steady stream of Japanese farm workers who made their way into California in the late nineteenth and early twentieth centuries. In the middle 1930s, as every reader of John Steinbeck knows, something like a quarter of a million refugees from the Dust Bowl went to California as well, earning the designations "Okies" and "Arkies" on the way. Shipyards and munitions plants as well as the armed forces absorbed many of those native migrants in the early years of World War II, and the result was an arrangement made with Mexico known as the bracero program, in which Mexican nationals could migrate into the United States on a temporary basis to work California farms. The bracero program officially ended in 1964, but the impulse set in motion then has scarcely slowed from that time to this. Mexicans have made up the largest farm labor pool by far from the early 1940s on, and there are no reasons to suppose that the pattern will change any time soon.

The East Coast migrant stream has a much shorter and simpler history. The first trickles of that stream appeared not long after the Civil War, when surplus farm labor, most of it black, began drifting north for seasonal work because the collapse of the plantation economy had left them marooned. The stream took on a more distinct shape in the

1920s, when thousands of acres of South Florida muck-land—including the environs of Immokalee, of course—were drained and opened to farming. The climate of the area allows crops to be planted and harvested on an almost continuous basis over the course of the season, so the opening of those lands made it possible for farm workers to spend the winter in Florida and then to drift north with the changing season in a trajectory that passes through Georgia and the Carolinas and either veers west into the upper Midwest or veers east into upstate New York. Migrant farmhands are like migratory creatures seeking a constant temperature, riding a seasonal tide north as warm weather moves slowly up the coast and riding it back down again as the first chills of autumn press south—one of the steadiest rhythms of nature.

The people who make up that migrant stream are almost wholly expendable as individual human beings, a fact they know all too well. But the stream itself is probably irreplaceable. There was hope once that mechanization would put an end to the need for migrant labor, but that is not likely to happen. It takes a human eye to distinguish the ripe from the unripe, and it takes a human hand to pick a fruit or a vegetable without damaging the plant that gave it life.

It is commonly estimated that one hundred thousand men and women work the harvest in Florida and that half of them join the migrant stream north. Their life is an extremely hard one. They have to face all the forms of cruelty that human beings know how to impose on one another as well as all the forms of uncertainty that nature introduces. It is truly backbreaking work, and the opportunities for savings or for establishing a homestead are so few as to be negligible even for the Americans. A vast majority of them, though, are illegal aliens, without papers or prospects, and their situation is even worse. Some limp home after several years in the fields to their own native species of poverty, but for many, time just drags on. "I've never gotten out of the fields," said a Haitian man approaching sixty. "I'm old enough to be out of the fields now." And when the human engine slows to the point of inefficiency, there are no pensions or benefits to fall back on, no savings accounts or home equities. Unless they are very lucky, they begin a life of poverty the very hour they leave the fields.

Two-thirds of those who lost money in the default of Fred's Barn were Haitians, a new population in the already rich ethnic mixture of South Florida. The law of succession in the ranks of migrant labor works almost exactly as it has in the industrial centers of the North, with incoming waves of newcomers, each one hungrier than the one before, taking almost as their birthright the lowest rungs on the occupational ladder. American whites have virtually left the ranks of migrant farm work, having been shoved out into other pursuits by the sheer poverty and desperation of refugees from elsewhere, and American blacks, too, are losing out in that sad competition. "I've lived here almost all my life," said one black woman who now resides the year round in Immokalee, shifting from the present tense into the past as she speaks of her family's migrant career: "I'm a migrant. We migrate from one place to the other. . . . My daddy was a vegetable man. He didn't like watermelons or nothing like that. He mostly would go up for the vegetable crop. So we followed the East Coast all the way up. We started off in South Carolina and ended up in New York. . . . Well, that was their life, and that's the way they earned their living."

In Immokalee and in similar agricultural centers, more than 80 percent of the farmhands are citizens of other countries: the vast majority entered this country illegally, and only a few speak enough English to navigate successfully in these peculiar cultural waters. Mexicans continue to dominate the migrant pool in number, as they have since the early days of the bracero program, but they are being pressed hard by workers from Guatemala, as well as from Nicaragua, El Salvador, and, in the last decade, Haiti. (Jamaicans come in substantial numbers to cut sugarcane, but for reasons we need not pursue right now, they constitute a special case.) So each new wave of migrant threatens to displace the one preceding it by its willingness to accept more hardship and less pay—wave upon wave of misery pressing up from underneath. "Let's face it," said one Immokalee farmer to a reporter, "why pay five dollars for a sack of fertilizer when you can get it for one dollar?"[5] Whether or not the speaker really meant to compare migrant workers with excrement, the image is blunt and to the point.

I V

The *Miami Herald* of March 22, 1981, said of the winter just then coming to an end: "It was the year of the new migrants, the Haitian stampede." The common estimate in those days was that fifteen thousand or more Haitians, virtually all of them illegal "boat people," had reached the eastern shore of Florida and that the majority of them had found jobs in the fields of South Florida—Homestead, Belle Glade, Frostproof, and, of course, Immokalee. The *Herald* report continued:

> In fact, the refugee infusion has been so voluminous that an entire Haitian village seems to be relocating in Immokalee. Of the estimated 1,500 Haitians there now, about 700 are from Jean-Rabel, a poor farming village of about 9,000 in northwest Haiti. Six months ago, Immokalee residents didn't have Haitians walking their streets. Now Immokalee has a Haitian minister from Jean-Rabel and a loyal congregation singing "Onward Christian Soldiers" in Creole.

Haiti was once the most prosperous colony in the New World, but it is now, by any useful measure, the poorest country in our hemisphere and one of the poorest in the

world. It is both the most rural and the most densely popu-
lated of Latin American nations. Of the rural population,
94 percent is judged to live in absolute poverty, and the rest
of the six million people who call Haiti home—excepting
only a small community of the much-too-rich—live so close
to the poverty line that they can be swept across it with even
the lightest shift of wind. Haiti is a mountainous country
with no more than 10 or 15 percent of the land under
cultivation, and what remains of that land is so leached and
exhausted and drained of nutrients that it yields but a fraction of what it once did. The countryside used to be lush in
hardwood forests, but virtually all those trees have been
felled for fuel, and with that layer of natural protection gone,
seven or eight million tons of already thin topsoil wash
down the bare slopes into the sea every year.[6]

The culture of Haiti is not a subject I need to go into
now, even if I knew enough to do so. But Haitian migrants
bring cultural outlooks with them to the streets of Immokalee that sometimes strike American sensibilities as passing
strange.

Anthropologists would presumably class Haiti as a polyg-
ynous society, meaning that both men and women are per-
mitted by custom to have more than one spouse at a time.
Whether or not that is the right technical term, one can
certainly say that the meaning of "marriage" is a good deal
more fluid and more flexible in Haiti than it is in Florida.
A man may begin with a legal marriage—one sanctioned by
the church as well as recognized by the state—and then add
a consensual union with someone in another household, all
the while maintaining a liaison with a third or even a fourth
woman. All the offspring of that dizzying round of life are
accepted by the man as his responsibility. He is their father
and their presumed source of support. Multiple marriages
are not as common for women—that would make for very
complicated households—but moving from one mate to
another in a pattern of serial monogamy is so. When a

Haitian migrant says to an interviewer, "I have six children and two wives," he is only relaying a simple fact of his life. And the same is true when an exchange like this one takes place in a legal deposition. "How many wives do you have?" asks Fred's attorney, making the most of what he knows to be sensitive ground. "Here I have one. When I was in Haiti, I had three." Next question: "How many children do you have or did you have by the three wives in Haiti?" Answer: "All together, I have ten children."

In another deposition Fred's attorney asks: "The three children that you have, were they by one woman or more than one woman?" "Two." "Two women?" "Yes." And then: "Do you know the names and ages of your children?" The witness is naturally incredulous: "They're my children. It is impossible for me not to know their names!" Thus the ways of Haiti encounter the ways of South Florida. The attorney is being shrewd, looking for adversarial profit in what he knows will look to a local jury as far too loose and untidy a marital arrangement. But he makes the very American mistake of assuming that anyone who could move so casually from mate to mate will of course be equally casual about parentage. Millions of Americans have been married twice. How many have been asked in a deposition: "Do you know the names and ages of your children?"

Haitian migrants also confuse their Immokalee neighbors with the richness and variety of their religious excitements. It is widely understood that they come from the land of vodun, a dark and sometimes sinister mystery to those who know the least about it, and the religion of their homeland, as is often the case with former colonies, is an ingenious mix of Catholicism from France, vodun from Africa, and new strains of evangelical Protestantism issuing from North America. Most of the Haitians of Immokalee would call themselves fundamentalist Protestants (as the singing of "Onward Christian Soldiers" in Creole would appear to suggest), but the people of South Florida generally do not

see the Haitians as belonging to one of the established religions of the host country. Mexicans are Catholic. Jamaicans
are Protestant. Haitians are, well, different.

People have been leaving Haiti in such numbers that the
term "diaspora" is commonly used to describe that population flow. The homeland is thought to contain between five
and six million people, but a million or more compatriots
have drifted off to the United States, the Dominican Republic, Canada, France, and elsewhere in the hemisphere. Haiti's
topsoil washes into the sea; its surplus population drains off
into other countrysides as if by the same gravitational pull.
For generations, moreover, "topsoil" would have been just
the right metaphor, because the vast majority of those leaving the country were middle-class professionals and skilled
craftspersons who considered themselves in exile from a
despotic regime. The largest group settled in New York
City, but Canada drew quite a number as well; it has been
estimated, for instance, that there are now more Haitian
physicians in French-speaking Quebec than in all Haiti.[7]

The best established of that earlier wave are true emigrants
by now. They flew in by daylight in the 1950s and 1960s
with their papers in order and their families intact, and they
are now for the most part middle-class urban dwellers. Some
may still speak of returning to Haiti someday, but most
know that their relocation is permanent. That is what happens when people settle into neighborhoods and jobs and
when children grow up more native to the host culture than
to the one their parents originally came from.

The newest migrant wave, however, reaching its crest
around 1980, was made up largely of single men from the
most rural parts of Haiti who landed at night on the beaches
of Florida without exit visas from home or immigration
documents from the United States after crossing seven hundred miles of ocean in open boats "without an engine." That
wave, by definition, is impossible to count. But to judge

from the number of people who were caught by the U.S. Border Patrol on Florida beaches, it is reasonable to assume that fifteen thousand or so came in 1980 alone and that fifty thousand to eighty thousand arrived altogether.[8]

The story is an old one. Poor people from Haiti have for years been exporting themselves to foreign markets for a season or two or even for a working lifetime to support families still at home. Cuba was a familiar port of call for migrant workers early in the century, while the Dominican Republic and the Bahamas relied heavily on Haitian labor up until quite recently. And in more recent times the target has been South Florida, known generically as Miami. Many of these people, too, have been marooned, and the odds of their returning to Haiti probably diminish with each passing year. But unlike most of their compatriots in New York City, they live like people in temporary exile and make very few efforts to learn the languages and ways of the host country.

Virtually all the Haitians in Immokalee regard Haiti as their true home, whether or not they expect to see it anytime soon, and virtually all of them feel responsible for the support of family members still living there. This is known throughout the impoverished countries of Latin America and the Caribbean—where there is neither enough land nor enough income-producing work to support the population—as the remittance pattern. A family decides to send one of its members abroad to earn money for the family's welfare, and it pays the expenses of the trip by drawing on its pooled savings, by selling off parcels of land or livestock, or by borrowing from moneylenders, usually at high rates of interest. However financed, the passage represents an immense investment to the hard-pressed family. One expert on Haitian migration notes that "a large amount of money, perhaps the entire economic base of the extended family, is being put at risk. Any bad luck may mean the family's economic ruin."[9] And the whole village's. Three out of every four households in a village on the Plain of Léogane, according to a recent study, had "at least one immediate family member living abroad," two-thirds of whom had traveled by boat to South Florida.[10] The prevailing estimate for all Haiti is that one-third of the households—*habitations*—have at least one member abroad.[11] The authors of the study on the Léogane village note:

> Today the desire to leave is universal; even young children expect that when they grow up, they too will go "over there" to "give life to their families." From early on children learn the value that as adults they will be responsible to assist the rest of their extended family. Parents explicitly view their offspring as economic resources, and their emigration, like schooling or apprenticeship, as an investment in their own future as well.[12]

As an old Haitian proverb goes, "A donkey has children so that he can rest his back."[13]

The sense of responsibility can be tremendous. The migrants are not being sent out into the world to seek their own fortunes or even to reduce by one the number of mouths that need to be fed at home. They are the family's emissaries—its delegates, its agents—and they are a major source of support for many people. One migrant in Immokalee said: "In Haiti, we come from poor families. You know when you leave that you leave at least fifty or maybe a hundred people who are suffering, hungry, with not enough food. That is why when you come here, the money you make you cannot keep." One common guess is that every migrant outside the country feeds and clothes four people at home,[14] so the above statement, if taken literally, is an exaggeration. But this means that a very large portion of Haiti's population is dependent upon remittances from abroad—estimated as $160 million a year by the World Bank.[15]

The man quoted above added:

> I came here to help my family. . . . You have a family. They created you. They suffered for you. In the future, you are supposed to extend your hand when it comes to your family. . . . From the time I was sixteen, I see that it was my mother who fed me, who sent me to school. My parents help me. Then, when I reach a point where I work, I'll send money to them and take care of them.

"My mother paid fifteen hundred dollars for me to come here," said one man who came to Florida at the age of twenty-one and who lists as his family responsibilities "my mother, my father, three sisters, four brothers, and two children" in addition to "a wife and three children here." That original investment, furthermore, is an obligation that may remain in effect for decades. Another migrant, now forty-five, said: "My mother has been sick for the last six months, and I haven't been able to send anything. If my father had been sick, it would have been a different story, but my mother paid for me to go to the Bahamas." That had happened twenty-two years earlier! A donkey has children so that he can rest his back.

In one of my interviews the interpreter forgot for a moment to translate directly from Creole into English and told me what a thirty-six-year-old migrant had just said: "He said he was born into a very, very poor family in the mountains. His purpose in this country was to come here and to be able to work and to help all his family." Indeed, "all his family" covered a large assembly of people. The interpreter, having now caught himself, rendered the next answer directly: "I have three children in Haiti and two sisters who have four and five children. I have a father and mother. I help my children and my sisters' children go to school. The youngest child lives with my wife. The other two children, by two different mothers, live with my mother." As the interpreter pointed out, reverting to the practice of summarizing his countryman's words indirectly, "It is a very heavy burden for him."

Nor is it atypical. Migrants from poor families generally tend to be responsible for more persons in Haiti than the national average of four would indicate since a larger share of the family's resources is required to sponsor the trip abroad and since poverty always seems to generate large family clusters. A donkey . . . "I got seven kids in Haiti, a wife and my wife's sister, and my father, my brother, and my mother. I'm living by myself here. I have responsibility for all my family in Haiti. . . . Yeah, and I got to help my sister and my brother too. I got three sisters, and I take care of two [children] for each of them. I take care of two [children] for my brother, too."

The remittances that flow from Florida to Haiti are used for all kinds of expenditures, especially those in which cash changes hands (purchasing land, livestock, seed, clothing, and household items; paying medical bills and repaying debts; providing uniforms, books, and tuitions for school). In addition, rural families in Haiti have no insurance or old-age benefits, no reserves even to bury their dead according to custom or to engage in the other ceremonies around which communal life revolves, and the migrant thus serves the family as a resource to be drawn upon in moments of special need. In some households sacrifices have to be made to ancestors, often on the migrant's behalf, and other spirits need to be propitiated as well. "From time to time the rain doesn't fall," said one migrant, using an old folk metaphor to speak of more than crops and harvests, "and you can't plant in Haiti. Then they send word that they are hungry."

Virtually all the Immokalee Haitians, as I noted earlier,

are "boat people." Of the 127 whose date of arrival in this country I have information on, 118 came in either 1980 or 1981, and the rest are clustered nearby: 1 in 1977, 1 in 1978, 4 in 1979, and 2 in 1982. This may be taken as more or less representative. In 1981 an interdiction agreement between Haiti and the United States essentially closed off this way of entering the country, so the original Haitian stampede was for all practical purposes over at the time of the default of Fred's Barn. But the Haitians of Immokalee found themselves in an awkward position. Even though they arrived in this country without papers and were thus illegal aliens, and even though a number of them were held for considerable stretches of time in a detention camp, the Carter administration decided to treat them as parolees seeking asylum and to issue them work permits. This allowed them to stay in the country for at least the immediate time being, but their standing was tentative and their prospects were uncertain, and since they were officially seen as a kind of political refugee, it was difficult for them to return to Haiti in the meantime.

I did not have sense enough to ask the Haitians I interviewed how much their passages had cost, but Fred's attorney, for reasons of his own, did so in a number of the depositions he conducted. On the basis of that very informal survey—and a scattering of other data[16]—we may presume that the cost ranged from ten dollars to fifteen hundred dollars, and sometimes more. Half the Haitians interviewed by Fred's attorney remembered having paid less than one hundred dollars (although it may be worth remembering that a number of those passages were actually arranged by someone else), and a handful described far more elaborate pooling arrangements. One migrant provisioned the boat he came on with "fish, soda, and drinks," and another paid for his passage by providing "a goat to eat on the boat."

V

Housing for migrant workers in places like Immokalee ranges from the deplorable to the adequate. With a handful of important exceptions, it consists of a few apartments in larger complexes, a few trailers, and acres upon acres of wooden shacks, built in rows or freestanding, perched on cinder blocks. "Slums" would be the right term for much of that housing stock. Rents were said to vary from $160 a month to $800 or so when I was there—high for that part of the world in any case but staggering when seen as a percentage of the average tenant's income. So people press into those narrow precincts as closely as the laws of volume permit in order to share the costs of rental. I have been in rooms where the furnishings, spare as they are, take up so much of the floor space that one needs to crawl across one bed to get to the next. (Some Haitians joke a bit ruefully that it takes their children a long time to learn to walk because they have so little room for practice indoors, and one local public health official, herself Haitian, describes this as a ranking public health problem.)

At one end of the housing range are profiles like the following, both of them drawn from a muckraking newspaper exposé: the seventy-five-year-old retired farm worker, blind and sick, who pays $160 a month for a "tiny and decaying roach-infested one-room shack" and has to walk a hundred feet to the nearest toilet facility and eight blocks to the Guadalupe Mission soup kitchen where he eats; and the sixty-two-year-old veteran of World War II who pays $160 a month for a single room measuring ten feet by ten feet, "barely enough for [his] bed, which is brown from encrusted dirt and stinks of stale sweat," with no heat, no cooking facilities, no water, and no protection from the termites that have eaten away portions of the shack's underpinnings.[17] At the other end of the continuum one finds spare but comfortable housing into which remarkable numbers of people have been gathered. A Guatemalan family of three, for example, shelters seven fellow villagers in its small house. Or another Guatemalan farm worker, who says of his housing arrangements: "I live here in a trailer camp with four couples—five with me and my wife. They are from San Juan Ixcoy in Guatemala. There is a new born there . . . [and] a teenager lives with us. . . . The motor home has three rooms, but we are in need: we divided each room in two spaces separated by a blanket."[18] The concentrations of people, then, issue from both desperation and hospitality, since few farm-working families can afford the space required to live in even the most modest comfort and each family is obliged by village tradition to provide shelter for kin and for fellow townspeople.

The Immokalee housing code, from which accommodations like the above are so dramatic a departure, seems sensible enough. It insists on a sound structure, free of rats and vermin, with both hot and cold running water; enough heat to maintain sixty-eight degrees; a stove and refrigerator, a sink and counter, and at least one cupboard; screens in the windows; safe electrical wiring; a secure roof; and a minimum of 150 square feet for the first occupant and 100 square feet for each additional one. Most housing units fail to meet one or another of those standards, as might be expected, but that last innocent provision is by all odds the most problematic. The usual reckoning is that Immokalee's housing units accommodate five persons on the average, and it is certainly safe to assume that the figure is much higher for farm workers. So thousands of people would become homeless overnight if the code were enforced rigidly.

Even when housing is clean and up-to-code in other respects, it is likely to be very compact. The Crawford Apartments, for example, known locally as Little Haiti, have ninety-six units, each 11 feet by 16 feet. They have no refrigerators or stoves—a distinct violation of the code—

but they are dry and solid and equipped with bathrooms, and at $175 to $200 a month, they are generally thought to be choice lodgings. The problem is that these units—176 square feet apiece—can accommodate but one person within the strict meaning of the code, and it is apparent to anyone who visits the complex that the rate of occupation is vastly greater than that. Fill an 11-by 16-foot room with four beds, a television set, and a bureau or two, and it is easy to understand why Haitian children might go for days without setting their feet on the floor.

When housing is bad, however, as is so often the case, the density of occupation serves only to aggravate an already dismal situation. One local estimate is that 25 percent of the housing units are without toilets and that 35 percent have no hot water. That is easy to believe for anyone who has made those rounds. I have been in a number of shacks where the windowpanes have been broken for weeks, where such plumbing as there is leaked constantly, where the air is thick with flies and mosquitoes and the indoor surfaces are alive with roaches, spiders, and an exotic variety of insect life. Most of those shacks sit on cinder blocks; this means that pools of stagnant water can gather underneath and serve as a perfect breeding ground for mosquitoes.

There is a chilling circularity to all this. On the one hand, a considerable portion of the housing available to migrant farm workers is really shameful, and a visitor can only marvel that landlords are able to sleep at night or to look at themselves in the mirror. The units are not only in violation of a code but in violation of every standard of decency that can be imagined. But at the same time the levels of cleanliness and hygiene one finds among that group of tenants leaves the impression—certainly to those who already have doubts about poor, dark aliens speaking odd tongues—that they simply do not care. And so the cycle goes. Tenants can see no reason to take good care of housing units that leak and invite rats, and many of them, burdened by too many hours in the fields and too many bodies at home, withdraw into a glazed, demoralized slump. The landlords, meantime, some of whom may have moved into the business with kinder hopes, begin to suspect that "they" have no respect for property and little interest in keeping their persons or the places they live in clean. "They live like animals in Mexico," one man said, meaning in his own way to be sympathetic; "why should it be different here?" Well, they don't live like animals in Mexico, as it happens, or in Haiti or Guatemala or El Salvador or anywhere else. They learn to live like that here. But it is an easily understandable mistake all the same.

VI

Three hundred and four people lost money as a result of the default of Fred's. In one sense, at least, every one of them was damaged by the event, both because of the loss itself and because of the manner in which it took place. The harm done varied from person to person, clearly, but we can begin by talking in generalities.

The poor are vulnerable in ways that go far beyond the fact of their destitution. The loss of a few hundred dollars under circumstances like these would mean little to most people in the long run, no matter how sharp the immediate privations, but the consequences for those who have lived for years in or on the edge of poverty have to be weighed on a different scale. The average loss at Fred's was around $900, and the range (with two peculiar exceptions that need not detain us here) was from a low of $15 to a high of $3,320. Haitian depositors—two-thirds of the total group—lost slightly less than $1,100 on the average with a low of $190 and a high of that same $3,320. It makes sense to think that the handful of people who lost $15 or $25 were less scathed by the event, but it is difficult to see any direct relationship between the amount of pain experienced and the amount of money lost when we move into higher altitudes. The Haitian who lost $3,320 said: "I cried. I felt so bad I cried. I worked so hard to save that money and carry buckets of tomatoes, bags of oranges. It was a long time before I could sleep because of this." A Haitian whose losses were just above the mean at $1,280: "It hurt me very badly in my heart. It hurt me because I had worked so hard to earn that money." And a Haitian whose loss of $640 was nearer the bottom of the scale for his compatriots: "I was sick at that time because I lost my money. Really, I was very depressed because of that. I spent two months really worrying. That was just like my blood."

So feelings can be sharp even when the sums involved appear to be relatively small. It does not take as heavy a load to endanger a frail vessel as it does a sturdy one, and the men and women who entrusted their savings to Fred's— durable and tough in so many other ways—share all the fragilities that go with being poor.

As painful as the event must have been for everyone who lost savings at Fred's, the Haitians have to be counted as especially vulnerable. Even during the best of times they experience all the disadvantages of being black, poor, and foreign in a country that ranges from ambivalence to inhospitality on each of those scores, and to complicate matters, few of them speak English or understand the ways of the country in which they find themselves. During the worst of times, as the period following the default of Fred's most emphatically was, they have few cultural or personal resources to fall back on. "That was a big problem for me," said one, "because I'm not in my country. I am a foreigner here. I am not in my country, and I don't know anywhere to go." One man walked seventy-five miles to Belle Glade, sleeping "in the bush" on the way, to seek out the only other Creole-speaking people he knew for help. The other people of Florida, even at their most generous, sometimes find the Haitians odd. They can be very expressive of both good moods ("When you're happy, you dance") and dark ones ("I died. You know, I was walking, I was yelling, I was crying. I was really crazy. I cried. I cried"). Not only do they view such sensitive concerns as health and illness through a Haitian cultural lens ("He thought the devil sent some kind of vodun to his father"), but they sometimes have little more than the vaguest appreciation that American medicine operates by different logics ("My husband was sick. That's why he left to go back to Haiti. My husband fell down in the fields, and a truck ran over him. I took him to the hospital. The doctor told me it was cancer, but I don't know. Maybe they were afraid that we couldn't pay. That's why they didn't do anything. Now a traditional healer is treating him with leaves and other things").

The Haitians in general often seem to their Florida neighbors to be a perplexing mixture of strains. They can shift from incredulity to wariness in an instant. The gracefulness of their movements and the gentleness of their humor are sometimes punctuated by the streaks of fierce rage that have marked the history of Haiti for centuries. They seem at once exotic and sinister.

Haitian farm workers, furthermore, are totally at sea— apt imagery, actually—when they are riding the migrant stream up and back down the East Coast. They are transported by crew leaders in barely serviceable buses, and during their time away they do not meet a single person who knows anything of their native language or anything of their native ways. They are a long way from home, too, both geographically and spiritually. Most Haitian migrants, as we saw earlier, are emissaries of families at home, with the result that few of them have any kin in Florida upon whom they can depend in times of crisis. It is their responsibility in life to be depended upon by others.

Of the 304 persons who lost money at Fred's, 296 (97 percent) later brought suit against William Gerald Crawford, Charlotte Crawford, and Fred Edenfield—the trustees of Crawford and Edenfield—for recovery of the funds lost as well as for consequential and punitive damages. I am about to turn to the impact of that loss on the persons involved, but before doing so, I need to pause for a moment to say a word about the data on which I will be drawing. A few numbers, then:

Of the 296 plaintiffs, 197 (66 percent) were Haitian, 45 (15 percent) were black Americans, 26 (8 percent) were white Americans, another 26 (8 percent) were Hispanic, 1 was Cherokee, and (if you have been adding as we go and notice that we are still one short), we do not know the ethnic origin of the 296th. Two-thirds of these people (197) were interviewed for this study, and even though no effort was made to draw a sample in the stricter sense of the term— our original intention had been to interview every one of the plaintiffs—the ethnic composition of the interviewed group was very close to that of the larger plaintiff population. Haitians, for instance, our main concern here, made up 66 percent of the plaintiff body and 66 percent (131 of 197) of the group interviewed. I interviewed 33 persons, 14 of them more than once, and the remaining 163 were interviewed by legal assistants acting on my instructions. I shall be referring to other plaintiffs in what is to follow, but my focus will be primarily on the Haitians, so you should know that the views of 131 of them are recorded here in 142 interviews (and in the handful of depositions conducted by attorneys for Fred Edenfield).

To even out the numbers, then, let's say that three hundred people—two hundred of them migrant workers from Haiti—lost an average of a thousand dollars to what everybody agrees was an act of outright larceny. It was a dark moment in the lives of all of them, presumably—frustrating, infuriating, depressing. That much any of us can understand out of our own experience. But I am relating this event in a book on traumatic disasters, and my task here, as it was when the suit was tried in court, is to convey my own feeling that most of the plaintiffs—and the Haitians among them especially—were truly wounded by what happened to them. "That's the only money I ever had," said one Haitian of thirty. "When I lost that money, I was hopeless."

Every plaintiff suffered short-term privations as a result of his or her loss, and many saw important dreams deferred. We asked all the plaintiffs we interviewed what they had planned to do with the savings they had deposited at Fred's. The Haitians, as might be imagined, differed from the others in the number who had intended to send the lost money home in the form of remittances, but in other respects the responses were similar. Some of the money had been set aside to finance trips north when the season shifted and to improve conditions of life on the road. "Getaway money" Fred had called it. A white southerner who lost four hundred dollars explained: "I was saving the money for going to North Carolina. . . . If you have money, you can choose where you want to live, but if you don't have money, you have to stay where they put you when you go north." Another portion had been set aside for a particular purchase—often a car, which, to poor people in general and to migrant farm workers in particular, has long been a symbol of independence and mobility as well as one of the few ways for migrants to move to other occupations. One man of Puerto Rican ancestry said: "I wanted to buy me a new truck, like a Dodge Dart. It's kind of a dream of mine." And a third portion was being held in reserve for the kinds of special need I noted earlier. "When you're in Haiti, you have your garden," noted one woman whose words open this chapter. "Here your money is your garden." That's a very Haitian way of making the point, but migrants speaking in other tongues mean the same thing when they speak of saving for rainy days (a meteorological commonplace in the life of every farmhand) or of building nest eggs from which a better future might someday emerge.

The immediate reaction for most of the migrants was a

sharp stab of astonishment that turned almost immediately into feelings of rage, despair, and, particularly among the Haitians, shame and humiliation. "It was the saddest day of my life. I couldn't pay the rent. I went to a friend's house and asked if I could stay there . . . but he told me that he wasn't going to be able to help me. . . . It made me very ashamed to ask that. I spent three days sleeping in an old car without anyone knowing because I was too ashamed. . . . At the time I thought that life had no meaning for me."

A large number of Haitians reported that they became "sick" upon learning of the loss of their money, using either that term or an equivalent. People spoke of physical discomforts—hives, weight loss, headaches, insomnia, inability to eat—and pains of a vaguer but nonetheless compelling sort. To express feelings of pain in somatic terms is, in part, a Haitian way of giving shape to experience, but it is familiar to every culture. It gives substance to otherwise impalpable hurts, converting the sense of feeling terrible into a more widely understood currency both to others and to oneself.

I had a headache for a week. I was amazed.

After that I was sick. That was such a big shock to me. You know, I worked hard to save that money, and when I lost it, I became sick. I got hives.

After I lost the money, I lost thirty pounds. I used to weigh one hundred sixty pounds. I was totally wounded.

The physical symptoms people reported and the pain accompanying them were both sharp and real, so I do not mean to suggest for a moment that those afflicted were inventing convenient locations for hard-to-describe ailments. But one can sense as an undertone in these reports a feeling of things breaking apart, of worlds shattering, of persons being broken by events that do not strike directly at the tissues of the body. "It hurt me badly in my heart," said one man from whom we have already heard, and a countryman added: "When the money was gone, my ideas were broken."

An even larger number of the Haitians described feelings of disorientation, depression, and the kind of numbed lethargy and listlessness of spirit that so often accompanies trauma. It is a sense that things are out of kilter, that the landmarks by which one normally finds one's way in the outer world have disappeared and that the inner compasses, too, have come to a stop. People come to feel that they are drifting in a dead magnetic field and that their bodies have gone limp.

> It gave me so much problems. I spent several days, I couldn't eat. I was so depressed. I was out of myself for several days.

> I felt dead because I didn't have nothing to do, no place to go. It was just like I was dead.

> I was very sick. I was very sick because I pick oranges. I worked very hard to save that money. When I lost that money, I was uncomfortable. I spent a week—I didn't even know where I was. I couldn't sleep at night.

> I was just like someone who lost his mother or his wife.

> I felt like I died. That's all I had. It was a very big tribulation for me. I had a headache. I couldn't eat. I didn't know where I was.

> I don't even know where I was. I can't tell you. I was up in the air.

Moreover, the sense of disorientation experienced by so many of the victims led to feelings of being even more out of control than is usual for people in their uncertain line of work. A very large number said things like:

I felt out of control and sick. I lost all my life.

Really, I was out of myself. I could not control myself. I worked so hard to save that money.

Well, I didn't have life, any life. I was depressed. I couldn't control myself. I was out of control at that time. In America, I didn't have any more money to take care of myself. And I worked so hard to save some money, and, you know, it was gone. So I was totally depressed.

At times that feeling of being out of control almost seemed to verge on the psychotic. I have already cited the man who said: "I died. You know, I was walking, I was yelling, I was crying. I was really crazy." And that was far from a unique reaction. "I got mad about that. I just talked. I was just talking like I was crazy." "When I lost my money, I was almost crazy. I came to this country, working hard picking oranges all day. I was working hard to make money to buy a little place for my family."

The volatility of those responses can be counted in some measure as characteristically Haitian, but that only adds a dramatic edge to feelings that are shared by most human beings who encounter so bitter an assault. The sense of being out of control, of course, is sharper among poor people in general and migrant farm workers in particular because they have command of so little in life even when things are going well. What people are reaching for the words to say, then, is that they feel disconnected, helpless, adrift, no longer anchored anywhere. That those feelings become experienced as somatic discomforts makes excellent psychological sense.

I have been dealing so far with the immediate effects of the default on the persons whose money was stolen, but it is crucial to add, especially in the case of the Haitians, that shock waves were felt many hundreds of miles away, where the families of the migrants—who could not be expected to understand what happened at Fred's—suffered their own species of distress. It had been a hard season in Haiti anyway ("It happened at a difficult time. The fields were not good. My family wrote and said they were sad and hungry and discouraged"). And as the legal action was making its deliberate way through the courts of Florida, the Haitian countryside broke into turmoil. I was completing plans to visit Jean-Rabel, the hometown of about a third of Immokalee's Haitians, when the *New York Times* reported:

> Witnesses to a brutal battle last week have given grisly accounts of peasants and sharecroppers fighting with machetes and metal spikes in a clash that killed at least 50 people. Casualty counts differed widely, and some reports ranged up to several hundred. The battle between peasants demanding land redistribution and sharecroppers working for landowners occurred in Jean-Rabel, in a fertile valley in the remote northwest.[19]

The most dramatic reports, as it turned out, were also the most accurate. Amy Wilentz was in the capital, Port-au-Prince, at the time of the massacre, and wrote:

> The streets of Port-au-Prince were in chaos. The army had already killed dozens during demonstrations, and now, on July 23, in the northwest near the dusty town of Jean-Rabel, hundreds of peasants who were organizing land-reform actions throughout the area were ambushed and macheted to death by others underwritten by local landholders. Their hacked bodies were left alongside mountain trails or thrown into the deep ravines that ring Jean-Rabel.[20]

So, once again, the poor are panicked into killing their own on a battlefield drawn by the well-to-do. The Haitians of Immokalee did not seem very surprised about all this, so far as I could tell, although it makes sense to assume that reports of the event would have reached them slowly and in discrete bits. That, after all, is one of the ways disputes are settled in Haiti.

A considerable part of the money the Haitians had deposited at Fred's, in any event, had been scheduled for shipment home, so it is essential to count the costs to those at home when filling out the book of accounts.

Important rituals, around which life revolves in places like Haiti, were not adequately observed: "My dad died," said one man simply. "I could not send any money for the funeral." Another said: "At that time I had a lot of problems. My grandma died, and Haiti sent me a letter to send something [to assure a proper burial]. I did not telephone or send. I did not have any money to send back to them. I was depressed. . . . I felt that way for two or three months."

Moments of crisis were not met:

My father was sick in Haiti. I didn't have no money to send for my father to see a doctor in Haiti. As a result, my father died.

I felt bad and I felt sad. Some kind of blood came to my eyes, and I could not see or sleep too good. The pressure because my son was in the hospital and I could not send money made me emotionally very sick. I felt because I am a foreigner to this country, he [Fred] should not treat me this way. . . . I had just gotten a letter from Haiti saying that my son was sick. I went to Fred's to get the money to send for him in Haiti. He was in the hospital. I could not get the money. My child died. I was going to use to send to my baby in Haiti.

My father just died. . . . When I lost the money, he was sick. And at the time I was going to send part of the money to take care of the hospital. And when Fred's Barn took the money, I couldn't find any money to send to him. I sent messages telling him that I didn't have any more money because where I left the money the person took it. I told him that I was sleeping on the street because I didn't have any money to pay rent. And since then he became worse because of the shock. . . . He died last October 21, and it was the biggest regret—

Relatives went hungry and without clothing, and the inability of the migrants to provide cash for other essentials of peasant life—seed in planting time, a scrawny pig or donkey—had lasting repercussions. But the most painful deprivation to most of the Haitians was that children at home were prevented from attending school because no money was available for tuition, uniforms, and the other expenses that attend education. Haitian peasants, like poor people everywhere, look upon schooling as the one chance for their children to advance in life. So when the migrants stepped cautiously onto the shifting deck of the first boat most of them had ever seen, cardboard suitcase in hand, the mission uppermost in mind had been to provide for the children's future. Although it is hard to make an accurate count with the data available, it is evident that the Immokalee Haitians were responsible for the education of many hundreds of children and that quite a number of them lost a semester or more of schooling as a direct result of the default of Fred's. "I'm the oldest and the only one here," said one man of thirty-six who was responsible for ten younger brothers and sisters as well as two aging parents:

It made me sad to know that my father had me here and that the children could not go to school. They understand that when I don't send money, I don't have it. But I was sad. They didn't swear at me, but they let me know that the children couldn't be in school. This saddened me. Since I'm the one who's here, I'm responsible. . . . When my father is not there, they all call me papa. It's as if I'm the father.

So the money stolen by Gerald Crawford brought a triple dose of misery, because the bad times visited on Haiti only added to the already profound despair of those in Florida. The sense of having failed, of having been found wanting, falls like a dark shadow over all the interviews, even though the words needed to describe that feeling may rarely have survived the translation process in their original richness. But it is not hard to sense the pain in such passages as these:

> That was terrible. I could not buy food for myself. I couldn't find anything to send to my family, my relatives in Haiti. What happened to me—I want to explain to you—I felt it was very bad. I had to work so hard to get that money. I could not support my family. That was very bad. I did not know what to do.

> The money that I had—I was planning to send some money for my children for school. . . . The money got lost and I didn't know what to do. My eyes were full of water, and I didn't know what to do. I think that was the worst thing that could ever have been done to me in my life.

Many of the Immokalee Haitians, then, felt a deep sense of shame and humiliation at having let down the family members who depended on them for help, and that feeling lasted long after other effects of the default had dimmed. Those at home, understandably, often expressed doubts about the good sense and even the goodwill of the migrants who had to write that they could not contribute anything to the family's welfare. Some were accused of "splurging." Others were scolded for having acted recklessly with the family money, and quite a few had to reassure loved ones at home that they had not deserted. For example, "I died a lot. I had no money in the bank, no place to go. It made me sad. My wife wrote to me, and I couldn't write [send money] for three months. She said I had abandoned her.

This made her very upset. She would have had the right to look for another husband, but she didn't."

Misunderstandings of that kind were resolved sooner or later ("excuse me, I'm sorry, I thought you had abandoned me" was the happy ending the wife of the speaker above is reported as having supplied), but the sense of shame is a continuing source of pain. So much is at risk. "Sometimes it is so bad that I can't eat," said one man, speaking of his embarrassment, and others expressed the same sense of being demeaned, of being reduced in stature, of being made to feel dirtied:

> My children and my brothers' and sisters' children didn't go to school for six months to a year. All the people who depended on me suffered because I could not send them money. In Haiti the honor of the person providing support to the family is diminished if you don't send money.

> I was not able to pay rent, and I had to move. It took me two months to find housing. My family in Haiti depended on me to send them money for themselves and for their children, to send them to school. They all felt like I was dying because all their hopes in me were ended.

A number of the losses suffered by the Haitians have to be understood as permanent, even if their immediate effects do not seem to rank as disastrous. Migrants everywhere in the world live on the hope that they will earn large enough stakes working away from home to start new lives. The Haitians of Immokalee, almost to a person, expected (a) to return home within two or three years of their arrival in Florida, having earned enough money in the meantime to buy land or begin a business in Haiti, (b) to become well enough established in this country to bring children and other family members back with them, or (c) to move back and forth at will, as migrant workers elsewhere in the world do. That dream can be postponed for very long stretches of time, of course, but it remains a sustaining hope, and the savings a migrant can manage to accumulate are an important part of it. So great a loss of funds, however, and the feelings of hopelessness that accompany it, complicate the situation enormously. Separations now seem endless. Children mature. Vital ceremonies like baptisms and marriages and funerals come and go. The meter of life continues to run at home, and the moments missed are simply gone forever. To miss two or three years of a child's growing or the final months of a parent's life is a permanent, irreversible loss.

As I noted earlier, most of those who lost money at Fred's experienced a sense of betrayal that loomed as importantly as the loss itself. That, too, is a finding often reported in studies of human disaster: The damage done by the event is bad enough, but the fact that it was the result of human agency—that other human beings caused it by acts of malice or inadvertence—adds appreciably to the feelings of injury. Locals of long standing, who viewed the Crawfords and the Edenfields as trusted neighbors, were very upset. One black woman of sixty, speaking of Fred, could hardly contain her disdain: "He's a sorry son of a bitch. For anybody to take a person's money, that's just plumb awful." But her neighbors were as moved by hurt as they were by anger. The two women below, both middle-aged, lost seventy and fifty dollars respectively—small sums even in their stretched circumstances:

> I mean it really hurted me. It really, really hurted me. Boy, for him to just do like that. You know, I had confidence in him that he would never do a thing like that, and then—No, he really deceived me, and it hurt me. . . . I just didn't want to believe that Mr. Edenfield or anybody done anything like that.

It changed my ideas about people. We been knowing those people all our lives. The Crawfords and the Edenfields, we've knowed them folks all our lives. . . . It just make you think about the whole crew. Is there any good in any of them?

Two Hispanics, one of Mexican and the other of Puerto Rican heritage, felt much the same way:

I knew Fred. . . . I trusted Fred for thirty years. . . . It really hurts that Gerald didn't care. We had trust in that gentleman.

Well, my problem really wasn't the money. It was the friend-ship. It's just the damage of the friendship. It's kind of—I thought all along we was kind of friends. It's like you're sitting there and somebody pull the chair out from under you.

The Haitians, once again, got a double portion of trouble. In the first place, "Fred" had proved an unreliable neighbor for them, as he had for the other migrants who put trust in him. Nor was there any question in their minds who was at fault. The store, after all, as I noted earlier, announced itself as the Barn of Fred. It was an extension of his person and of his household, and as such it was well within the space his sense of honor and responsibility was supposed to occupy.

I was in Haiti. I had children and I had a wife, and I was told that here it was better than in Haiti. So I came here to help my children. And when I got here, Immigration got me and kept me for fifteen months in jail. The minute I came here I started working at picking oranges. I make twelve hundred sixty dollars. And then I saw everybody giving their money over there, and I put my money there. And when I went to get it, I found out that the money wasn't there. After spend-ing fifteen months in jail, the money was lost and I know that I will never make it again. I felt like I was crazy because I

knew I wasn't going to be able to make it again. Fred took
the money. And I knew he wasn't going to give it back to me.

That way of putting the case makes better sense than all the
talk of corporations and trustees and consequential damages
and breaches of fiduciary duty that American lawyers used
to debate the issue. There is this thing called Fred, and it
acts like—it proclaims itself to be—a human being with
motives and personality. "What kind of person do you think
Fred is?" I asked a Haitian man of thirty-two. "He is skillful
as the devil" was the answer. A man of about the same age
said: "Because that man stole my money, there is a poor
person in misery. Is this a human being who God created?"

All this is compounded when these real people—visible
members of the community with names like Fred and Gerald—try to make themselves invisible by crouching behind
a palisade of lawyers and legalisms. Gerald pleaded *nolo
contendere*, becoming a creature with no voice. Fred hired
an attorney to speak for him and not only claimed that he
bore no responsibility for the debts of the establishment
that bore his name but, when the assets of the store were
attached by court order, presented himself as one of the
most deserving of the store's debtors.[21]

In the second place, though, this "Fred" was not only a
personality, a thing of greed and cunning, but a representative of a whole country: "Ah, well, I was about to die. I was
so afraid. You come to a new country. You are a newcomer.
You are working hard to save money . . . and then someone
comes and does something like this. That was a miracle to
me. I couldn't believe it. The American people were supposed to help us." In a sense, the default at Fred's was experienced not only as an act of larceny and a personal assault but
as an augury of things to come. As we shall see in chapters
to follow, the sense of being betrayed is often generalized
into a feeling that people everywhere, not just a particular
one or two, cannot be relied on. That is a hard realization

for anyone, but an almost desperate one for people who live on the edge of poverty. "It's kind of got people leery of trusting anybody, you know," said a black farm worker. And a Hispanic neighbor noted: "We feel that there are not honest people here in Immokalee that you can trust. I was going to dig a hole under my house to save my money there."

Too, the sense of injustice brings a pain all its own. "I was angry. And I thought, How could they get away with it? It's not the money. It's just the thought of someone taking something. How can someone do something like that and get away with it?" This from a woman who lost $150.

Two dialogues to end with. The first is between a Haitian plaintiff and Fred Edenfield's attorney:

You seem to be tapping your left eye, and I was wondering what was the matter.

Yes, I'm sick.

Is that from the money that you lost at Fred's Barn, or an infection in the eye?

Because of the money. When I lost the money, I feel like a was crazy, like I was lost.

Are you still crying over it today?

Still. And as long as I don't receive the money, I won't feel right. I'm poor. I have children in Haiti. I have my children's children to take care of. And to lose the money to a rich man in a big country like that—for a rich man to do that to me. . . .

The second is between the woman whose words I used to begin this account ("You don't take poor people's money, you just don't do that") and a visitor with a tape recorder.

It seems particularly fitting that she should provide our closing as well.

> We was coming by all those restaurants, and we thought we saw Gerald Crawford. And everybody had been telling me he was in jail.

> Oh, he's out, he's out.

> I *knew* it was him. I told my daughter, I said, "that's him." I said, "That man is not in jail, that's him."

> Well, he was sentenced to thirty months.

> Thirty months!

> And he served about a year and a half.

> Thirty months! Thirty months! That's all he got for taking that money? Thirty months?

> Yeah. That's ten thousand dollars a month.

> Oh, Jesus. My brother stole a TV and got three years for it. . . . Thirty months! Thirty months! [She's crying now.] Oh, Jesus, thirty months. Oh, my Lord, that's not right. That's not right. Thirty months! Oh, Jesus, that's not right.

No, it isn't.

3

The View from East Swallow

PROLOGUE

In the summer of 1985 the operators of a Royal Petroleum service station on the corner of South College Avenue and East Swallow Road in Fort Collins, Colorado, discovered that they had been experiencing significant inventory shortages over a period of several years. They solved the leakage problem by replacing three "incontinent" underground tanks.

Later that year David and Patricia Losser, who lived in the first house down East Swallow Road, were alarmed by a sharp smell that seemed to fill their home. It turned out not to be natural gas, as they at first supposed, but vapors drifting to the surface from underground pools of petroleum. By year's end the Lossers had been forced to evacuate, and in the months that followed, waves of concern began to radiate in slow-motion ripples down East Swallow Drive as people came to understand that a plume of petroleum was moving eastward with the sureness of a glacier. Before long sixteen families living within the affected area (together with a handful of others who owned property in the neighborhood) brought suit against Royal Petroleum and another oil company.

East Swallow Drive is a pleasant residential street with neatly spaced ranch-style houses and comfortable backyards. To a stranger visiting in 1989, the only evidences of turmoil on that block-long stretch of homes were a fierce and incongruous chain link fence around what had been the Losser home marked by a sign warning of "danger" and an occasional monitoring well protruding from a private lawn or a public street.

The residents of East Swallow lived for the most part on modest incomes. Roughly half of them (averaging seventy-one years old) were retired, and the other half (averaging a shade under fifty) were well into what most of them would call their middle years. So it was an older group, as such neighborhoods go. Only two of the sixteen households contained younger children, and the parents in both cases were in their forties.

The East Swallow neighborhood belonged at the very center of the American social landscape occupationally: a machinist, a bookkeeper, a construction foreman, a teacher; a handful of people in sales, government service, and clerical work of one kind or another; another handful trying to make a go of home businesses.

And it belonged at the center of the American social landscape geographically. Most of the retired residents came from small towns in the Middle West (South Dakota, Iowa, Nebraska, Missouri), and while the younger residents often came from farther afield, most of them had spent their adult lives in that part of the country and expected to continue to do so. Even though the neighborhood itself was relatively new, many of the residents were living in the first homes they had ever owned, and most were living in the last homes they expected to own.

So it was an altogether familiar grouping of Americans, acquainted with hard work, tuned to small-town values, entitled to the feeling that they had earned whatever comforts and securities had come their way.

The report to follow is in most respects like the others in this volume. The troubles that visited East Swallow were of a different sort from the ones that plagued Grassy Narrows and Immokalee, but the resemblances, as we shall see, are sharp and important.

I visited East Swallow on two occasions and did some interviewing of my own, but as was by then my habit, I called upon a very able associate to do the rest of the data gathering. She conducted long interviews with thirty-one of the thirty-three people over fifteen years of age in the neighborhood, using an interview schedule that Robert Jay Lifton and I had devised for the purpose, and then, because neither of us was satisfied, she conducted follow-up interviews with twenty-three of the original thirty-one. I also had access to twenty-eight depositions, some of them of considerable length, taken by the petroleum company's lawyers.

I wrote a memorandum on the strength of my own experiences in East Swallow and the eighty-two transcripts that were by then available, and it was filed with the District Court of Larimer County as expert testimony. Up to that point the research process had been entirely familiar.

I mention all that now, however, because once my report had been filed, I asked twenty-one East Swallow residents to read copies of it sitting at home with tape recorders in their hands. When one of them was struck by a particular passage in the report, he or she was to mark the spot on the margins of the copy being read and then dictate a comment into the tape recorder. My official reason for putting so many people to so much trouble was that it would arm me with a kind of information I might need later in court. The report I had filed, of course, was a sociological profile of the plaintiff group, and I thought it would be useful to know how accurately that profile reflected the particular feelings or circumstances of each person individually.

I had other reasons, too. I had long wanted to ask a group of people whose lives I had described what they thought of my portrayal. My hope was not just to get a seal of approval on my handiwork (although I was certainly interested in that as well) but to bring the people I was writing about into the composing of their own story. I offer the results of that experiment here as a minor methodological innovation in the writing of fieldwork. Comments evoked by a reading of the report appear as footnotes in what follows at those points in the flow of the argument that originally brought them to mind.

To accommodate that objective, though, the report has to appear here in roughly its original form. This means that the present tense is used in what follows to describe events and feelings that belong to a time now past, while comments of a later date are consigned to brackets.

A REPORT ON
THE PEOPLE OF EAST SWALLOW

The residents of East Swallow, seen as a group, have been damaged appreciably by the gasoline spill and the events that followed. The apprehension and stress reported by virtually everyone in the neighborhood are a product not only of inner psychological struggles but of the fact that a good part of the immediate social world on which people depend for security and coherence—home, neighborhood, wider community—has been harmed in decisive ways.

*   *   *

The degree of dread and anxiety expressed by the plaintiff group is so sharp and so widely shared that it becomes a sociological finding as well as a clinical one, if only in the sense that it can be said to form the prevailing social temper—the culture, even—of the whole community.*

It can take the form of a tension so profound that it results in something approaching real physical distress:

> That bothers me more than anything. And I just tie up in a knot. My muscles are tight and tense and I am nervous. I can't relax, I can't enjoy myself. . . . I just tie up in such a knot that my muscles hurt. It's my muscles and my legs and my thighs and my back and my neck and shoulders. It's such a tension and I can't let go. . . . It hurts. It just plain—you can't see stress—it just hurts.

> Physically ill? Sleepless nights, if that's physically ill—yes, I have had them. Being nervous, upset, sometimes sullen, snappy—if those are physical symptoms, then I'll clarify it: Yes, I have had them. But I haven't had a big lump grow on the end of my nose. No parts have fallen off.†

---

*"When you're talking about the ongoing anxiety that everybody seems to feel around here, one thing that strikes me about that is that it's been going on for so long that you almost think that it's a normal state of affairs. For me, anyway, it just seems like something that I have to adjust to or accommodate to, and it just becomes almost like a part of myself."

"The other observation about this is that once you've been subjected to stress like this, you're less resistant to stressful situations in other aspects of your life. So in the workplace or church or wherever, things that once were pretty mundane seem to be critical—you're on edge, you are tense, you feel stretched, you know, and it happens more frequently. . . . In this situation what is happening is that every little thing—not every little thing, but lots of things—tend to cause me to feel uneasy. And I think, in large measure, over the last four years or so since we've learned of this situation, that other experiences are exacerbated by the sort of weakened resistance to the sort of shifting world around you."

†"I would say that not only does it *approach* real physical distress, but that it actually *is* physical distress. It becomes an actual illness. You get the flu. You can't function. You don't sleep. If you do sleep, you wake up very tired. . . . As the

It can take the form of an apprehension so deep that it almost dominates one's spirit.

> I don't know if I have come across with this yet or not, but I have a lot of fear, a lot of fear. I have fear for my family, I have fear for myself. I have a lot of anger. . . . I went from a human being that I felt I was an average, good, human being—caring, loving. I'm full of anger. I'm full of frustration. I'm full of fear. I have a lot of emotions. I feel that my life has gone from a normal to a real hellish, hellish situation.

> I fear for myself having been exposed to it, for my parents who are still exposed to it. Everyone in the neighborhood. I fear an explosion. That something may set off a spark and blow the entire thing up. I fear for my parents' health, my future health, what effects this may have on me.*

It can take the form of a sense of helplessness and a feeling of upset so overwhelming that it makes strong, resolute, and

---

stress level goes up and as the fear goes up, even though you may be in bed and you may actually not remember not sleeping, you wake up in the morning as if you've spent the night running."

"I've noticed in myself a lot of tension, a lot of back-of-the-neck, shoulder strain where there's just strain, where your neck hurts. At the meeting the other night the more [the lawyers] described the judge and his views and the progress of the case and that sort of stuff, the more I felt uneasy—I guess what you might call gastrointestinal distress. I even felt like I was having heart palpitations, you know, irregular heartbeat or something, just the kind of stuff where your heart's in your throat, quite literally. . . . Well, I don't know, that seems to me to be stress-related, pretty much related to the incident of talking about this dispute. And again, two days later we were talking about it and I'm sitting there and began to feel the same kind of tightness in the neck and shoulders that I had the time before."

"I think a thing to add that I have noticed more and more is that there's just a total sapping of energy. And it seems to affect me all the time, whether it's trying to get up in the morning to go to work or even do things that are supposedly recreational. It seems like increasingly everything requires a great and deliberate effort. And it wasn't that way in the past."

*"How do we know that sometime down the line—ten years, twenty years down the line—we won't both develop cancer or some other dread disease that we don't even know about yet just because of having been exposed to breathing these vapors for twelve years? We don't know. I don't think medical science can

remarkably capable men cry (this is from the deposition of a burly man of fifty used to controlling the spaces he occupies):

> No, we never wanted to sell that house. We wanted to stay. But—you got to excuse me. Shit. Excuse me. You know, hell, I can't explain this, Richard. I am like a bawling baby anymore. It is just something that happens, and I can't control it. I'm sorry. . . . But this has been pure hell. I've never experienced anything like this in my life. I never dreamed it would happen to me, but, goddamn, it did. I want to tear things up. I want to argue with people. I want to fight. And that's not me.*

And it affects the youngest members of the community every bit as much as their elders. The comments below were both made by mothers, the first speaking of a fourteen-year-old son, and the second of a six-year-old son.

> Well, he asked me the other day, "How are we in danger? We're just fine here." I said to him that we are breathing fumes and they are not good for your health and we could come up with a disease of some kind or cancer or something and he had a funny look on his face. Maybe it finally hit him. He's old enough, and you're hearing this and it's sinking in.

> I have told him that there is a gasoline spill, and we will move out to my sister's house upon indication. And they want to know why. We told them because we believe that the house is unsafe to live in. That it makes us sick and we want to stay where it is healthier. . . . [W]hen they were at my sister's

---

say with any degree of certainty at this point, and one of the scary things about it is that you just don't know."

*"This situation has never brought me personally to tears, but it has lowered my self-esteem to all-time new lows. This helplessness that's mentioned here—being not able to do anything about it. I don't feel very good about myself and this inability to do anything. Even when I try to convince myself, you know, that it's not my fault, that I can't, I somehow have this feeling that I either shouldn't have been here, or I should have been able to extricate myself better."

house and we were going to town for the day, he would say, "I don't want to go to the gas house." That's his words.

The intensity and persistence of such feelings will be no source of surprise to social and behavioral scientists familiar with accidents involving toxic poisons [or, of course, to readers of this book]. The evidence from communities that have been affected by toxic contamination together with other findings that have recently emerged from the new field of risk assessment is now quite compelling: people in general find accidents involving toxins a good deal more threatening than both natural hazards of even the most dangerous kind and mechanical mishaps of considerable destructive power. Toxic poisons clearly unnerve human beings in new and special ways.

For one thing, it is by now a familiar finding that toxic emergencies are often harder to deal with than natural ones because they are not framed by distinct beginnings or ends. The danger one is exposed to has no duration, no natural term; and as a result one remains in a permanent state of alarm and anxiety.

The plaintiff who spoke the lines below understood that point very well indeed, even if he had other things on his mind as well:

> And again, it's that uncertainty, you know. Somebody said: "Aren't you glad you weren't in the earthquake?" Well, I am. But on the other hand, if we'd been in the earthquake, it'd be over with and then you go on. . . . A few seconds and it's over with. And you start rebuilding. The good Lord kicked you in the teeth and said: "Hey, you're not as big as you thought you were. Now I've put you back down a bit and here's your chance to go again." He's always giving you a chance to come back. But this just goes on for ever and ever.*

---

*"My memory tells me that we got your report roughly around the time of the San Francisco earthquake. My aunt lives in San Jose . . . and she described the same exact feelings that we have as happening to her while the earthquake was

Moreover—another familiar observation by now—most forms of toxic poison are without substance and cannot be apprehended by the use of any of the unaided senses, and for that reason they seem especially terrifying. Gas fumes can be smelled from time to time in East Swallow, so we are not talking here about something completely beyond the reach of the senses.

Deadly smells, skunk smells. A few weeks ago we had, every day, a skunk smell downstairs just for ten seconds or so. It's like there's a ghost in the house . . . and it comes through and you can smell him and then he's gone. But you know he's still there.

Well, I've been awakened at night with the smell of gasoline, in the summer in particular. You don't know whether it's a backfiring, passing car or whatever it is. You don't know, actually, whether it's a dream or not, and you awaken and you smell [it]. So the answer is that I can't say for sure, but I know I've spent a lot of sleepless nights, a lot of flopping around.*

---

going on. It was a very long earthquake—I think it was thirty seconds, or something like that—but she had these feelings for thirty seconds, and they were terrifying, they were horrifying. There was nothing she could do and there was nowhere to go and there was nothing to make it stop. . . . And what struck me, of course, is that she had that feeling for thirty seconds. She had follow-up fears like 'Is there going to be an aftershock? What's happened to the substructure?' and those sorts of things for another period of time after the earthquake. But she didn't have it for four years at a stretch. She had it for thirty seconds. She doesn't have it forever."

"I think that the source of most of my frustration is that we feel like this has gone on and on and on, and it's never going to end. It's such a helpless feeling to be in the middle of a situation like this and to want to make other plans for what to do with your life. And you can't do it because you're tied up with not knowing whether or not you can sell the house, whether or not you can move. Do you need to be in town? Can you leave? If this was a disaster that was over and done with—a tornado or an earthquake—we would know where we stand and we could go ahead and get on with our life."

*"Yes, this is my quote and it fairly accurately describes what life was like back last summer when the windows were open and you'd think everything would be fine—weather was great, most days, you know, the air smelled sweet, it was

Neither of the above speakers lives directly over the liquid gas plume, but they and others who live at its edge share with neighbors who live right above it the realization that the occasional whiffs are really no more than intimations of all the things that might be wrong down there. The presence of odors does not begin to tell you the size of the problem, and the absence of odors is not—and under the circumstances cannot be—sufficient reassurance that everything is under control.

> You know, when you see something, when you see something coming after you, you can get out of the way. But when something is invisible, what do you do? You don't know how it's hurting you.

> I have become more worried since our last readings. I wasn't until they put the machine in and read our house twice a month. And I noticed that ours kept going up. As a matter of fact, towards the end, we were one of the higher readings. And it concerns you most because you don't know. Now, you know, if you could *smell* it, explicitly really smell it . . . then you would know. But it's a lethal weapon that you can't smell, and so you don't know what's happening. You don't know whether you're well off or bad off.

The intangibility of the gas fumes is not the only problem faced by the plaintiffs, obviously, since the uncertainties

---

fine. But then this thing would come in, this feeling, this dread, this knowledge would come in and get you. Sometimes it was triggered by a smell, and you don't know for sure. As I said in my quote, you don't know what it is. You know that gasoline is out there. You know other people are smelling it in their homes. You know that you've smelled something really strange in your home from time to time, and it wakes you up at night, this new smell. I mean, 'man, that's a good one!' And you do flop around. You do start thinking, my gosh, what have I gotten my family into here? Not very responsible and so on. I think from time to time in the background you may hear a dove cooing. We have a dove in the house, and it's not so that the dove will die first if there's gas in the house, but we have this bird and she sings sweetly and it's comforting."

introduced by the long, drawn out legal proceedings complicate matters greatly. People must live with the fact not
only that they may have been exposed to toxic poisons some
time ago but that they may still be exposed to them now
and will continue to be in time to come.

For all practical purposes, then, the accident is still in
progress, and it involves agents that are all the more dreaded
because they cannot be detected by the usual human senses.
People worry that the accident still in progress may yet
result in explosions:

> When I think I want to do something within the house or
> out in the yard I hesitate. What if I should drill holes to put
> in a post? What if I ignite something? I stop and hesitate.
> I'm very careful about that—about any trash around, any
> matches around, or anything like that. I don't want to start
> an explosion on my property.

> Scared. Scared. And especially when I found out later on
> that the fumes were on this side of the street. It's the fumes
> that can blow you up. The gasoline won't explode, but fumes
> will. . . . And you just sit here, like on a time bomb, waiting
> for whatever, I guess.*

And people worry that the accident still in progress may
have done—and may yet do—lasting harm to themselves

---

*"I, too, am frightened. I constantly think about this so-called recovery system
next to our house. The monitoring station for this system is in our backyard, and
from our house we can see the warning light, and when it comes on, you know,
signaling some kind of a malfunction in the system, it scares me to death because
I don't know what the problem is. Many nights I've gone to bed when the light's
on and been unable to sleep, wondering if the place was going to blow. I also
think about the possibility of the gas pooling at the end of our driveway, and it
scares me. I wonder when and if that's going to go on."
"I live over the liquid plume, and that's certainly one of the things we think about
a lot—the fact that there could be some kind of an accident which would blow
the entire neighborhood up."

or their loved ones.* The point is not that most plaintiffs have reason to suppose that dreadful things have already happened to them, although the great majority of them express real concerns about what the future has in store for them medically and some are convinced that the health of those who live in their households has already been affected. The problem is that they can never know what is happening to them or has already happened to them, and so they remain—despite themselves, as often as not—on constant alert:

> I know when they tested in the soil there was hydrocarbons next door in the ground, so I know it's there. I know it's locked in the soil. And the thing that bothers me here . . . is that every time something happens, especially to the children healthwise, you wonder if it isn't because of this or if it isn't aggravated by this. . . . A cold isn't just a cold. It becomes "Is this gasoline-related?" And then you get on this guilt trip wondering if it's on account of that.[†]

---

*"I worry about the toxins being absorbed in my body. Just because I can't touch, see, or hear (if you please) the sounds of gasoline vapor does not mean that those vapors are not present every day or that they will not intensify at some future date. If they intensify at some future date, they just increase the likelihood that these toxins will someday affect and shorten my life and the life of my son."

[†]"Ted and I have both been tested by a neuropsychologist, and he found cognitive impairments. He found more in Ted than in me, but he did find them in both of us. So now we know that we were not wrong when we felt that we were not functioning as we should have been functioning, that our abilities were being impaired to some degree by this situation in which we're being forced to live. . . . But as you say here, even after you *know* it's happened, we don't know *what's* happening. So we still remain in this state of constant alert, constant fear. We know now that we have these impairments, but we don't know whether they're permanent, we don't know whether or not they're not permanent, we don't know whether they'll get well. We feel now like they're worse than they were when we were tested, so all these things make it worse and worse all the time."

"The last few days I've been experiencing some neck pain, some joint pain, some muscle pain—feeling almost like my bones are coming through my skin. I'm not otherwise sick. I don't feel bad enough, really, that I need to go to a doctor about this. But it has crossed my mind. Yes, what if this is some kind of symptom that is caused by having gasoline contamination on our property or in our house? . . . What if some of this is being caused by gasoline contamination? That does cross my mind."

I mean no tests have been done on my property. I don't
know whether it's contaminated or not. . . . I have a regular
physical every year. No big deal. I'm always overweight but
healthy, you know—that kind of stuff. But the last time I
went in I had a raised liver count on one enzyme. No big
deal. Just one thing. Just barely. But then you think "Oh
shit, could it be from the—" I mean I'm not supposed to be
exposed to it, but maybe I am.

All of these feelings together form a community climate
that is the context for the other points I plan to make here.

Members of the plaintiff group report a very strong sense
of being out of control, of being caught up in forces that
capture them and take them over. They feel helpless, pushed
around, worked over, pummeled.*
   These feelings of helplessness and vulnerability are so common in moments of crisis, as we noted earlier, that they are
one of the identifying psychological symptoms of "trauma"
and a prominent feature of what is now widely called "the
disaster syndrome." But they have a special urgency in places
like East Swallow—first because toxic poisons are still absorbed into the very tissue of the neighborhood, leaving the

---

"It's only been in the last year that I've noticed what seemed like allergic reactions—
my nasal passages plugged up, coughing, throat congestion, and so on—which
would come on suddenly and last for quite a while or hang on for days at a time
sometimes. I've never had that sort of thing in my life. And it was only after talking
with the Thomases and some other people who had similar symptoms that I began
to think, gee, maybe this really is due to those low-level gasoline vapors that are
hanging around here. But you can never know for sure."
   ". . . just little things that people have, like a cold—all of a sudden we start to
wonder if it's related to the gasoline and if it has some other hidden meaning or
some other particular effect on us."
   *"Sometimes I think I'm standing on the edge of my own life, watching other
people in charge making what should be my decisions and my choices. And you
feel so darned helpless. You're stuck and you're trapped in a situation not of your
own making or choosing and you can't do one thing about it."

persons who live there vulnerable, and second because the slowness of all efforts to find redress leaves them more or less frozen in place, unable to take charge of their own destinies or even to cope effectively. Plaintiffs speak of being "hostages" or "prisoners," of being "besieged" and "trapped":*

> A disaster. I'd say it's a neighborhood of pretty unhappy, hurting people, stuck in a situation that they can't get out of. . . . We feel helpless. We feel trapped. We feel—you have no control, no control.†

It is hard to think of a more basic tenet of the American way—and maybe even especially for those who come from small towns and farms, as the majority of these plaintiffs do—than that individuals should be independent and self-reliant, free to chart their own lives, to take care of their own families, and to command the spaces they earn title to.

---

*"Of the words up here—'hostage,' 'prisoner,' 'besieged,' and 'trapped'—I think I personally like 'trapped,' because trapped is definitely how I feel. Going on day to day with existence, with work and carrying on a routine, but trapped in it. Not thinking about being able to do anything different, even having the ability to do anything different. I know, we develop this kind of small-business mentality where we depend basically on ourselves. What we have, we have achieved because we've worked hard. If we did something more, we worked a little harder. We did a good job, we succeeded. Cause and effect. But we're in a situation now that we can't work ourselves out of. Don't really know how to handle it. It isn't just a matter of buckling down, doing a little bit extra, nose to the grindstone—whatever other clichés I can throw in there. We cannot seem to work ourselves out. And that was the only way that we have ever known to confront a situation. So that's why I come back to the word 'trapped.' "

†"I would concur that we are living in a neighborhood of unhappy, hurting people. My neighbors, basically, are afraid to even talk or communicate for fear that anything we say is going to be admissible as evidence in court, and it makes it very hard for us to communicate with one another about our true feelings about the devastation, the psychological devastation, as a result of this gasoline leak. I do not feel comfortable in going to my next-door neighbor and say, 'Hey, today I am really feeling anxious and I'm really feeling angry about this damn lawsuit.' If I do, and they're asked to say, 'Well, what have you heard about this lawsuit from your neighbors?' they will be forced to testify on anything that I say or tell them. We are becoming a neighborhood of very closed, almost paranoidlike people, and people's tempers are just on the surface."

Most of the people of East Swallow have lived by that ethic and have worked very, very hard to achieve its benefits. To find one's family, one's home, even one's livelihood jeopardized after so many years of sacrifice can be demoralizing if not crippling—all the more so if one has reached or is on the verge of retirement. Lungs and homes and struggling businesses are all made fragile when an accident like the gasoline spill takes place, but it is important to remember that a dream and a promise—emerging from the very heart of this country—are endangered, too. Such an outcome can damage the spirit, and it clearly has done so here.

That, at any rate, is the background one has to keep in mind when one hears people speak of the uncertainties with which they now live:

> But then there's no choice, so you're caught in a situation where you have no control. You're completely uncertain about health risks as well as the stability of the investment you have in the home, you know, so that first few months after we learned of the spill was a time of stress, worry, anxiety, and, frankly, not a whole lot of sleeping.

> We could sort of chart our own destiny . . . [but] we just feel like we're kind of adrift in the sea right now, and that there really isn't anything that we can do because our lives are just on hold, waiting for this problem to be resolved. So we've really lost control of the whole situation, and our options are so limited.*

---

*"I really think this whole business comes down to a matter of the illusion of control, where you really think that you're in control in your life. You believe that you're making decisions, that you're guiding your own destiny, that you're going the way you want to go, that you and your family discuss these things and make choices. And I suppose that's never really true. Certainly, when you get in a situation like the one we're in, you can see that it is just an illusion that you're in control; things are going on around you that you don't have a hand in. But that innocence, that sense that you really can be in control—making choices, captain of your own destiny, and all that stuff—that's an important value to have and a wonderful feeling to regain. And once in a while, now, we get a glimpse of what

Or when one hears of the frustration they experience as a result of the fact that they are unable to reach out and help shape the world around them:

> I've always kind of been one of these hotshot tough guys, so to speak, that thought I could handle just about everything. . . . It got to me. The dam broke. I was so damned beside myself, I cried, I screamed, I did whatever. I don't know what all happened. And then after I thought about it—I don't know how many days—I turned into a bawling and babbling idiot, and I'm still that way a lot of times. You know, I'm not used to not being able to correct the damned situation.

Or of the embarrassment and stress and even shame they experience when they feel they have not adequately cared for their own families:

> It's made me think if I were more successful I could just move my family away from this and deal with it at arm's length. . . . [I]t's really made me second guess a lot of things that I've done and made me feel less than adequate about my ability to take care of my family.*

> It's like everything's on hold until we can get out of here and get on with our lives. . . . That's been much of my stress, because I feel I've taken a lot of pride in my life of being able to provide for my family and work. And in the last two or

---

that will be like, you know. You feel in control again. Once in a while you kind of forget these things a little bit, and that's a great feeling. But then you're snapped right back to the reality that, no, wait a minute, other people may be in control of their lives, but certainly there's evidence that you don't have any say over what's going on here."

   *"This was touched upon [earlier], but I think it bears reiterating. At least for me, [there was] a real sense of failure that I couldn't have somehow anticipated this or if I was more successful that I could've handled it quicker on my own . . . you know, moved my family away and then taken care of it. But it tends to make one feel not very good about oneself."

three years we've gone downhill to the point where that's just been a constant worry.

And, in general, of the feeling—shared in one degree or another by almost every plaintiff—that one's very life is in suspension, on hold. They feel that their feet are no longer planted on secure ground, that they are no longer connected to a secure place, that they are being held in midair by circumstances that keep them captive, that their very lives have stopped:*

That's one real dramatic change that the gas spill brings to your life—your life ceases. You just don't do anything except wait for the gas spill situation to end so that you can begin doing normal things again.

. . . I would say you could kind of sum that up by saying I have lost my life. And that sounds real melodramatic, but that's exactly how I feel. As far as I am concerned, the gas companies—both of them—have deprived me of my ability to live a life. They have chosen. They dictate. They tell me, indirectly, exactly what I can and cannot do, which is noth-

---

*"I agree, you just sort of live your life on hold. I'm always saying, 'God, will it ever end so we can get on with our lives?' You can't really make any plans, you just sort of live your life in limbo. Sometimes it's almost unbearable. It's like you really don't live, you just sort of exist, and you wait and you wait and you wait for it to end. But it doesn't, so you just struggle through each day and you worry. You know, it's really, really a pretty sad way to have to live."

"I'm forty-four going on forty-five, and these are supposed to be the prime years of my life. A few years ago . . . things just seemed to be going right. And now everything has been just put on the stop button, and that's where it stays. These years have been taken away. Even if this is worked out and I can find a place to live and to work that is the same as this or equivalent to this and is equitable, they're still not going to be able to restore the last four years to me. I feel like we've been robbed. And four years, the way this is going, just may be the tip of the iceberg."

"And here we are. For five years we've been through nothing but problems, problems, problems, and the stress of it all is very, very sad. It makes you wonder what's gonna happen next, what we're into, when we'll ever get out of it. We've just been living in a dead space. The time has just gone dead on us."

ing. My entire ability to choose a lifestyle has been taken away from me.

The residents of East Swallow who were exposed to the effects of the gasoline spill complain—with considerable justice, one has to assume—that the value of their homes has declined precipitously as a result of recent events.* In one sense, of course, that is a financial matter and outside the scope of this report: plaintiffs have invested large amounts of capital into the dwellings they occupy, and they are understandably concerned about the safety of those investments. For many, maybe most of them, it is not just a matter of losing a valuable possession; it is a matter of placing a life's savings at risk.

Well, it doesn't make me feel sick or it doesn't make me feel nervous to the extent that my hands shake, but when we think about the loss of our property, the value of our property, it concerns us very much. Most of our estate is in that home. . . . [I]f we would lose our property, if it would be

---

*"Now my wife and I have thought about this question of the value of our home very carefully, and to be quite frank with you, we cannot imagine how this house has *any* value. We've thought about what to do—how to get out of it, how to sell it, how to recoup, how to bounce back, how, how, how to make something out of this on our own. And we cannot think of a way to do it. . . . The value of this home has not 'declined precipitously,' as you indicate. It has gone to the bottom. . . . It has no value. And we can't think of a way to make it have value other than through the lawsuit that we're pursuing."

"When we bought this house, we intended to spend probably the rest of our lives here. We were hoping that we wouldn't ever have to move again. And now we find—in talking with our realtor a few weeks ago, we asked him what the value of this house would be if indeed it could be sold at all, and he said, 'I wouldn't touch it.' He said, 'I don't think it can be sold right now because of the contamination.' And he was very up front about it. So that means, in effect, that we have lost a considerable amount of money, not to mention the psychological stress that we've been under because of the contamination."

"Since the time of my deposition the house has been professionally appraised, and the report lists the property—because of the existing gas situation—as having no value. That has put a stigma on our home that will make it unacceptable as a place of residence for a period of time unknown to me."

condemned and we move out, it's possible that we would lose everything we own.

Well, we feel that the value of our property has taken a nose dive. It is our only security. We don't feel that it's salable. If we can't sell it, we can't relocate, we can't move, we can't expand or change. We feel that we're sort of stuck.

But it is also clear that the people of East Swallow have invested a great deal more than money in their homes. They have invested great quantities of time, energy, skill, devotion, pride. They have invested a part of themselves, in short, and when something happens to that property, the part of the self that was thus invested is at risk. People experience damage done to the homes they cherish as damage to themselves.

It is well understood by social and behavioral scientists who are familiar with accidents of this kind that the loss of a home can be profoundly traumatic. I wrote in my report on the Buffalo Creek flood of 1972, for example, that a home in which a person has made a real personal investment "is not simply an expression of one's taste; it is the outer edge of one's personality, a part of the self itself. And the loss of that part of the self . . . is akin to the loss of flesh." Other researchers have come to the same general conclusion. A well-known study of a tornado in Texas, for instance, reported that people who had lost their homes felt as though "they had lost part of themselves." And an equally well-known study of an urban relocation project in the East End of Boston was entitled, simply, "Grieving for a Lost Home."*[1]

---

*"One of the more interesting things in the report that I found was the quote about the house being the outer edges of one's personality, a part of the self itself. The threat to our home has bothered us so much. I used to think that maybe Margy and I were kind of out of line to be so wrapped up in our homes, so involved in it. To see that this is something that's recognizable and that other people have suffered, other people feel, makes us feel a lot better. . . . This house

The East Swallow plaintiffs have not—yet—lost their homes, and I do not mean to suggest that they have suffered in the same way as the people of Buffalo Creek. But the feelings they experience are of the same kind. Those who assume that they will need to move elsewhere to resume a normal and healthy life are grieving for lost homes even while they remain resident in them. And those who expect to remain are acutely aware that damage may have been done to their homes and has certainly been done to the land on which they stand. In either event, the damage is experienced as an insult to and an assault on the persons who live in it. To a sociologist, then, the complaints expressed by the residents of East Swallow speak of injuries to their sense of personal security and pride as well as injuries to their purses. And such injuries are felt all the more sharply in places like East Swallow because so many of the residents expected to live out their lives in the shelter of those homes.

The woman who said in an interview, "I have sadness thinking that we might have to leave; we've put a lot of work into this house and I really don't want, really, anyone else to live here," is very clearly speaking of something far more than a possession. The home she thinks she will have

---

was a hobby. Basically, from the time we got in here, we changed it, we remodeled it, we shaped it, we molded it; we took out ceilings, we took out walls, we added on here, we added on there. It wasn't just a matter of, you know, that we kept it up nicely. It constantly changed, and therefore, it stayed new, and it stayed vital and kind of exciting. There was always something new to do, a new project to do, trying to find that perfect balance. . . . [But] with this we basically stopped working on the house. We maintain it, especially outside, but definitely don't want or feel that we can put any more money or time in it. . . . We see things running down, and it's not the way that we wanted our house to be—it's not the way we wanted our lives to be—and it hurts. . . . And we're still here. If we moved away and didn't have to watch it, I suspect it wouldn't be so bad, but it's kind of like having somebody in your family with some slow degenerative disease and you're sitting there watching them fade away. That might sound melodramatic, but that's the way we feel. We feel like the house is dying around us, and there's so much time and energy and money and love that's been put into it, it's really, really sad to see."

to leave is a part of her, an extension of her person. The two persons quoted below, a wife and a husband in early middle age, share that feeling deeply:

> Our home has always been our castle. We feel very good about it, and it houses everything we have. Our whole lives are right here. We've always felt good about it. And now to feel that it *isn't* good—that's hard to deal with. . . . And I have this feeling that if I move away then somebody else is going to come in and they're going to benefit from everything I put in it. And it's *mine!* I don't want to give it to you!

> It's become—it's a dwelling, it's not what it was. It was kind of—I don't know—it was sort of an integral part of our life, it was almost like a friend. It's just a house now. When everyone else was, you know, building up a little equity and then moving onto the next new trendy neighborhood, we just kind of stayed where we were and shaped it to ourselves.

To many plaintiffs, it is almost as if the home, once having been a living thing, is now dead or dying.* There is no point in breathing any kind of personality or distinctive character into it, of continuing the process of shaping it to one's needs and preferences, because no one knows how much it has been depreciated in any of the several senses of that term. In this respect, too, life is on hold:

> [Y]ou hate to put all the work into it and not know what's going to come out. I mean there's things I'd like to do. I

---

*"One of the problems we have is that in the bottom floor—essentially a sort of half basement in the sense that it's got windows that are just barely above the ground level—we have tiles that are coming off the floor in various places, and that's a problem that has gotten progressively worse over the last two years. And I always wonder why they are coming off at this time. Is it just simply that the glue or whatever adhesive that was holding the tiles on is just aging and cracking? Is it that the tiles are just for no good reason kinda curling up and coming off? Or is it perhaps that there is a slight amount of hydrocarbon vapor permeating the concrete and loosening the tiles and making them come off?"

mean I'd like to paint the house. I'd like to dig up a couple
of trees and plant some others. But by the same token, I
don't know what's going to happen. I'd hate to put in all
that work and then the place blow up or something.

Just lethargic. We used to always do things in the house.
Obviously we don't want to do it anymore because of the
situation. At Christmas time we went out and bought a
limited edition print. We can't do anything permanent in the
house, so we'll get a nice picture. We had it framed, we got
it back, it was finally done on about our anniversary. It's
sitting in the bedroom on the floor. Haven't put it up. Just
haven't felt like doing it. . . . Why bother, you know.*

The long and anxious wait for some kind of resolution,
moreover, is made all the more difficult by the fact that, to
begin with, people are afraid of their homes and see them
as places of danger, and yet, paradoxically, are afraid to leave
them for anything more than a few short stretches of time.
It can be a painful dilemma. On the one hand, the home
may be so perilous that it is unfair to expose other people—
children particularly—to it:

I don't want [my children] to be in here at all, really, any
more. I feel that they're better off if I visit them. It's a fear
that is intangible.

I used to do a lot of babysitting for friends. Younger people
that would like to go out, I would babysit their kids and
they would bring them to my house. Then I thought if there

---

*"I'm not as attached to the house as some of the people quoted [here], but I
feel like I'm in a quandary because I would either like to be able to sell it and get
out of here, or I would like to be able to upgrade it and remodel it and make it
more suitable to our present needs. And I feel just like the quote: Why upgrade
it? It would be money wasted. That's exactly the way I feel. . . . So essentially I
feel I am obligated to live in a house that's not quite the way I want it, and at the
same time I cannot sell it or get out of it without a tremendous financial loss. So
it's like being between a rock and a hard place rather literally."

are fumes around here that I am not detecting, could they
possibly be harmful to somebody's child? . . . So I don't keep
these children any more.

I would like to use my yard for parties and things [but] I just
don't feel like—you always kind of have to think: "Should I
expose other people to possible contamination by having
them over?"

On the other hand, people are afraid to leave the house
exactly because they appreciate how many things could go
wrong in their absence. The speaker above who described
her reluctance to invite her children to the house also said:

I've gotten to be more or less of a recluse. I'm frightened to
leave for fear something might happen. . . . Like I was almost
a prisoner. Almost a hostage, more or less. Keeping me here
because I'm frightened to go away. . . . I'm scared to death
to leave this property.

That is a familiar feeling in the neighborhood. "You cannot
go out of town and really be at peace of mind about whether
your property is going to be there or something else is
going to happen until you get back," said one man at his
deposition. "What are you worried is going to happen?" he
was asked. "Fire, explosion, whatever," was the answer.
Another neighbor said:

And it's an awful feeling to leave your house and in your
mind wonder: "Is the house going to be here when we come
back?" We don't dare take a vacation, we just don't dare.

So people find themselves trapped in homes they no
longer value or even trust. What ought to be a hearth, a safe
haven, a source of pride, a place of comfort, now becomes
something spoiled, dangerous, and even hateful—a process
Michael Edelstein calls "the inversion of home":[2]

Well, yeah, [my feelings] have gone a hundred and eighty degrees in that we just don't enjoy the home any more. It's not a thing of pleasure. It's just a big albatross to us. . . . There just isn't any enjoyment there. Well, it's just turned into a complete nightmare. I don't think any of the neighbors enjoy their homes any more. And we're all just looking forward to the day that we can turn the key and walk away.

The house doesn't have the love and the care and everything that goes into making a home anymore. The yard doesn't. Our whole lifestyle has changed from tender loving care to being with something you're fearful of, something you resent, something you lose interest in.

One resident of East Swallow—speaking, without having that in mind, for all her neighbors—summed the matter up perfectly:

One of the major ways is by not feeling that we could live there safely. . . . Also the fear of the vapors, the fear of the gasoline odors—never knowing how strong they may be, never knowing when they may appear, never knowing how strong they may be, never knowing if they become explosive. You don't have friends over, you don't have your children have their friends over, you don't want to encourage others to expose themselves to harm. You don't enjoy or even have any desire to maintain your property and increase its value because you feel that it has no value because of the gasoline spill and the contamination underneath it. Why make it more refined? Why upgrade it? It would be money wasted.

Sociologists and other social and behavioral scientists have known for a long time that a secure sense of community is important to the well-being of people in general. Individuals may vary in the strength of their need for communal structures, but the longing for and dependence on some form of communality can be said to be natural for hu-mankind. It is a fair rule of thumb, moreover, that people who come from rural and smalltown backgrounds, as most of the East Swallow plaintiffs do, feel a greater need to gather together into continuing communities than is the case for people of a more urban background.

The East Swallow neighborhood is not a long-standing, traditional community as is the case for New England vil-lages, Appalachian hollows, or even the midwestern farm communities from which so many of the plaintiffs have come. Most of the residents seem to favor neighborhoods in which a fair degree of social distance is observed and a sense of individual privacy respected, but, at the same time, in which one can count on a caring and warm human sur-rounding. "We did not socialize . . . a whole lot," said one woman, "and yet if somebody went someplace and needed to have a paper picked up or mail picked up, any of us would have been willing to do it." And another woman, expressing views common to the majority of her neighbors, said:

> I don't have what you call a back-door policy of neighboring, you know—run in and out, chummy all the time. No, I can't say that. We are all friendly and speak to one another and usually at the mailbox or something like that. No, we're not chummy neighbors.

Still, it is clear that most of them are what the mountain folk of Appalachia often call "neighbor people." That is, they seek communal settings in which persons can be counted on to look after one another, to share a feeling of neighborli-ness, and together to form a buffer zone behind which they can feel safe and comfortable. It is an old dream for many, and especially those who move to new neighborhoods with the expectation of spending their final years there. So the story of East Swallow is not that of a place with a long past, now disrupted; it is the story of a place with an emerging future, now threatened. The loss is of a different kind, but it is a sharp and painful one all the same.

A sense of community depends upon a sense of place. A community is grounded. It has location. It belongs to, is a part of, a given territory.* Nothing could be clearer from the available evidence, however, that the residents of East Swallow see the space in which their community is located as soiled and contaminated in some profoundly disturbing way, and such a perception can hardly help but disrupt the feelings of communality that are so crucial a part of neighborly living. It is "a disaster area," "a misery," "a dump." Not every resident of East Swallow would agree with the young woman who called it "the most horrible place in the world," but all would acknowledge that they are now part of what seems to be a blighted, half-ruined landscape.†

Something foul has worked its way into the very atmosphere of the community. Everything seems dirtied, contaminated, polluted:

---

*"The phenomenon that surprises me so much is that each of us has neighbors—each of us who live on the north side of Swallow at least—has neighbors to the back of us or to the side who are measurably just as close to the plume, in just as much danger as we are, and who don't see it. The function of living on a street that faces the other direction somehow acts as a barrier in mind if not in geohydrology. The vapor plume can and does extend under their homes, and yet they don't see it. . . . Those of us only a few feet away [from them] are tense and nervous, and those people who have yet to see the problem aren't. And yet they're in tremendous danger."

†"On the concept of neighborhood, what used to be a bunch of people in homes in a neighborhood of their choice has become a group of people who now have dwellings that are basically situated at a toxic waste site. It will never be the same. This neighborhood cannot be the same, regardless of cleanup efforts, be they successful or not. If there's a wholesale migration from the neighborhood following a successful conclusion to this litigation, or merely people giving up and dwindling away with the unsuccessful conclusion to it, the neighborhood will never be the same. And if some people choose to stay or are unlucky enough that that's their only alternative, they will never ever feel the same about the neighborhood again. That neighborhood died with this problem. It hasn't necessarily been buried yet, but the neighborhood is dead."

. . . The neighborhood, I mean it's really deceptive. It's like looking at someone who has cancer and you think they look healthy on the outside but you know they are not. That is the way this neighborhood is. I like the house, I like the location, but I don't like the fact that it's on contaminated ground.

Everyone in the community assumes that substantial quantities of gasoline are still to be found in the land under their feet, gathering in dangerous pockets underground, continuing to migrate, and ready to do further harm.* The place is not only contaminated, then, but dangerous, requiring people to live with thoughts like these:

At one time my sprinkler system became disengaged . . . so consequently, the west section of my lawn started to dry out. And then I really investigated and found out and had it repaired. But in the interim I was scared to death someone would throw a cigarette on my lawn . . . and cause the neighborhood to go up. Really, I was frantic.

The uncertainty, I think. . . . For instance, they are doing work over on the Foothills Fashion Mall, which is south of our home, and they have an enormous trench dug over

---

*"[W]e don't know for sure exactly, at this point—I don't know anyway—where the gasoline really is. Last summer's charts showed that it was under Matthew Street and down the middle of Swallow and part of the way into the cul-de-sac; at that point the vapor, the liquid plume, hadn't migrated underneath our property. But that doesn't mean that that's true now. That was a year ago. . . . But with the instability of the subsoil in this area, it makes it very difficult to know exactly where it is. . . . And that's difficult to live with because you don't know whether the place is real dangerous. I mean, if I go out in my front yard and I dig a hole to plant a bush, am I going to set off an explosion? Or am I going to have stuff oozing all over my front yard? I don't know that, you know, and that kind of stuff is difficult to live with."

"I, too, have a lot of apprehension and fears. As long as any gasoline remains underground within the proximity of my home, I have the fear that that gasoline and petroleum can possibly, and maybe very likely, for all I know, migrate just a few feet across the street and come on into the cul-de-sac, and we would also be sitting over a liquid plume. I fear that, with the rise and fall of the groundwater, this is very likely to happen."

there—I would guess six feet or so deep. I saw a man standing in it. . . . He was working down inside this trench and
he was smoking a cigarette. . . . And, frankly, I was terrified
to be walking by while he was smoking. . . . I mean it was
very scary not knowing whether I was going to explode
walking by.

It is easy to appreciate that when one lives with such
preoccupations as those, uncertainty and fear become the
prevailing moods of the community—a constant, nagging,
persistent worrying about what has happened in the past
and what might yet happen in the future. "We're living
over a time bomb," people say; "we're sitting on a stick of
dynamite," we're "standing in quicksand."

On the one hand, the residents of the neighborhood have
forged a new closeness in the process of facing such adversity
together. The event "has certainly brought us closer together
as a neighborhood," said one resident, "it's been, really, a
positive thing in that sense."* But that blessing, on the other
hand—if indeed one can even call it that—has a bitter edge.
For one thing, it increases the size of the circle of those
whose troubles one must share and take into account:

And since the gas spill, we have been forced to become more
intimate. And, in a way, that's actually going to make it worse,

---

*"Well, I do think that you've hit this business pretty clearly on the head here
with the idea of neighbor people. People seek communal settings. I think people
have enjoyed knowing their neighbors in this community and, in a kind of perverse
way, have enjoyed the opportunity that the gasoline spill has given us all to break
down barriers and get to know other people. But then you know them, and you
know the tremendous strain everybody's under. You can see the progress of this
tension and stress on people. I was thinking—it was last night at a meeting,
looking at these folks—that we've known them for four years and they looked like
they've aged ten years. And you know, I'm not sure I'm happy to be in on that
kind of a stress product. But it is nice to get to know people, and people do want
to know each other and they do want to have that feeling of friendliness and you
do get a sense of community when . . . you can feel good about the fact that there's
a connection among us all. And that's real good. So, yeah, I think about all that
sort of stuff, and I think we are neighbor people."

because now when I worry, I don't just have [my family] to worry about, I have the Owens and the Browns and the Overtons and . . . If you don't have a neighborhood that is homogeneous and engages in coffee klatch type activities, then you wouldn't know all those things about other people. And you wouldn't know how badly their lives have been affected by the same thing that's been destroying my life.

And, maybe more to the point, neighborhood gatherings are so focused on the spill and the miseries it later caused that the normal affairs of everyday life—the kinds of things neighbors usually discuss over the back fence—scarcely ever enter the conversation. The accident has moved into the center of the community's sense of itself:*

> I think as far as the neighbors are concerned, it's brought us closer to them than probably we would have. That's kind of a mixed blessing, you know. I mean it's been nice to get to know all the other people here, but the circumstances for it are not always pleasant, so a lot of times when we do get

---

*"Yes, it's true that we know our neighbors better now than we used to, and we feel like there is a common bond that unites us. On the other hand, it has also served as a reminder of what it is that we're all going through. The first summer that we were all involved in this litigation, the Bremers had a party, and it was for the people who were involved in the lawsuit. And we all went, and it was kind of fun, you know. We had a barbecue, and we all got to talk to each other and all of that sort of thing, and it was really kind of a good party. But then last summer, when there was another party that was going to be for the same people, I just didn't feel like going because I felt like—oh, you know, it's just a reminder that it's been a whole year and we still haven't gotten any farther than we were before, and we still don't know any more than we did then, and we're still stuck in the situation. And I don't want to get together with these people and just commiserate. I mean, that's not an awful lot of fun. And I think it was a feeling almost of avoidance rather than wanting to be with this group of people; it's because being with them reminds us of the futility of this situation and the helpless feeling."
"We're kind of unique in the neighborhood in that we moved into this house and found out about the gas spill a few weeks later. I have no sense of what the neighborhood was like before the spill, but it's certainly brought us closer together and made us a cohesive group. You know, sometimes I realize I don't even know what these people are like. I met them after this disaster, and I only see the angry, hurting side of them."

together it's—instead of fun or chit chat, it's commiserating a little bit about our problems and that sort of thing.

In part, then, the neighborhood came together and became stronger in the course of what most of its members consider a real struggle, and the irony of the situation is that the success of that community may very well mean its dispersal.*

People in society are insulated emotionally, so to speak, by layers of human warmth that surround them like concentric circles. The first of those circles, obviously, is the one occupied by the family niche. And the second, just as obviously, is occupied by the immediate neighborhood. Both of these inner layers of comfort and support have been greatly damaged in East Swallow by the spill and the events surrounding it. The home no longer has the feel of a family hearth.† and the neighborhood is now held together in the most fragile of ways—not by the bonds of communality but by the urgency of a disaster.**

The third circle of support is supplied by the wider human community, and I turn to that matter now.

---

*"We know more and more about each other, and we find out more and more that we feel the same pains and we've suffered the same ways. So . . . we are, certainly, facing the problem of: If this ever ends and we get out of here, and if we don't all move to the same block, it's going to be very difficult to maintain a relationship on a neighbor level. [W]e're going to have these friendships that we've formed very abruptly terminated or, if not terminated, at least dramatically changed."

†"I certainly agree with the statement that the home no longer has the feel of a family hearth. For some reason, when I was reading that, the image that came to mind was something like a devil with a trident coming out of the hearth, representing, in effect, the gasoline fumes. The safety that one normally associates with home is certainly largely being destroyed by the presence of the invisible gasoline fumes."

**"The point is also well taken—and I agree with it—that the bond of the community is more than inherent friendship; it's just essentially caused by the urgency of disaster as is stated here. . . . In my case, I feel constrained even about talking on that subject because I know that a neighbor could be turned as a witness against me if I actually tell him anything substantive. So . . . I have to feel always very careful about what I say because whatever I say can be held against me, and I think that really gets in the way of friendships."

* * *

I noted earlier that the gas spill produces even greater amounts of pain and stress (a) because, for all practical purposes, the accident is still in progress, and (b) because the toxic gasses doing the harm are so impalpable and ghostlike. That is a clear finding not only in East Swallow but in virtually every other community that has experienced a comparable event.

It is clear, too, that people who are victimized by such events feel a special measure of distress when they come to think that their affliction was caused by other human beings. And that sense of injury becomes all the sharper and more damaging when those other human beings respond to the crisis with what is seen as indifference or denial.* One of the clearest findings to emerge from the data now available on the people of East Swallow is that everyone—and this time I really mean everyone—shares the view, whatever else may be said about the matter, that the oil companies have acted irresponsibly if not cruelly both at the time of the gas spill and since.†

Persons who manage corporations (or, more to the point,

---

*"In all of these years that the spill has been going on, not once has anyone said. 'Hey, we spilled gasoline under your street and, gee, we're sorry and we'd like to help you clean it up.' Nobody has ever said that. It's been a matter of seeing how much they can cover up and how much they can get away with and how they can still come out smelling like a rose without ever putting out any effort to alleviate the problem. I just don't think that's right."

†"Indeed, the toxic gases every day continue to impact my life in a harmful way. Today it's the vapor plume. Tomorrow it may be the liquid plume. The anger probably is intensified greatly by the fact that the gasoline company—companies, I should say—are trying their hardest to show that there's no problem living in an area that's been contaminated by gasoline. This truly reflects their indifference to other human beings. This level of insensitivity makes me angrier and angrier and angrier every time I think about it. . . . They have the feeling like they're up there and we're down here—that they're gods and we're peasants, and that it's perfectly OK to have disrupted totally our lives. . . . They are not looking at how terribly we have been impacted both psychologically and physically from this gasoline spill."

perhaps those who are hired to defend them) generally speak of them as if they were *things*, bloodless and inorganic. But victims of accidents rarely forget, even when company officials manage to, that corporate decisions are made by human beings and that corporate policies reflect the views of human beings. When Ken Anderson et al encounter Royal Petroleum et al, it is people meeting people.*

The first reaction people have to that kind of distance is often one of puzzlement and amazement. It is hard to believe, at first, that anything of the sort can happen:

> I was just so flabbergasted that these people had put gas underneath our house and were lying about it for awhile. And even when they stopped lying about it they still didn't want to do anything about it. I just couldn't believe that. It was so frustrating to me. It still is, but back then I just couldn't believe it.

But that bewilderment can ripen into a real fury when people realize that no human response is likely to be forthcoming. It is experienced almost as a form of betrayal. One problem is that the oil companies sometimes seem as if they were a bit out of control themselves:

> Well, they're playing with my life and everybody's life here, in trying to figure out a way to do something that they don't know anything about. And I think it's unfair to us.

Incompetence, however, is far and away the gentlest charge people are ready to level at the oil companies. Because the

---

*"This is one thing that I noticed in the depositions of myself, my wife, and my daughter. All three of us, at times, referred to the lawyers taking the depositions as 'you, the people who caused this,' and the lawyers were very quick to point out it wasn't them, it was the corporation. But I think the lawyers should take it upon themselves to realize that they're representing the goddamned people that did this and they oughta recognize that they're part of the problem just like everybody else that spilled the gas."

point is so important—and the language in which it is expressed so telling—let me just let the plaintiffs speak for a moment without interruption:

> We have never seen a soul [from Royal Petroleum or any other defendant]. Not us. Not one. No, no one, no one. I guess no one cares. That's my opinion. You know, "I'm going to make money up here on the corner and I don't care if you get blown up or not." That's true, I think. I don't understand people like that. . . .

> Anger, resentment. . . . I'm sure from what I've heard and read that even if you get on to a gasoline spill immediately there's not much chance of cleaning it up totally . . . but just to have made some concerted effort to have cleaned it up would have made me *feel* better about the gasoline company. That at least they had some empathy and care about the contamination in a residential area. They seemed to be so callous. . . . They seem to have no moral conscience.

> I get angry, I really get furious, because here we are, six little families on, like, an island, on Swallow Road, and we are going through all this stress and nobody gives a damn. The city doesn't care, the Court doesn't give a damn. The people you represent . . . should be helping us. We're not young people, none of us. We're middle-aged and elderly, and all we wanted was to live here and mind our own business. And look at the mess we're in, through no fault of ours. . . . Why aren't the people who are responsible for it trying to help us instead of making us go through this? Why aren't they just saying, "We're sorry, it wasn't done deliberately. What can we do to get you out of there and put you back where you were before this leak?" That's all we've ever asked for. . . . My God, there is only that one little block. Why haven't they done anything to help us? Why are they fighting us?

> My feeling about their attitude [is that] it seems to be a total amorality. . . . "We're making our money. So their kids get

leukemia. So they get liver cancer. It's okay. We're getting a dollar twelve a gallon for gas."

I mean the blood is pounding in your neck when you listen to these people from the oil companies explain—almost whining, you know—that they just have invested so much money and they can just not afford to take care of these problems, and oh, my gosh. Well, what about the people who are living here in this neighborhood? I mean, talk about investing. We haven't invested ten percent or five percent or three percent of our assets. We've invested sixty, seventy, eighty, and ninety percent of our assets, and some of the people here are eighty years old. . . . It makes you angry. And frankly, [my wife] and I have said to each other that probably the oil company is just waiting for these people to die, thinking that their heirs will not care as much and won't want to carry through in trying to get this thing resolved.

Such feelings can infuriate people (often to the point, it may be worth noting, that they create new energy for exactly the kind of legal action the corporation feared to begin with). But to be treated in this way demeans people, diminishes them, devalues them. It is very hard for people to resist feelings of worthlessness when other human beings whose power they once respected and whose good will they once counted on regard them with contempt.*

And the situation becomes even worse when people come to feel—as many do in East Swallow—that those powerful others almost act as if it were *their* fault, as if *they* had reasons

---

*"One of the things in this country that is so powerful and important is the feeling of efficacy in your local government and your state government and so on. And if there's anything that has been permanently ruined in this neighborhood, it's the feeling that you can go to your government and petition and get a fair shake in any kind of timely way. I mean, I guess we might get the court to finally hear us out, but certainly the city council and the county and the department of health and the fire department and the state and the United States Environmental Protection Agency and others have just been unwilling—I guess unable—to do anything about our claim."

for being ashamed of the conditions in which they find themselves.*

> I'm angry at the gas company from the standpoint that those people have never, ever come—or let me rephrase that—those people never came and said, "hey, we have a problem here, we made a mistake." Nothing. The more I go into this, the more I get the feeling that we're being laughed at, that we're being—like we are basically the bad people.

The people of East Swallow, then, must face life with not only the layers of emotional insulation represented by home and neighborhood in disrepair but the next outer layer represented by the wider community in disarray as well. To induce or encourage that sense of distrust and suspicion is a terrible thing for one human being to do to another.

It is time for a brief word of summary, but one of the plaintiffs has done it better in a moment of conversation than I could manage in a week of writing:

> Well, it's hard to think of anything else. I mean those are good questions. Are we angry about this? Yes. Are we worried? Yes. Sleep well? Most nights, but not every night. Affect our personal relations? Yes. Neighborhood affected? Yes. Are there going to be health problems? Everyone knows there are: some-

---

*"One of the silliest things that has come out—I mean, it would be laughable if it weren't so serious—is the idea that somehow the people who live on East Swallow are responsible for the fact that the gasoline companies spilled the oil. I mean, it's like we conspired together—this whole neighborhood of twenty-two families conspired together—to somehow embarrass the petroleum companies because of the fact that they spilled gasoline under our street. . . . Talk about turning things around! It's an Alice in Wonderland situation."

"Now, when they realize that we're actually going to sue them . . . they try and convince us with various and sundry legal tactics that we are foolish and stupid and don't have any basis for our belief that they have done us harm. They are trying now, apparently, to convince us that no problem exists just because you have gasoline under your house and that no one is going to believe us that we do have problems. They appear to be making a really conscious—a conscientious and a conscious—effort to convince us that we are essentially out of our minds."

body's going to get sick over this stuff, that's just statistical. Think about that very much? Darn right. So what's the conclusion to it? I mean it's unpleasant. I didn't do it. I can't get rid of it. I'm out of control. I don't like it. I like you personally, but put an end to it now, if you would please, go ahead.*

AFTERWORD

The comments inserted as footnotes in the body of the report, selected from a much larger mass, appear at those moments in the flow of the argument that originally brought them to mind. It is an interesting set of addenda, not just because those comments strengthen and add flesh to the body of the report but because they add perspectives that would otherwise be missing.

Most of the people of East Swallow accepted the invitation to comment on the original report by speaking into the recorder informally ("This is Joan Wheeler," one of them began, "and if it's OK with you, I'd like to visit a bit and I'll do all the talking, OK?"). On the whole, plaintiffs seemed to approve of the report ("I like it a lot, and it makes me feel a little more hopeful that at least somebody can understand all the complexities of this situation. Thanks a lot").

---

*"I'm really ready for it to be over. I'm really ready for the gasoline companies to come forth and say, 'Hey, we're sorry. We spilled gasoline. Let us make it up to you. Let's get this thing settled. Let's get it over with and let you get on with your lives and go ahead and do what you want to do.' That's the way people should treat each other. I'm really tired of this whole situation, and I just want for it to be over so that I can move out of this house and get into a neighborhood where I feel safe and where the air and soil are clean. That's all I want."

"I'd just like to add that as I look back over these past four years, it's like being in an unending grieving process. We've suffered one loss after another since moving into this house and into this situation. . . . It just doesn't end, and it seems like we can't recoup from one loss till we're experiencing another. So we grieve, and we hurt, and we're angry, and we're stressed out and sick and tired of it all. And the tragedy of it is that there's not one darned thing we can do about it. We're the victims, and I'm fast learning victims have little or no rights."

But not without reservations. One of the younger men, disappointed to see so little quantification of the sort he took to be the soul of science, told me in the gentlest way of his concerns:

> My general impression of your report is that it's accurate. I guess after I first read it I thought maybe it was too general, perhaps, and I was maybe a little skeptical. But I think—well, I'm sure, after talking to a number of the plaintiffs—I see the things that you have said are pretty clearly manifested in their behaviors and in particular in the things that they have said to me. So I'm feeling very confident that you've made a good general profile of this group. . . . One of my concerns in reading it the first time was the concern about methodology. And you know, someone said, "Well, he related the process of the homeowners on this road, on Swallow Road, pretty well to theory," and so on. But I don't know. I don't see much theoretical stuff in here, and I guess there really aren't any data either. These are just some ideas that you have after reading from each of these people and based on your expert judgment, and . . . I feel more comfortable now, some weeks later, than I did on reading it the first time. Still, I would like there to have been like, you know, how many people expressed feelings of anxiety. But I guess from your testimony it's everyone. Well, anyway, those are my thoughts about that.

He is exactly right, too. Any number of other sociologists, tuned to a tidier tradition of research, would have tried to find ways to represent the feelings found along East Swallow in numerical terms. I began that way, as a matter of fact, even though I never expected the resultant numbers and proportions to constitute more than a fraction of the report. But exactly as the above speaker suspected, I came to think that the outlooks and pains that emerged from the interviews were characteristic of virtually the whole community.

People occasionally pointed out that passages in the report, focusing generally on prevailing community tempers, did not reflect their own circumstances accurately. "I'm not as attached to the house as some of the people quoted here," said one man in a comment quoted on page 120, and a neighbor distanced herself from what she understood to be the views of her fellows with lively emphasis: "I guess I really have no emotional attachment to this house. Actually I hate it. I don't have a sense of this place as being 'a home.' Sure, I'd hate to lose what we have invested in it, but frankly, I can hardly wait to get out of this place."

Sometimes commentators would reveal things about the community that had not been apparent in any of the initial rounds of interviewing. The two persons whose comments appear on the bottom of pages 112 and 128, for example, spoke of a degree of wariness and even distrust—one of them described the neighborhood as "closed, almost para-noidlike"—that was new to me. Now it happens that these two speakers live side by side at the outer edges of the affected area, and I have come to think from a few moments of check-ing around that the feeling was a local one, not typical of the neighborhood. Still, no matter how one read it, this was new information that would not have surfaced otherwise.

Sometimes, too, commentators offered insights of un-common acuteness. The person whose remark on the mental borders of the neighborhood appears at the bottom of page 124, for example, is making an extremely telling observation, one I wish I could claim as my own. Had the thought been pressed home to me earlier, I would almost surely have orga-nized my discussion of "community" differently; indeed, were it not for the fact that the rules of this presentation require me to stick with my initial draft, I would do so now.

Far and away the most compelling finding to emerge from this last round of data gathering had to do with the number of people who learned from the report that their feelings were not the peculiar reactions of strange and isolated individuals but the reflections of a general community mood. One couple had learned from contacts with a psychologist that their reactions to the spill were not idiosyncratic:

> Both my husband and myself realized that we were under a great, great amount of tension and stress and that we needed to get help. So we took it upon ourselves to go in to see a psychologist, and we have been working with him on helping us to relieve some stress and tensions. The thing that has come out of that is that we both realize that hey, we aren't going crazy. The tensions and stress are very, very hard on both the mind and on the body.

Most people, however, learn that lesson from their fellows when things go right—and not at all when they do not. "My wife and I thought that maybe we were kind of over-reacting or letting our imaginations run wild until we read where some of the others on East Swallow were having the same thoughts and reactions that we were," said one resident. And a married couple—husband and wife reacting separately—noted:

> My first comment concerns the fear and stress and anxiety that's reported by virtually everyone in the neighborhood. Until we had a chance to look at this report, we really didn't know how many of our neighbors were feeling the same thing that we were.

> It was somewhat unsuspected by me that not only am I in this state of total and complete psychological turmoil, but many of my neighbors, if not all of my neighbors, are in the same condition. Even though you know how *you* feel, you, of course, can never understand or know how someone *else* feels unless you ask them. And because of the way the situation has been, only recently have we really come to understand that it isn't just us that feels so helpless. It's everyone.

When I visited Fort Collins, I sat for several hours with a group of nine plaintiffs in a local living room, and that is the gathering referred to here:

> I was greatly relieved to see what other people said. A lot of things that I thought myself are expressed here by other people from slightly different angles, different words. But it was kind of reassuring to see these same thoughts from other people. Up until we met with Dr. Erikson at the Bremers— I was a member of that group—I wondered a lot of times that the things that I personally had been feeling maybe were out of line. . . . I was wondering if the enormous feelings that I was having were not wrong. That meeting, and now seeing this report and what other people said, gives me a little reassurance that I wasn't feeling something that other people were not feeling. . . . I don't feel now that I was out of line, I guess; that's the big thing.

I would have thought that the firming of the communal circle described by so many of the plaintiffs would have enhanced that kind of sharing. It seems apparent on second glance, though, that the conversations within the circle must have been so attuned to legal matters, so fixed on instrumental concerns, that more intimate feelings stayed submerged. That's a good lesson to remember for all of us who visit places like East Swallow and then pass on to other pursuits with data pressed between the covers of closed notebooks.

On June 19, 1990, as the trial moved into its third week, the suit was settled on terms the senior attorney for the plaintiffs—a laconic, understated Coloradan—described as "satisfactory." That outcome is what the oldest of the plaintiffs had dreamed of a few weeks earlier: "I hope that someday it will be over and I can live in peace. Thank God, no more secret tears."

4

Three Mile Island:
A New Species
of Trouble

On the morning of March 28, 1979, one of two generating units at a little-known place called Three Mile Island experienced an odd sequence of equipment failures and human errors, resulting in the escape of several puffs of radioactive steam. It was a moment of considerable potential danger, as we all were soon to learn. And it was a moment of considerable uncertainty as well.

When the uncertainty was at its height, the governor of Pennsylvania issued a calm and measured advisory suggesting that pregnant women and preschoolchildren living within a five-mile radius of the plant might want to evacuate, while others within a distance of ten miles ought to consider taking shelter in their own homes. In effect, the governor was recommending that 3,500 people living in the shadows of the reactor relocate for at least the immediate time being and that everyone else stay put.

Instead some 150,000 people were alarmed enough to take to the public highways, and they fled, on the average, a remarkable hundred miles. For every person advised to leave home, almost 45 did. This was not the largest evacuation in human history by any means, but it seems to have involved the widest imbalance on record between the scale of an advisory and the scale of an actual evacuation, and it involved the longest average flight as well.[1]

Three young geographers from Michigan State University called this "the evacuation shadow phenomenon," meaning by it the gap between what official wisdom called for and what the people at risk, acting on wisdoms of their own, actually did.[2] Specialists as well as laypeople often try to span that gap by stringing a makeshift term across it. "Overreaction" is much in vogue these days. So is "irrationality." But to describe the gap in that way after the fact is to give it a name without saying anything useful about it at all. The important questions to ask are: Of what did that shadow consist? What were the wisdoms on which the evacuees acted? And the best answer to both questions, clearly, is: a deep and profound dread.

The accident at Three Mile Island is a particularly instructive one since we know only in the most approximate way how much radiation was released or how much harm, if any, it did. So in one sense, at least, the feeling generated there was pure dread, perfect dread, the very essence of dread. It was not a reaction to anything the senses could apprehend: the smell of smoke, the sound of breaking timbers, the sting of burning eyes, the sight of falling bodies, or, in general, the contagious sense of alarm and excitement that erupts among people who share a time of danger. There was no panic, just quiet withdrawal over a number of hours. Each of those 150,000 (or at least the ones who made the decision to withdraw on behalf of other family members) was reacting to an individual reading of whatever portents could be found out there in a silent landscape.

What the evacuees feared in this instance, of course, was radiation, but it might well have been some other form of toxicity. I want to suggest, in fact, that radiation is but one strain of a whole new species of trouble that we are sure to see more of in years to come. Recent events at Three Mile Island and Chernobyl, say, both of them involving radiation, are of a kind with recent events at Love Canal and Bhopal, both of them involving toxic substances of another sort. And they are of a kind with the mercury spill that visited Grassy Narrows as well as the gasoline spill that worked its way into the ground under East Swallow.

I

The first thing to say about this new species of trouble, to return to a theme sounded earlier, is that it is a product of human hands.

The ancients feared pestilence, drought, famine, flood, plague, and all the other scourges that darken the pages of the Bible. These miseries trouble us yet, to be sure, but it is fair to say that we have learned ways to defend ourselves against many of the worst of them. Some (certain epidemics, for example) can now be arrested or even prevented altogether. Others (hurricanes, tidal waves) can be seen far enough in advance for people to move out of their path, thus neutralizing much of their lethal force.

The irony, though, is that the technological advances that have afforded us this degree of protection from natural disasters have created a whole new category of events that specialists have come to call technological disasters—meaning everything that can go wrong when systems fail, humans err, designs prove faulty, engines misfire, and so on. Earthquakes, floods, hurricanes, volcanic eruptions, and tidal waves would be classed as "natural"; collisions, explosions, breakdowns, collapses, and, of course, crises like the ones at

Chernobyl and Bhopal, Buffalo Creek and East Swallow, belong on the roster of the "technological."

Technological disasters have clearly grown in number as we humans test the outer limits of our competence, but more to the point, they have also grown in scale. This is true in the sense that events of local origin can have consequences that reach across huge distances, as was the case, say, with Chernobyl. It is also true in the sense that news of it is broadcast so quickly and so widely that it becomes a moment in everyone's history, a datum in everyone's store of knowledge, a part of our collective consciousness, as was the case with Three Mile Island.

The distinction between natural and technological disasters is sometimes hard to draw exactly. When a mine shaft collapses in Appalachia, it is often a collaboration of restless mountain and careless people; when an epidemic spreads across Central Africa, it owes its virulence to both tough new strains of bacillus and stubborn old human habits.

However hard it may be to draw in actuality, though, that line usually seems distinct enough to victims. Natural disasters are almost always experienced as acts of God or caprices of nature. They happen *to* us. They *visit* us, as if from afar. Technological disasters, however, being of human manufacture, are at least in principle preventable, so there is always a story to be told about them, always a moral to be drawn from them, always a share of blame to be assigned. It is almost impossible to imagine a commission of inquiry, called to discover the causes of some dreadful calamity, concluding simply that it "just happened." We look for responsible human agents, and we find them (although Paul Slovic found a newspaper article in California the headline of which announced that a high rate of leukemia in West Sacramento had been "blamed on chance" by an expert asked to investigate).

Now there is a sense in which it *did* "just happen." This is not because the fates are full of mischief sometimes but because accidents are simply bound to happen sooner or later as human systems become more and more elaborate. When geologists describe a floodplain as being of the kind that is likely to be inundated once in every fifty years, they are not using a logic all that different from that of engineers who describe a core melt as the kind of disturbance that is likely to happen once in every twenty thousand reactor years of operation. The flood is an act of God; the core melt, a human mistake. But both have been written into a kind of script. Both are "natural" in the sense of being foreseeable, even inevitable. The flood lies beyond our control, we say, because nature is simply like that. But core melts can also be described as beyond our control because human systems, too, are simply like that. We know in advance that hands will slip and machinery fail some predictable fraction of the time. This makes of them what Charles Perrow calls "normal accidents."[3]

Technological accidents, though, are almost never understood as the way the world of chance sorts itself out. They provoke outrage rather than acceptance or resignation. They generate a feeling that the thing ought not have happened, that someone is at fault, that victims deserve not only compassion and compensation but something akin to what lawyers call punitive damages. This feeling can become an absorbing passion for survivors and, for some, almost a way of life. To understand the feelings and reactions that technological emergencies provoke, then, it is crucial to distinguish the crises that are seen as the work of nature from those that are seen as the work of humankind. The default of Fred's Barn in South Florida cannot really be called a technological crisis, I suppose, but it was most emphatically a product of human misadventure. So all the disasters and near disasters discussed in this volume were caused by human hands.

II

The second thing to be said about these new troubles is that they involve toxins: They contaminate rather than merely damage; they pollute, befoul, and taint rather than just create wreckage; they penetrate human tissue indirectly rather than wound the surfaces by assaults of a more straightforward kind.[4] And the evidence is growing that they scare human beings in new and special ways, that they elicit an uncanny fear in us. One of the surest findings to emerge from the new field of risk assessment is that people in general find radiation and other toxic substances a good deal more threatening than natural hazards of virtually any kind and technological hazards of considerable danger that do not involve toxicity.[5]

Example: The incident at Three Mile Island gave rise to a round of discussions about evacuation plans at other nuclear power plants, among them the Shoreham Nuclear Power Station on Long Island. In the course of that debate Suffolk County officials commissioned a survey to ask Long Island residents how they would react to a mishap at Shoreham. If an accident occurred, one question read, and everyone living within five miles of the plant were advised to stay indoors, what would you do? More than 40 percent of the residents living within a ten-mile radius of the reactor— together with 25 percent of the entire population of Long Island!—announced they would flee. And if pregnant women and young children were advised to evacuate? Then 55 percent of the people within ten miles and more than a third of the total Long Island population would leave. These are the mildest advisories that can be issued, and the latter, of course, was the one broadcast at Three Mile Island. More urgent ones, the survey indicated, would swell the number of evacuees still further, adding to the severity of what would already be utter deadlock.[6]

These are expressions of *intention*, it is important to note, and not reports of actual *behavior*, so they need to be viewed with the usual caution. But the percentage of people who expect to evacuate Long Island and the percentage of those who did in fact evacuate the neighborhood of Three Mile Island are nearly equal, and that degree of corroboration compels an additional measure of respect.

To throw a more recent log onto that small but sturdy fire, telephone surveys done in response to the government's proposal to build a high-level nuclear waste repository at Yucca Mountain in Nevada only confirm what other readings of the human mood have revealed: that people in general have an uncommon dread of things nuclear.[7]

That conclusion is clearly borne out by the few experiences we have to draw on in recent history. In a number of places where radiological and other toxic disasters have struck, the dread lingers long after the incident itself has been officially declared over. Fear of radiation was so strong in the regions surrounding Chernobyl several years after the 1986 accident there that government officials spoke (scornfully) of "radiophobia." In Goiânia, Brazil, where a small release of cesium 137 killed four persons and contaminated hundreds in 1987, officials were alarmed to discover that the apprehensions of many residents seemed to grow rather than decline with the passing of time. Even at Three Mile Island, where there is still no evidence of lasting physical damage, levels of anxiety remain a good deal higher than the experience of other kinds of disaster would give us any reason to suppose. The same is true of Love Canal, which has been carefully studied, and other sites around the world where toxic substances were released into the environment and may have found their way into human tissues.

This evidence, added together, is still far from decisive. Risk assessment studies remain few and scattered; surveys like the ones conducted on Long Island and in Nevada are both infrequent and inconclusive; and the world can count itself fortunate that accidental laboratories of the kind found in Goiânia, Bhopal, and Chernobyl are as rare as they have been. In that sense the information available to us has to be seen as a few brief glances into the heart of things. What we have are not hard scientific conclusions so much as hints, intimations, auguries. But they are nonetheless important because they may be the leading edge of a wave building just beyond the sight of shore.

III

Most technical experts seem to assume that increased experience and familiarity will act over time to reduce the dread and sense of mystery. Those feelings seem entirely illogical after all: Fifty thousand persons are killed every year in traffic accidents without provoking any deep aversion to automobiles, so why should we be so afraid of nuclear power plants and toxic waste dumps, which, on their face, do much less damage? This thought encourages a hope on the part of some experts that people will one day become as resigned and philosophical about radiological accidents as they are now about hurricanes or earthquakes. One of the most thoughtful pronuclear physicists has noted how much easier it is to "scare" people than to "unscare" them, but his reading of human history has persuaded him that people will sooner or later overcome this apprehension as they did their initial fears of electricity.[8]

Perhaps. Time alone can tell. In the meantime, as we wait for the passing of years to deliver that verdict, we have many reasons to suppose that toxic emergencies simply nourish dread, that they are, in their very nature, a thing of darkness and foreboding, that the fear, in fact, may grow rather than diminish. We will dismiss this fear as irrational if (like most experts) we assess the danger by calculating the odds of an accident and then estimating the number of casualties likely to result from it. But there are other reckonings at work out there in the world. Maybe radioactivity and other forms of toxicity can be understood as naturally loathsome, inherently insidious—a horror, like poison gas, that draws on something deeper in the human mind. That may seem like odd conceptual terrain for a sociologist to be wandering around in since social scientists have no warrant to speak of "primal fears" or "the wisdom of the body," as psychiatrists like Robert J. Lifton are invited by the logic of their discipline to do. So let me just offer the proposition that toxic emergencies really *are* different, that their capacity to induce a lasting sense of dread is one of their unique properties.

But why should toxic crises create so much alarm? What makes them seem so different? Why should the people of East Swallow, say, exposed to what even they recognize as modest levels of toxicity, live in such fear? In seeking some answers to those questions, I will be calling on the voices of a handful of people who lived through the emergency at Three Mile Island. The voices are those of plaintiffs in a legal action speaking several years after the event itself, so we have no right to assume that they represent the feelings of everyone in the neighborhood. We do know, however, that the outlooks expressed here are widely shared at Three Mile Island and, moreover, that they are common to other places studied by social scientists where toxic contamination has struck.[9]

One reason toxic emergencies provoke such concern is that they are not bounded, that they have no frame. We generally use the word "disaster" in everyday conversation to refer to a distinct event that interrupts the accustomed flow of everyday life. "Disasters" seem to adhere to Aristotle's rules of drama. They have "a beginning and a middle and an end." They "do not begin and end at random." They have "a certain magnitude" yet are "easily taken in by the eye." They have *plot*, in short, which is "the first principle and as it were the soul of tragedy."[10]

An alarm sounds the beginning. It is a signal to retreat, to take to storm cellars, to move to higher ground, to crouch in the shelter of whatever cover presents itself. A period of destruction then follows that may take no more than a brief, shattering moment or may last many days. Sooner or later, though, the disaster comes to an exhausted close. The floodwaters recede, the smoke clears, the winds abate, the bombers leave, and an all clear is sounded either literally or figuratively. An announcement is then heard that the emergency is over and that the time is now at hand for cleaning up and restoration. The time has also come for that extraordinary moment when a fire marshal or a sheriff or whoever is in charge of such ceremonies casts a shrewd eye over the devastation and estimates for the press how many dollars of property damage was done. The pain may last, of course; dreams may continue to haunt and wounds prove difficult to heal. But the event itself is over, and what follows will be described as "aftermath." "In the wake of the flood," we will say.

Toxic disasters, however, violate all the rules of plot. Some of them have clearly defined beginnings, such as the explosion that signaled the emergency at Chernobyl or the sudden moment of realization that opened the drama of Bhopal; others begin long years before anyone senses that something is wrong, as was the case at Love Canal. But they never end. Invisible contaminants remain a part of the surroundings, absorbed into the grain of the landscape, the tissues of the body, and, worst of all, the genetic material of the survivors. An all clear is never sounded. The book of accounts is never closed.

The feelings of uncertainty—the sense of a lack of ending—can begin the very moment that the event ought, in logic, to be over. Here is the report of a family that left the vicinity of Three Mile Island upon hearing the governor's advisory and traveled several hundred miles:

So we got in the car and headed South and we got as far as—I believe it was Durham, North Carolina, where we stopped first. And we didn't know how bad we were hurt. I remember when we went to the motel, I remember sleeping with my hands between my knees, and I was just trembling, worried sick about what this had done to our family and the ones who were still back there.

That uncertainty can continue for months, years, even generations. Others may look in on the scene from a safe remove in time or place and think of the emergency as over. But the ones who were there reckon the situation differently.

What damage would it have on me or my unborn child? What damage was done to the ground, the surrounding areas? What damage was done to the people who lived around the area at that time and still live there? . . . What reaction did it have on my daughters, my sons? What took place over there that we are not aware of?

I had felt sure at that time that we had gotten quite a bit of radiation, and at that point you don't know if you're going to die next week . . . but because of this, was our life going to be cut short? Just exactly what was going to happen? We still don't know. Are the kids going to get it? Is my husband going to get it? It's nothing to dwell on, I can tell you, because if you dwelled on it every day you'd be crazy.

For many people, to be exposed to radiation or other forms of toxicity is to be contaminated in some deep and lasting way, to feel dirtied, tainted, corrupted. "It will always be there, the contamination," said one woman of sixty, speaking of both herself and the world around her. A neighbor of hers, a man of forty-eight, added: "I don't feel that the stuff is going to leave. It's still here with us. It's in our bodies, in our genes, and later on we're going to pay for it."

Those comments sound like echoes of the voice from East Swallow we heard earlier: "How do we know that sometime down the line—ten years, twenty years down the line—we won't both develop cancer or some other dread disease that we don't even know about yet just because of having been exposed to breathing these vapors for twelve years? We don't know. . . . [O]ne of the scary things about it is that you just don't know."

Radiation and most other toxic substances are without body. One cannot taste them, touch them, smell them, or see them, and for that reason they seem especially ghostlike and terrifying. Moreover, they invert the process by which disasters normally do harm. They do not charge in from outside and batter like a gust of wind or a wall of water. They slink in without warning, do no immediate damage so far as one can tell, and then begin their deadly work from within—the very embodiment of stealth and treachery.

The widely observed prohibition against chemical warfare might be instructive here. Chemical weapons clearly have a special place on the human list of horrors, but why that should be so is not at all obvious. In World War I, for example, shrapnel proved a good deal more lethal than gas, but no one seems to have suggested that it be outlawed on that account, presumably because it does such a straightforward job of ripping through flesh and tearing bodies apart. So the moral case must lie in the way the two work rather than in the amount of damage they do. "Gas is a perfidious, impalpable, and cruel abomination," said an Allied report shortly after the war[11] ("that hellish poison" Winston Churchill called it), and that puts the case plainly enough. It is furtive, invisible, unnatural. In most of its forms it moves for the interior, turning the process of assault inside out and in that way violating the integrity of the body. A sociologist, again, may have no warrant to suggest that this aversion stems from something elemental in the human spirit, but in this instance, at least, we have historical records to draw on, for poison has always represented the epitome of evil and treachery in the way we tell the story of our past.

"Why is asbestos poisoning seen to be more fearsome than fire?" Mary Douglas and Aaron Wildavsky wonder in their influential book *Risk and Culture*.[12] And Henry Fairlie, writing in the *New Republic*, asks: "Why do Americans seem to be more concerned about the risks of pollution than about the budget deficit, economic stagnation, and even war?"[13] The mood of these questions is a kind of puzzled disapproval, but the best answer to both of them would have to draw on the considerations I have just raised. Toxic poisons provoke a special dread because they contaminate, because they are stealthy and deceive the body's alarm systems, and because they can become absorbed into the very tissues of the body and crouch there for years, even generations, before doing their deadly work. A number of people from Three Mile Island, as we have seen elsewhere as well, note that it is as if they had "a time bomb ticking" within them.

IV

All of the above may suggest that people will not so easily become "unscared" of radiation and other forms of toxicity with the passing of time. And if that is what fate has in store for us, a new set of questions rises quickly to the surface: What happens to people who experience this kind of dread over long stretches of time? What will be the consequence if that dread finds a more and more permanent place in the human imagination?

People exposed to disasters are very apt to develop a sense of being out of control, of being caught up in forces that capture them and take them over. Feelings of helplessness and vulnerability are so common in moments of crisis, I noted earlier, that they are recognized as one of the identifying psychological symptoms of "trauma" and a prominent feature of what is often called the disaster syndrome. Two more witnesses from Three Mile Island:

> Fear, that's what it is. Afraid. You're sitting at the edge of your seat. It's like we're in their hands. It's like we're being manipulated by a couple of stacks.

> I don't know how to explain it. I just feel insecure. I just feel scared, afraid. It's just like being in an airplane and you're afraid because you don't know [anything about] the pilot.

Survivors of severe disasters, that is to say, experience not just a sense of vulnerability but a feeling of having lost a certain immunity to misfortune, a feeling, even, that something terrible is almost *bound* to happen. They come to feel, as I pointed out in my report on Buffalo Creek, that the blow visiting them "was not just a freak act of nature or a vicious act of men but a sample of what the universe has in store for them."[14] One of the crucial jobs of culture, let's say, is to help people camouflage the actual risks of the world around them—to help them edit reality in such a way that it seems manageable, to help them edit it in such a way that the perils pressing in on all sides are screened out of their line of vision as they go about their daily rounds. Daniel Defoe has Robinson Crusoe muse:

> This furnish'd my thoughts with many very profitable reflections, and particularly this one, how infinitely good that providence is, which has provided in its government of mankind such narrow bounds to his sight and knowledge of things; and though he walks in the midst of so many thousand dangers, the sight of which, if discovered to him, would distract his mind and sink his spirits, he is kept serene and calm, by having the events of things hid from his eyes, and knowing nothing of the dangers which surround him.[15]

This kind of emotional insulation is stripped away, at least for the moment, in most severe disasters, but with a special sharpness in events like the ones we have been considering here exactly because one can never assume that they are over. What must it be like, having just discovered through bitter experience that reality is a thing of unrelenting danger, to have to look those dangers straight in the eye without blinders or filters? Let's return to our witnesses from Three Mile Island:

> Scary. Like you pull in the driveway, and you think "when I walk into the house will there be some kind of radiation lingering?" It came into your house and it's going to stay there. You think "is the food in the refrigerator safe to eat?" So you still have that insecure feeling of wondering what is going to happen at TMI. Are they telling us everything? . . . You always have that insecure feeling. I'll always have it.

> And the radio, to this day, plays all the time in my house. I have to know if anything happens. . . . Something like that just hanging over us constantly. I hate it. I just hate it.

People stripped of the ability to screen out signs of peril are not just unusually vigilant and unusually anxious. They evaluate the data of everyday life differently, read the signs differently, see patterns that the rest of us are for the most part spared.

> My mind is like a little computer. It's always ticking. . . . I figure it even ticks when I'm asleep. I listen more to what people say to me. It's hard to trust. Only the ones close to you it seems you can trust. I'm not being paranoid or nothing. It's not like that. It's just that these last couple of years . . . I see more now, I listen to more of what people say. I read between the lines more.

Once victims reach that level of awareness, evidence that the world is a place of constant peril appears everywhere. It is a rare morning newspaper or evening broadcast that does not contain news of acid rain, polluted beaches, tank car derailments, newly discovered toxic waste dumps, or malfunctions at nuclear power plants (all of which are stories in the news as I write these pages). The following stories, for example, were among scores clipped from the two newspapers I read within a few days: "Plutonium Hazard Found at Nuclear Power Plant," "Polluted Lake Belowground Worries EPA," "Entire Town in Ohio Evacuated in Gas Leak," "Dioxin Found in Milk from Paper Cartons," "Oil Spill Shuts 30-Mile Stretch of Hudson River," "Pollution Poses Growing Threat to Everglades," "Mill Town Agonizes over High Dioxin Readings," and "Nuclear Reactor in Spain Catches Fire." If these are the kinds of data your mind is sensitive to, the kinds of data your eye, made sharp and canny by events of the recent past, is good at taking in, the gloomiest of forecasts can seem amply supported.

It will come as no surprise, surely, that people who share such an outlook can easily lose confidence in officialdom, not only in designated spokespersons but in certified experts as well. Bruce Dohrenwend, who headed the task force on behavioral and mental health effects of the President's Commission on the Accident at Three Mile Island, thought that the sharp decline in respect for and trust of public officials was "one of the major findings, perhaps *the* major finding" of his various inquiries, and that conclusion is certainly supported by other research.[16] For one thing, officials and experts can lie. Here's a prim, middle-aged woman, made blunt by a sense of urgency: "I think—should I say it?—I think that's bullshit. I really do. I think it is. That's how I feel about it. 'Everything's under control.' Bullshit. Nothing's under control. I don't believe anything they say, if you want to know the truth. I do not believe anything I hear from them." To make matters worse, people who have been sensitized by exposure to a toxic emergency can lose faith not only in the good*will* but in the good *sense* of those in charge of a dangerous universe. It is not at all obvious that "they" can tell the truth even when they want to, for they do not know what is going on either. They, too, are out of control: "It's like a child having a grenade in his hand and you lay it out there for him to play with. Sooner or later he'll figure how to pull the pin and blow his brains out. That's what they're doing down there with nuclear. That's all there is to it. Just playing with it."

Nor is that feeling confined to the immediate neighborhood. *The New Yorker*, reporting ten weeks after the catastrophe at Bhopal when the casualty estimates had reached two thousand dead and two hundred thousand injured, put it well (an excellent example, incidentally, of the event that becomes a moment in everyone's history):

> What truly grips us in these accounts is not so much the numbers as the spectacle of suddenly vanished competence, of men utterly routed by technology, of fail-safe systems failing with a logic as inexorable as it was once—indeed, right up until that very moment—unforeseeable. And the spectacle haunts us because it seems to carry allegorical import, like the whispery omen of a hovering future.[17]

The most important point to be made here is that when the dread is lasting and pronounced, the spectacle of a failed technology can become the spectacle of a failed environment as well. This is an outlook born of the sense that poisons are now lodged in the tissues of the body, that the surrounding countryside is contaminated as well, that the whole natural envelope in which people live out their lives has become defiled and unreliable. "Dead ground," said one person from Three Mile Island, speaking of the land he was standing on. But he did not mean that it was inert and lifeless like a moonscape. It was, for him, alive with dangers, a terrain in which fresh air and sunshine and all the other benevolences of creation are to be feared as sources of toxic infection.

Imagine having to see the natural world through so dark a glass as these four women do:

> I don't even hang wash out anymore, and usually I'm a fanatic on hanging wash out. I don't want to bring in what maybe is out there.

> I used to lay out in the sun, but ever since TMI I don't lay out in the sun anymore, because you're thinking about the radiation. . . . What's to say that the stuff isn't coming over and just coming right down on me?

> Well, one of the things was—you always felt that to get out into the fresh air was so much better than to be inside. Well . . . it's healthier inside now than outside. So we just spend more time inside. And when you do go out you have the feeling: should you be there? is it going to harm you?

> I do not want my grandchildren romping in my back-yard. . . . I just don't know what's there. I can't see what's there.

Indeed, everything out there can seem unreliable and fearsome. The vegetables in one's own garden can no longer be depended on ("I went down there and I cut [the asparagus] off and threw it into the weeds. . . . The stuff around here that was growing in the ground was not fit to eat because it was radiated"). The river can no longer be depended on ("The water's polluted and doesn't even freeze up anymore"). The ground itself can no longer be relied on ("We had a very nice yard. Now nothing grows. The land is bad"). People feel that something noxious is closing in on them, drifting down from above, creeping up from underneath, edging in sideways, fouling the very air and insinuating itself in all the objects and spaces that make up their surroundings.

"Well, why don't you move to a safer location?" they are asked. But that is to misunderstand, for there *is* no safer location. The point is not that a particular region is now spoiled but that the whole world has been revealed as a place of danger and numbing uncertainty:[18] "The whole country. There's no place in this country that you could go to that isn't slopped up. . . . There isn't a safe place that you could go to that the drinking water isn't bad. The food you get is all poisoned. There's radiation. . . . It isn't like it was when we were kids."

It is important to note (once again) that these voices express a fear and a view of the world shared by a portion of the people of Three Mile Island—and, for that matter, of the people living in other emergency sites where researchers have posted themselves to listen. I am not trying to suggest that all survivors of a toxic emergency see things as they do. The portion that does, however, is large by any measure. And the fact that waves of people share a common dread not only in such well-known places as Love Canal and Three Mile Island, Chernobyl and Bhopal but also in lesser-known disaster sites like Centralia (Pennsylvania), Legler (New Jersey), Times Beach (Missouri), and Woburn (Massachusetts)—never mind Grassy Narrows and East Swallow—should tell us that something important may be happening here, for the apprehension that appears to be so widely spread throughout the population can easily erupt into the feelings expressed above.[19] It ranks, at the very least, as another "whispery omen of a hovering future."

5

Being Homeless

In one of its older meanings "home" refers to a land of origin, a native soil. It is the place to which one really belongs, even though quartered elsewhere; the place to which one dreams of returning, if only to be buried with one's ancestors or to rest in old and familiar ground. Home, as we learned from the Haitians of Immokalee, is the place where "one is a person," and that can remain true even when one lives out one's life and is buried elsewhere. The Haitians of Immokalee, in that sense, are a long way from home.

But no one would call them homeless. "Home" in a second and more common meaning refers to a residence, a dwelling, an abode—an enclosed space to which one has a kind of natural title and over which one exerts some measure of control. Literally or figuratively a home is built around a hearth. That is where the family huddles against the cold, where it cooks its food (an essential activity for the human digestive system), and where it gathers at mealtime. We are, after all, the only creatures on earth who schedule our hungers so that we may feed together.

One can find asylum in a barracks or a dormitory, a prison cell or hospital ward, a crisis shelter or a flophouse. One can double up in the margins of someone else's household. But a true home—a place of one's own—is an extension of the individuals who live in it, a part of themselves. It is the outer envelope of personhood. People need location almost as much as they need shelter, for a sense of place is one of the ways they connect to the larger human community. You cannot have a neighbor (or be one) unless you are situated yourself. You cannot be counted a townsperson unless you have an address. You cannot be a member unless you are grounded somewhere in communal space. That is the geography of self.

In certain cultures one can be located by having a defined place in a fluid group, as happens, say, within a nomadic band. People carry the means of shelter with them and then make their homes within a bounded encampment. In most cultures, however, to have a place is to occupy a fixed habitation, if only for a time—to be anchored somewhere in social space. And when that combined sense of dwelling and location (both of them implied in the term "homestead") is missing, one is deprived of a measure of personhood. That, too, is the geography of self.

In at least that one important respect, then, to be homeless is to live on the outer edges of the human circle, if not to be excluded from it altogether—to be of another kind, maybe even of another species. The homeless feel left out, understandably, and we, in our turn, find it hard not to distance ourselves from them by distinguishing their kind of being from ours. The mother of a homeless family of six tried to explain this to a congressional committee. Once you become homeless, she said, "people look at you like you don't even register as a human being any longer. If you're on welfare, you're at least on the bottom of the scale, [but if] you tell people that you're living in a *shelter*, they do not hire you. They do not hire people who are living in a shelter, for whatever reason. It's like you no longer exist as a human being."[1] Now this was a clean and neatly pressed woman, sitting with her husband and children. But for those who have long lost the means to wash and groom and stay tidy, the situation is clearly worse. "Dirty, ugly, disagreeable to all the senses," wrote Dickens of Jo, the street urchin in *Bleak House:* "Homely filth begrimes him, homely parasites devour him, homely sores are in him, homely rags are on him. . . . He is not of the same order of things, not of the same place in creation. He is of no order and no place; neither of the beasts, nor of humanity."[2]

The homeless are a thing apart, living outside the vast traceries of kinship and community that make up the social order. That makes them pathetic, to be sure, but in a curious way it also makes them dangerous. They are not likely to attack, being too numbed and depleted and cowed for anything like that, so most of us know as we pass them by that we need not fear for our persons or our purses. But people who live outside the human circle look as though they are not constrained by the understandings that obtain within it. They are a negation of the very idea of society, so the apprehension and revulsion we can scarcely help feeling at the sight of such degradation are a fear of disorder, of infection, of contamination. They are (to borrow a wonderful phrase from Terrence Des Pres) "disturbers of the peace."[3]

Homelessness in America has long been regarded as a condition peculiar to single men who have been cut loose from their social moorings and drifted noiselessly from the settled shore. The term "derelict" so often used to refer to homeless men once meant just that: abandoned hulks left to twist and turn in the open seas. Sociologists have been interested in those men since the early days of the discipline, intrigued by their isolation from the rest of society, by their high rates of alcoholism and mental illness, and by the hesitant forms of fellowship they often developed among themselves.[4]

The new homeless are a somewhat different breed, brought to the streets by different circumstances. There are many more of them, for one thing, and a growing portion is made of up single women and women-headed families. A generation ago homeless men tended to gather into urban pools where spare and inexpensive shelter was available in skid row hotels and flophouses and where a man could find work for the few hours it took to make enough money for his immediate needs. But the skid rows are now gone, and the new homeless are dispersed across the urban landscape. They are younger on the average and poorer—younger because improvements in Social Security benefits have removed many of the aging from the rolls of the homeless, and poorer because opportunities for intermittent unskilled work like handloading and packing have largely disappeared as a result of automation. They may have a higher incidence of mental illness, too, since many of the people who would have been absorbed into mental hospitals and similar institutions a generation ago have now found their way to the streets.

What does this population look like? Estimates of its size vary from several hundred thousand to several million, depending on the definitions and methods that guide the count and sometimes on the ideological moods that impel it. The very imprecision of the term "homelessness" lends it a certain mystery. The ranks of the homeless include people who live without roofs over them a good part of the time, people who find refuge in crisis shelters a good part of the time, and people of such precarious means that they slip into and out of homelessness with even minor shifts in everyday fortune. Americans are used to measuring the size of a social problem by counting the people exposed to it. How many people have AIDS? How many are without work? How many are illiterate or disabled or dependent on drugs? Assessing the size of any of those populations is a technically difficult business at best, but keeping a running count of the homeless is impossible. They "cannot be tagged like geese and their patterns of migration charted," note two of the most serious students of homelessness,[5] and most of the other ways of tracking people as they make their way across the surfaces of the city are of no help here. Crisis shelters and flophouses presumably keep tally of the people who pass through them, and the ragged of the streets, curled over steam grates or crouched into doorways, are at least visible to the eye should anyone care enough to try taking a census. But the rest slip into and out of homelessness without a trace. They press into the already overcrowded corners of other households or find niches elsewhere in the interstices of the city: on rooftops and under bridges, in boiler rooms and basements. So it is an elusive, shifting population. Peter Rossi, as shrewd and experienced a reader of the available data as can be found anywhere, concludes that something like three hundred thousand people are homeless on any given evening, while James D. Wright, another seasoned hand, puts the total closer to half a million. The number who endure homelessness at some point in the calendar year, however, is well over a million (a million and a half is Wright's guess), and the number who are poor enough to be in constant risk of homelessness reaches several million.[6]

The ranks of the homeless continue to be dominated by single men, but while that group once represented close to 100 percent of the whole, it now represents something like 60 percent. About 15 percent of the homeless are now single women, 5 percent are single children, and 22 percent are family members—for the most part single mothers and their young offspring. Almost 40 percent of the new homeless, then, are women and children, a striking change.[7] But that statistic, for all its apparent concreteness, describes one point on a curve sloping upward, for there are many reasons to suppose that the number of family groups moving into homelessness is now increasing and will continue to do so.

Of the new homeless, 40 percent appear to have significant problems with alcohol or—a growing menace—drugs. About a third are thought to suffer from depression or some other form of mental illness. And 40 percent have been jailed at least once in their lives, with close to half that number having served time in state or federal prisons for what we may safely presume to have been felony offenses.[8] The incidence of physical problems among the homeless, too, has to be measured on a different scale from the ones in use for other population groups since skin ailments, traumatic injuries, upper respiratory troubles, liver and cardiac diseases, infestations, anemia, infections, hypertension, and a host of other woes are so widespread as to seem commonplace.

The sheer volume of those numbers is in large part due to the single men in the homeless population since that group contributes more than its share to the prevailing rates of alcoholism, illness, and so on. But even then it is hard to know what to make of those numbers, for the correlation between homelessness, on the one hand, and all the above frailties, on the other, is a complicated one at best. Heavy alcohol use clearly can burden people to the point where they sink into homelessness, but the humiliations and deprivations that accompany homelessness, just as clearly, are reason enough for turning to drink. And so with mental illness. It is easy to see how a poorly functioning mind can lead to homelessness, but at the same time it is also easy to see how the life of the homeless and the trials that lead to it would affect the sturdiest of temperaments. After all, what kinds of mental reflexes would one expect from individuals who spend their days maneuvering in terrains where privacy is almost unheard of, where eye-level contact with caring human beings is rare, and where danger is a constant? And who knows what effect sustained periods of malnutrition and dehydration and sleep deprivation—never mind panic and despair—have on the minds of the already vulnerable? The relationship between physical ailments and home-lessness may be easier to sort out, since some of the condi-tions found widely among homeless people seem to predate their fall from social grace and can thus be listed as contrib-uting causes. But many of the miseries treated in clinics to which the homeless turn can only be attributed to neglect, exposure, and all the other ravages of that brutal way of life.

So the correlations point in two directions at once. Those experts who think that the disabilities and fragilities of the homeless explain their presence on the streets can find all the empirical solace they want in the data now at hand. And so can those experts who take the view—a somewhat lonelier and braver one, it should be said—that the disabili-ties and fragilities of the homeless are among the grim penal-ties people pay for landing on the streets.

To speak the language of causation at all, however, may be to miss the point. If I declare with confidence that drink-ing or madness or something else causes homelessness, and if you declare with equal confidence that the reverse is in fact true, we both will be correct enough on the face of it. But we both will be forgetting that the chemistries of the human mind are a good deal more subtle than that. Here's a brief tale briefly told:

They were in a despairing mood when they opened the bottle, hoping that it would help. But before the first drops of alcohol had even reached their bloodstreams, a chance comment from one of them reminded the other of an earlier exchange of words that had been festering like a small sore for several hours. A quarrel erupted that served not only to darken the mood and endanger the relationship but to increase the speed with which the bottle emptied. This so absorbed their energies that they missed an appointment that might have produced a day's work or an evening's shelter, and the chagrin they felt when they remembered may have been among the reasons why one of them took an awkward swing at the other. No harm would have come of this, probably, since neither of them, by now well into their second bottle, could move with much precision, but a police officer engaged in some other pursuit happened to be passing by. Words were spoken, a knife emerged from the folds of someone's clothing, a revolver was drawn, and . . .

An aimless story. We do not even know its ending. But how can one reach into so contingent a tale to assign causes and effects? Do we blame the mood? The relationship? The bottle? The missed opportunity? An accident of timing? All those pieces of the narrative disappear into some larger whole like the threads of a fabric. They reinforce one another, define one another, forming a continuous loop that spirals toward whatever outcome this miniature story eventually turns out to have. And the same is true on a larger scale. All one can say in the long run is that where one finds homeless people one also finds a high incidence of mental illness and alcoholism, a fearsome array of physical disorders, life histories marked by family dysfunctions and brushes with the law, and all the other liabilities that are a part of life on the margins of society.

Why do people become homeless? Because they lose out in the competition for a shrinking supply of low-cost housing. If that seems like something less than a powerful insight, it nonetheless draws attention to the fact that markets rather than the more subtle fates we have been talking about so far determine how many people will be without homes and— up to a point at least—how those people will be distributed across the social landscape. That raises two questions.

First, why should there be a shortage of low-cost housing

in this richest of lands? What happened in the 1970s and 1980s to change the ability of the economy to absorb those people who are now homeless? To begin with, the price of building new housing stock (or even of maintaining the old stock) went up so high that private capital shifted into more promising ventures. The costs of remaining in what housing remained, understandably, also went up, not only because competition for space drove rents higher but because taxes, interest payments, and the price of fuel rose as well. Government subsidies for housing shrank appreciably during that same period as a matter of deliberate policy, while—the other side of a hard coin—favorable tax rates were inducing various forms of upscaling and gentrification. Meantime, hundreds of thousands of rental units disappeared altogether as a consequence of arson, abandonment, land clearance, or just plain collapse.

So large numbers of people were destined to be without homes as a simple consequence of reduced supply, raising the second of our two questions: What kinds of people among the millions who were economically and temperamentally eligible for that quota turned out to be the most likely to help fill it? Among the newcomers to the ranks of the homeless were:

- Members of single-parent households, many dependent on public relief, who had been shaken loose like precariously attached leaves when tremors from the market shook the tree
- Members of working families who were cut adrift by layoffs or plant closings and found it difficult to reconnect
- Single women fleeing abusive family arrangements
- The mentally disordered who, a generation earlier, might have been hospitalized, as well as former convicts who had no marketable place in the legitimate world

(and may also have been without the skills or the contacts or the frame of mind required for success in the illegitimate world)

- Old people without Social Security coverage or adequate pensions
- Young people who had run away from (or had been cast out by) their families and were being absorbed into the life of the streets
- Legal and illegal immigrants from Latin America, the Caribbean, and Asia, as well as Native Americans leaving reservations—the people who suffer most when the number of jobs for the unskilled shrinks even further

People drift into homelessness because they are fragile and burdened and largely without resources (although it is important to repeat that many of the fragilities that most impress observers when they try to trace backward down the lifelines of the homeless in a search for motives were a derivative of the process of drift as well as a contributing cause of it). People drift into homelessness because they do not have families to take them in, thus depriving them of what has been the natural safety net for people in want throughout the history of the species—in some cases because they have no relatives left, in others because they have worn out whatever welcome they were once entitled to, and in yet others because they have taken to the streets in the hope of escaping intolerable living conditions or the abusiveness of a parent or a mate. And people drift into homelessness, finally, because in addition to everything else, they are luckless. Those who live on the edge of destitution, of course, do not have any emergency reserves to fall back on, and when something happens—a missing check, an illness, a theft, a misunderstanding, an eviction, an arrest, a car accident, a pregnancy—the whole structure of their lives is endangered. When the vessel begins to take on water and to list, the measures necessary to right it again, some of them but routine details, can be frustrating and exhausting. You need to take four different buses to visit the only vacant apartment on the current listing with a rent you can afford, and if you miss one of those connections, it may be days before you get another chance. You need to round up three children on half an hour's notice to take advantage of a sudden opportunity, and if you fail to do so, it can mean a payment delayed or a night's shelter forfeited. You need to arrange for the storage of your household effects as the result of an eviction proceeding, and if the plan you work out fails or the person you counted on defaults, you may lose everything you own to vandals or landlords or garbage collectors.

The resources of this land are so apportioned that hundreds of thousands of persons are without housing on any given day, a million or so are lost from sight in the creases of society without anything that could reasonably be called a home, and several million are so poor and vulnerable that homelessness is but a misstep away. The language most of us use to describe those who become homeless points to their vulnerabilities and to the accidents of fate, and that is fair enough. But it is important to remember when we think about the problem that the rates of homelessness are so sensitive to manipulation that we may be said to *create* homelessness by the way we set incentives, the way we allot tax burdens, the way we tune the economy. Homelessness is a cost we are willing for one portion of the population to pay in the hopes of benefiting another. It is a matter of policy.

I have tried in the discussion thus far to offer a rough sketch of the problem of homelessness in America, drawn on the work of specialists who know a great deal more about it than I do. Much of that work, appropriately enough, relies upon the statistical records to which the homeless contribute as they drift through shelters or apply for benefits or otherwise leave a mark of their passing. Those data are the bases on which we estimate how many people are homeless at any given time, what paths they traveled to get there, and how their numbers are distributed by gender, race, age, marital status, and the like. Those form the statistical silhouette, as it were, of the ranks of the homeless.

When one wants to consider how it must *feel* to be caught up in those currents, however, one needs to turn to the work of observers who actually went to the shelters or the streets to talk with homeless people and to watch them pursue their everyday rounds. The homeless, as we have seen, make up a hugely diverse population, so each foray out into the field focuses on a different sector of a vast universe. To use three of the best of them as examples: Jonathan Kozol's celebrated study draws principally on mothers struggling with welfare hotels in New York; the work of David A. Snow and Leon Anderson on single street adults, most of them men, in Texas; and that of Barry Jay Seltser and Donald E. Miller on families passing through crisis shelters in Los Angeles.[9] These are, by definition, partial views, as the authors in each case are the first to note.

This chapter, unlike the others in this volume, draws wholly on the work of others, and in the paragraphs to follow I plan to borrow from a useful set of interviews conducted by Seltser and Miller. They talked to one hundred persons altogether, all but one of them parents—the majority single mothers—living with children in Los Angeles crisis shelters.

The group was made up almost entirely of newcomers to homelessness, meaning that most of them were frightened, sensitive, tightly wired, alert. Few of them had yet slumped into the kinds of apathy and depression and numbed despair that one often finds among the more seasoned of the homeless, and almost all of them expressed hopes for the future that most observers would probably describe as unrealistically high.

These interviews, then, are encounters with people on the edge. Some of them will move back into more secure housing once their present emergency has been resolved, although many of the ones who do recover will be shaken back out of the tree the next time something goes wrong. A number of them will fail altogether and move into homelessness as a way of life. In either case, though, this is an interesting group to meet because in a sense the ones who succeed as well as the ones who do not will soon be drifting out of radio range. Those reabsorbed into the ranks of the precariously housed will be therefore out of touch, and those who become a more permanent part of the homeless population not only will be hard to locate but are likely to develop the kind of mute, dulled inaccessibility one finds among the chronically traumatized.

Most people in the sample place themselves, as one man put it, "right on the precipice between here and the streets." They have found temporary housing in a shelter—that's the "here" of which he speaks—but they know that to be no more than a temporary solution to a lasting problem. The world they came from is one in which everyday existence depends on a heavy expenditure of energy as well as a measure of good fortune. One woman, dependent upon state aid to feed herself and her infant child, describes how much work it is to live on welfare:

> [The aid helps, but] it keeps you stuck right where you are. It's not enough to get out because of the cost of living, and it's not enough to stay where you are. It's enough to just make you crazy, because it's only barely survival, and when you are scrounging for money and survival, there is nothing else you can accomplish. It takes everything you have—every ounce of energy, every ounce of concentration or focus—so

you find that your life is consumed by getting through the day.

Living like that involves a form of calculation that few of us have to face on anything more than an occasional basis. Another single woman, this time with two children, offers a lesson on accounting among the very poor:

> So I lost my place, because I basically couldn't keep up with it. . . . See, I have just enough to make it, and I know each time this check comes that I can do a, b, and c, and get just enough groceries until the fifteenth or the food stamp day or whatever. And you decide you're going to get your kids some decent sneakers and clothes. You say, "to hell with it, I'll take a few bucks and I'll make it up." And then you get a medical bill, and you pay that because it isn't covered. And then it's a domino factor, where you've taken x, y, and z from the rent money. And you can't catch up. I guess they assume that people would use [any extra] for beer or whatever, and they want you to have just enough to get by.

And if anything goes wrong in that brittle round of life, the bottom can fall out altogether. Here are two tales worth hearing, the first from a black man of forty-three, married for ten years and the father of an infant, and the other from a white woman of fifty-three, survivor of several marriages now living with three of her seven children. These two are older by quite a margin than most of the persons in our sample, but their stories are typical. The man:

> Well, for me it started when I lost my job. I was working for a realty company as an assistant manager, and they sold the building. They fired everyone who was working for the company, and I was out of work. That was in '86. I drew my unemployment, had odd jobs in between time. And then [my wife] lost her job because she became pregnant, and it's

just been a continuous downhill run for us. We depleted our savings. Then we had to move out of the apartment because the new management wanted to renovate, so everyone was given eviction notices. And things just kind of went sour all at once. . . . So what tried to do was move in with some other people, and that was the *biggest* mistake I ever made. Friends, supposed to be friends. . . . I've tried it with three different friends, moved in with three different friends, and none of them worked.

Now the woman:

I had come from Texas about July, August. My children were all in this area. I was divorced. There was no reason to stay there, so I came here. I registered for Kelly Services right away. I've always done that because they would always put me on a full-time, six-month assignment, so I wouldn't have to worry. We rented an apartment, my two older sons who are not married and my little one and myself. . . . It was real nice. Then just a chain of circumstances. I broke my leg, and Kelly, of course, was not going to send me out on assignment on crutches. And I broke my leg at home, so there was no workmen's comp. . . . And then the car broke down, and my son, who is a security guard, needed it. You have to have transportation or they remove you, which they did. There was no way of getting there on a bus. And then the next one, the one that was 22, got involved in drugs. He is now in jail. And we got an eviction notice, naturally. The landlord wouldn't go along with anything, he wouldn't work with us. We were evicted the 23rd of December. I'd never been in a situation like this before, and I went to welfare. They gave me three checks for $210 . . . and when it was gone I proceeded to sell all my belongings that I had that was of any value because I thought "What am I going to do here? It's going to be living in the car now." It was terrible.

So the fall from grace feels like a thing of contingencies, a history made up of details each one of which is small in scale. It is a fall from grace without motive, logic, meaning, rhythm. There are no critical moments around which a dramatic narrative can be spun, no decisive turns of fate that can lend it a tragic quality. It is, as we just heard, a free fall, "a continuous downhill run," "a chain of circumstances."

It is hard for the newly homeless to find sound bearings in the world they now enter. For one thing, the unthinkable happens all the time:

One time we didn't have nowhere to go. I don't know if you ever heard of Tent City; it's like a camp-out. We went there one time. This guy was nice enough to give us a sleeping bag and let us stay there in his little tent thing. The next morning we woke up, and my son's face was all swole up where the mosquitoes had bitten, and that scared me to death. I thought: right now I'd kill to get him inside, to get him out of these streets. . . . He was disfigured. He was disfigured, I'm telling you. It scared me to death.

We were sitting one morning [in a shelter] and I was reading the bible at five, six o'clock in the morning. And I looked up and there was literally a maggot crawling out of this baby's diaper. I just jumped. They acted like it was an everyday thing, but I just flipped out. And then one of the men came up with a flashlight, and they were finding them all over the floor.

It was depressing what you see in the [welfare] hotels. You see children half taken care of. You see mothers on drugs. You see beatings, you see child abuse. . . . You see murder, people get killing in a room. It's every day. Every day you'll see a child beat up. You see all this every day, and you say "Where's the way out?"

When one realizes where one is, the result can be a panic that borders on disorientation and disbelief. Most of these people have lived near the edge of poverty before, so they know something of deprivation and want. But this new world is a grotesque wonderland where nothing can be taken for granted and the rules of everyday life seem inverted.

This has been like a great panic to me. I'm known as the type of person who can handle anything, but since I've been here I've been fearful all the time. I walked the streets wondering: "What am I going to do? I got two girls. There's no way I can make them sleep on the street!"

You don't know what a mental strain it is to know that, okay, I'm not in the cold tonight with my child, but where in the heck am I going to sleep tomorrow night? There was one night I remember very, very clear. We thought we had made an arrangement with a friend that we could stay overnight, and it fell through at eleven o'clock at night. It was very cold outside, and my daughter—I actually went into tears sitting on a park bench. . . . I think I was delirious or something, because it really scared me to death.

That was really something. It was cold. You go downtown and you see people sleeping in cardboard boxes. You just have to pick a spot. I *never* thought I would be that way. Never.

It's a very strange feeling not to have enough money to buy food. It's really a strange feeling. It's hard to deal with. . . . Fear is something I've dealt with—on the level of terror almost—at the thought of being without a roof over your head. . . . To me, one of the basic fundamentals of life is having a roof over your head, no matter what. So there's panic and fear, a sense of disbelief. It just doesn't seem possible, yet there you are dealing with it. A nightmare!

Many of the homeless, as one might easily imagine, begin by blaming themselves for the circumstances in which they find themselves, even though, when they are pressed, it is difficult for them to figure out how they might have managed otherwise. What is one supposed to do about a broken leg or a stolen car or a beating or an eviction notice? So it is a generalized feeling of guilt, a sense of incompetence and unworthiness. The first speaker here is speaking about the father of her four children, and the second about herself:

> I think he takes it a little more to heart than I do, because he sort of feels like "Well, I'm not doing what I supposed to, I'm not holding up [my end of the bargain]. I've got to provide everything for my family, and I've always got to have things right for them." And I just tell him: "The only way I can see to look at it is that this is an experience that God wanted us to go through, and this is His way of showing us how to make it through. This is a learning experience." He responds, but then he slips back into "Well, I'm not doing this and I'm not doing that."

> With me being pregnant, it's not too good. I'm okay when I know I have a place to stay, but the closer we get to going into the street, the crazier my mood swings get. I keep on thinking to myself "I have this daughter of mine. I can't even get a roof over her head. I should just give her up to somebody else who can take care of her." Because it makes me feel inadequate. It feels like I'm not doing a good enough job being mom.

But none of the doubts these unfortunate people have about themselves can match the contempt with which they think they are being treated by others. People who lack confidence in themselves often have a way of seeing that assessment mirrored in the words and looks of those with whom they deal, so we may want to make some allowance for that very human habit when the time comes to make judgments. But the main point to be made is that the sense of being despised and rejected and set apart as loathsome—"contaminated" may even be the right word—is a palpable part of the world of the homeless.

It begins with agency personnel. These, we might as well assume, are good people doing hard and draining work. They are not crankier or meaner than workers in other offices, nor are they quicker to judge. But a larger logic seems to govern exchanges between the homeless and the persons assigned to help them. The homeless often act with a sharpness born of panic and frustration and a sense of injustice, and agency personnel, in their turn, overwhelmed by the sheer numbers with which they must deal, need to protect themselves from all that urgency and despair. So the exchange reflects a social situation more than it does individual moods or biases. It is a meeting of social forces as well as personalities. It is a cultural composition.

"These people make you feel like you are white trash," said a white father of twenty-eight, adding diplomatically, "whether you're white or black."

> I know I'm homeless. I know that I could have prevented getting homeless, but I was in a no-win situation. . . . But they make you feel like you're the scum of the earth when you come and ask them for help. . . . It's bad enough that you have to come to a place like this because they know you've hit rock bottom, but then they're treating you like trash.

One man interviewed by Jonathan Kozol for *Rachel and Her Children* knew that feeling all too well. They make you feel like "trash," he said, a problem of "waste disposal."[10] One black mother of four from the Miller and Seltser sample seemed to catch the nature of the encounter with an eye that was wistful and philosophic as well as angry:

> I thought: "I'm a grown person and I can be treated like an adult. I'm going to respect you and I would like for you to

respect me. This is not the way I'm planning on staying, so
you don't have to treat me this way. . . . [Y]ou don't really
know my whole situation, you just answer the phone." Most
of them, their general attitude is: "Why don't you get a job?"
They deal with the outside, but they don't deal with the
inside. And the inside, there's more to it than just getting
jobs, especially when there's child care and transportation
problems. And money. There's a lot of things inside of the
picture book, but they look outside and they judge from the
outside of it.

That's it precisely. How can agency personnel, deluged by
oceans of troubled people, afford to look for the inside?
    The rest of the world seems to look upon the homeless
in the same way. Some of them sense a general attitude of
disapproval and disdain, a reaction they find easy to understand in that they cannot help sharing it themselves in part.
A white mother of one says:

Yes, there's a pressure, there's a self-consciousness involved.
If I buy something at the store and I'm pushing it around in
the cart, I suddenly have this self-consciousness: I don't want
to appear to be homeless. Because people do look at you.
And everybody's so conscious of homeless people now that
if you even look remotely like you might be carrying around
too much with you, people look at you—especially when
you have a child. So you have to be sure that it doesn't look
like you're schlepping everything around. That might seem
silly, but I'm sure I'm not the only one who experiences that
fear. We've all seen the other people with the shopping carts
and everything. There's that. And there's feelings of inade-
quacy, as I've mentioned. Feelings of rejection. You feel like
a heavy weight as far as judgment is concerned.

For others, however, the attitude of the world in general
has a sharper sting. A black mother of seven children: "People are under the impression that, if you're homeless, you're

either an alcoholic or a dope addict, not that hard times hit
and you were trying to make ends meet. It's like you are
lowlife. Like you are the scum of the earth." The man who
spoke of "white trash" a moment ago had a brief story to
illustrate his complaint: "When I was growing up, everybody said: 'If you get down and out, don't go stealing. Go
ask somebody to sweep the parking lot.' So me and my kid
went up to ask this store if we could sweep the parking lot.
They called the cops on us! Was going to have us thrown
in jail!"

All this fuels the already overwhelming feeling that one
has lost membership in the larger human community. One
now lives outside the circle in which compassion and respect
can be taken for granted. One now belongs—like Dickens's
Jo—to a different order of being. Many of these people,
mind you, are new to shelter life, having been without
homes for no more than a few days or a few weeks, so we
are not listening here to people with any long experience
of homelessness. "There is this feeling of being disconnected," said one woman, "of not being in the mainstream
of society. There is this sense that the world is passing you
by." And the same woman of fifty-three who broke her leg
during a family-wide free fall put it well: "You're kind of
ashamed to go to church. You're kind of ashamed to go
anywhere. I feel like a forty-fifth class person." As we noted
in earlier chapters, one finds these feelings wherever people
have been battered by the force of some severe calamity.
But one also finds them in places where people feel abandoned, cut adrift, separated from the larger flows of human
life, treated like a form of refuse. For that, too, is a form
of battering.

The feeling of being outside society is, of course, a state
of mind, but it is, in certain ways, a problem of practical
mechanics, if only in the sense that appliances and conve-
niences that the rest of the world takes entirely for granted

are no longer within reach. There is a wonderful moment in Aleksandr Solzhenitsyn's *One Day in the Life of Ivan Denisovich* where a prisoner in a Siberian work camp—always outside, always cold—simply gives up trying to explain himself to someone sitting in an office. After all, he concludes, "How can you expect a man who's warm to understand a man who's cold?" The parallel is far from exact, but the homeless often feel that the everyday circumstances in which they try to make a life are so far outside the experiences of other people that they cannot really be expected to understand. Everyday cleanliness, for example: "It was bad . . . when we were living in the car. And the biggest problem was taking a bath and ironing my daughter's clothes. Because if you don't send her to school, people are going to report you and then they're going to take her away." Or being without refrigeration: "I had to go to the store every day, because I didn't have a refrigerator or anything. It was a lot of hassle, a lot of pain, because you have to carry the children everywhere you go, and they was tired. So it was like if you didn't have a strong mind, it could be very tiring on you. I think that's why a lot of people give up. They don't have any way out. They just get so depressed." Or any of the details of life:

> It's hard to look for a job when you don't have clean clothes. It's hard to look for a job when you wake up and you've got to make sure that your family is secure. . . . My first objective every day was to make sure my daughter had Pampers and milk, then my second objective was to make sure she [my wife] had something to eat and I had something to eat. And last but not least that we had a place to stay. If I accomplished those feats, then I have done my day's duty. . . . I've had to hustle. Like selling cans, picking up aluminum, just walking down the street seeing guys building apartments asking if they need some help. . . . Some days we were at it all day, hour after hour. Simplest things. Day after day after day after day after day.

This may be more of a problem for those, like the man above, who have not yet learned the ways of the street or developed the habits of mind and the emotional reflexes— the sense of detachment and distance—that are a part of that round of life. A relatively seasoned campaigner, one of the few in our sample with some experience of the homeless life, said: "As far as the streets are concerned, I have a master's degree that you can't get in nobody's university. I wouldn't trade it for the world." This was a black mother of six who just turned thirty. But most of the people she met in the shelter had scarcely begun their education. The first speaker is a black man and the second a white woman, both of them parents:

> The greatest problem that people struggling have is lack of information, lack of knowledge of resources. I've talked to people that have been sleeping in the park, that has gone hungry, that didn't even know about the food banks. They didn't know about the cold weather program, they didn't know about the homeless shelter. . . . Most is mouth to mouth, people that are in a similar situations to yourself. That's where you pick up your most valuable information.

> It was about four o'clock in the morning. It was freezing cold. I didn't have no coat for Allison, no coat for myself, no coat for my husband. And they made us go outside. And I mean that was the scariest. These were like street people for years. Sometimes people have been doing this, living on the street, for years, and they know. They're streetwise. But we've always had a home. We had no experience.

And that is one of several ironies: Fate can leave you without a home, but you have to learn to be homeless! In the long run the process of becoming homeless is not at all unlike the process of becoming an inmate described by Erving Goffman—the irony being that the kinds of institutionalized patient from whom Goffman learned the process forty years ago are now among the homeless.

When one ponders the scene from a distance, homelessness looks like an enduring feature of the human landscape, and the ranks of the homeless appear mute, dulled, inert, adrift. They seem a thing apart, caught in currents unlike those that impel the rest of us. But the slide into homelessness, even when it sounds gradual and inexorable in the telling, can be an acute and traumatic moment to those who experience it. Whether gradual or abrupt, however, can leave marks on the spirit as crushing and as immediate as a collision or any other sharp turn of fate.

That is why the words I used to describe the people of Buffalo Creek not long after as acute an attack as can be imagined could nonetheless be applied to those who drift homeless across a more chronic terrain. A homeless shelter or a welfare hotel, too, can look "as if it had been painted in shades of gray," and the people one finds in them often act "as if they were surrounded by a sheath of heavy air through which they could move only at the cost of a deliberate effort." That, as I noted earlier, is the look of trauma.

PART TWO

6

Hiroshima:
Of Accidental Judgments
and Casual Slaughters

On the morning of August 6, 1945, and again on the morning of August 9, atomic bombs were exploded a few hundred yards above the cities of Hiroshima and Nagasaki.

I

A single B-29, lazy in the morning sky, passes over the center of town at an elevation of twenty-five thousand feet without attracting much attention. A few seconds later the whole area is lit up with a bluish white glare, which is quickly transformed into a huge fireball and a thick column of smoke beginning its climb into the sky. Heat rays from the initial flash blister roof tiles for a distance of several hundred yards, char telephone poles more than a mile away, and burn exposed human flesh as far away as two and a half miles. The heat rays are followed in an instant by a seemingly soundless blast wave that smashes everything standing for a considerable distance and fills the air with bits of debris. A period of relative calm follows as the day darkens under clouds of dust raised by the blast. And then a conflagration, a virtual whirlwind of fire, bursts into motion and rages out of control for the rest of the morning and afternoon. In the meantime, minute particles of carbon as well as fission fragments and other debris are sucked up into the colder air overhead, where they condense and return in the form of an oily black rain, slick and full of radioactive fallout.

In a matter of hours, nine square miles of Hiroshima and five square miles of Nagasaki—the latter somewhat more protected within a ring of hills—are reduced to dust and ashes.

As many as 140,000 people in Hiroshima and 70,000 in Nagasaki died on the day of the attack or in the weeks immediately following, and the death toll rose by another 130,000 or so before five years had elapsed. Hundreds of thousands of others, of course, were severely hurt, some of them never to recover, and to this day people die from injuries or illnesses that can reasonably be traced to the effects of the bombs.

Those caught near the center of the explosion ran a high risk of being incinerated by the white flash or of being blown apart by the force of the blast. And those who happened somehow to escape the direct effects were crushed under millions of tons of wreckage, lacerated by flying splinters of glass and wood, or engulfed in the fire storms that soon followed. The farther away one was from the center and the more effectively one was shielded, the better were one's chances of survival; but the bomb shot out its deadly shafts in every direction, and no one within a matter of miles was truly out of range, truly safe. Even a mile or more from the center people moved along in a daze with their skin peeling off in loose folds like layers of clothing and charred so badly that one could not tell at first whether one was looking at them from the back or the front. A considerable part of the death toll, too, must be charged to the radiation, for among its more sinister effects are the slowing down of the natural processes of regeneration and the lowering of resistance to infection.

The other effects of radiation were felt later. At the time of the attacks large numbers of people suffered from nausea, vomiting, fever, anorexia, diarrhea, and what is delicately translated in the most thorough audit of these troubles as "general malaise."[1] No one knew what these symptoms signified, of course, nor were people much better informed about the matter a few weeks later when many of them began to notice that their hair was falling out, that they were developing high fevers, that they were experiencing strange lesions and ulcers as well as discoloration of the skin, and that they were not only bleeding from the nose and gums but leaving evidence of internal bleeding in stools, urine, and sputum.

It is not clear how many people died from the effects of radiation within the few weeks of the attacks themselves, but the long-range effects certainly became evident. Infants then in utero were destined to die in considerable numbers, to experience more growth disorders and chromosome abnormalities and to have higher rates of microcephaly and mental retardation than their peers. Young children exposed to the effects of the bombs failed to grow as tall or to become as robust as nonvictims, and they matured more slowly. And both adults and children were to experience abnormally high rates of blood disorders, cataracts, leukemia, and other malignancies.

By the awesome standards of today's weaponry, these bombs were primitive little devices, but the destruction of Nagasaki and Hiroshima was, for all intents and purposes, complete. Not only had most of the landscape been turned into scorched ruins, but the two communities no longer had the vital resources, the necessary reserves to manage their own recovery. More than half the population was dead or disabled, and the rest were so dazed, so hurt, so in shock that they were not able to maintain useful connections with one another. To the extent that communities can be sensibly thought of as organisms, as living systems, these had simply disintegrated.

The great majority of families had been weakened by the loss of at least one member, yet the burdens on those families had increased considerably and continued to do so in the years to follow. Many had members who required years of expensive medical care or who remained infirm forever. And many never got over the fear that some dark poison was lodged deep in the tissues of every survivor, ready to erupt into new malignancies or to pass along the family line to generations yet unborn.

The destructive power of those miniature bombs, then, was appalling, beyond comprehension in any useful human sense. And the question often asked since is: What could bring a fundamentally decent people to do such a thing? What kind of mood does a fundamentally decent people have to be in, what kind of moral arrangements must it make, before it is willing to annihilate as many as a quarter of a million human beings to make a point?

II

The bombings of Hiroshima and Nagasaki are among the most thoroughly studied moments on human record. Together they constitute the only occasion in history when atomic weapons were dropped on living populations, and together they constitute the only occasion in history when a decision was made to employ them in that way.

I want to reflect here on the second of those points.

The "decision to drop"—I will explain in a minute why quotation marks are useful here—is a fascinating historical episode. But it is also an exhibit of the most profound importance as we consider our prospects for the future. It is a case history well worth attending to, a compelling parable.

If one were to tell the story of that decision as historians normally do, the details arranged in an ordered narrative, one might begin in 1938 with the discovery of nuclear fission or perhaps a year later with the delivery of Einstein's famous letter to President Roosevelt. No matter what its opening scene, though, the tale would then proceed along a string of events—a sequence of appointees named, committees formed, reports issued, orders signed, arguments won and lost, minds made up and changed—all of it coming to an end with a pair of tremendous blasts in the soft morning air over Japan.

The difficulty with that way of relating the story, as historians of the period testify, is that the more closely one examines the record, the harder it is to make out where in the flow of events something that could reasonably be called a decision was reached at all. To be sure, a kind of consensus emerged from the sprawl of ideas and happenings that made up the climate of wartime Washington, but when we look back, it is hard to distinguish those pivotal moments in the story when the crucial issues were identified, debated, reasoned through, resolved. The decision, to the extent that one can even speak of such a thing, was shaped and seasoned by a force very like inertia.

Let's say, then, that a wind began to blow, ever so gently at first, down the corridors along which power flows. As it gradually gathered momentum during the course of the war, the people caught up in it began to assume, without ever checking up on it, that it had a logic and a motive, that it had been set in motion by sure hands acting on the basis of wise counsel.

Harry Truman, in particular, remembered it as a time of tough and lonely choices and titled his memoir of that period *Year of Decisions*. But the bulk of those choices can in all fairness be said to have involved confirmation of projects already under way or implementation of decisions made at other levels of command. General Leslie R. Groves, military head of the Manhattan Project, was close to the mark when he described Truman's decision as "one of noninterference—basically, a decision not to upset the existing plans."[2] And J. Robert Oppenheimer spoke equally to the point when he observed some twenty years later: "The decision was implicit in the project. I don't know whether it could have been stopped."[3]

In September 1944, when it became more and more evident that a bomb would be produced in time for combat use, Franklin Roosevelt and Winston Churchill met at Hyde Park and initialed a brief aide-mémoire, noting, among other things, that the new weapon "might, perhaps, after mature consideration, be used against the Japanese."[4] This document does not appear to have had any effect on the conduct of the war, and Truman knew nothing at all about it. But it would not have made a real difference in any case, for neither chief of state did much to initiate the "mature consideration" they spoke of so glancingly, and Truman, in turn, could only suppose that such matters had been considered already. "Truman did not inherit the question," wrote Martin J. Sherwin, "he inherited the answer."[5]

What would "mature consideration" have meant in such a setting as that anyway?

First of all, presumably, it would have meant seriously asking whether the weapon should be employed at all. But we have it on the authority of virtually all the principal players that no one in a position to do anything about it ever really considered alternatives to combat use. Henry L. Stimson, secretary of war: "At no time, from 1941 to 1945, did I ever hear it suggested by the President, or by any other responsible member of the government, that atomic energy should not be used in the war."[6] Harry Truman: "I regarded the bomb as a military weapon and never had any doubt that it should be used."[7] General Groves: "Certainly, there was no question in my mind, or, as far as I was ever aware, in the mind of either President Roosevelt or President Truman or any other responsible person, but that we were developing a weapon to be employed against the enemies of the United States."[8] Winston Churchill: "There never was a moment's discussion as to whether the atomic bomb should be used or not."[9]

And why should anyone be surprised? We were at war, after all, and with the most resolute of enemies, so the unanimity of that feeling is wholly understandable. But it was not, by any stretch of the imagination, a product of mature consideration.

"Combat use" meant a number of different things, however, and a second question began to be raised with some frequency in the final months of the war, all the more insistently after the defeat of Germany. Might a way be devised to demonstrate the awesome power of the bomb in a convincing enough fashion to induce the surrender of the Japanese without having to destroy huge numbers of civilians? Roosevelt may have been pondering something of the sort. In September 1944, for example, three days after initialing the Hyde Park aide-mémoire, he asked Vannevar Bush, a trusted science adviser, whether the bomb "should actually be used against the Japanese or whether it should be used only as a threat."[10] While that may have been little more than idle musing, a number of different schemes were explored within both the government and the scientific community in the months following.

One option involved a kind of *benign strike*—the dropping of a bomb on some built-up area, but only after advance notice had been issued so that residents could evacuate the area and leave an empty slate on which the bomb could write its terrifying signature. This plan was full of difficulties. A dud under those dramatic circumstances might do enormous damage to American credibility, and moreover, to broadcast any warning was to risk the endeavor in other ways. Weak as the Japanese were by this time in the war, it was easy to imagine their finding a way to intercept an incoming airplane if they knew where and when it was expected, and officials in Washington were afraid that it would occur to the Japanese, as it had to them, that the venture would come to an abrupt end if American prisoners of war were brought into the target area.

The second option was a *tactical strike* against a purely military target—an arsenal, railroad yard, depot, factory, harbor—without advance notice. Early in the game, for example, someone nominated the Japanese fleet concentration at Truk. The problem with this notion, however—and there is more than a passing irony here—was that no known military target had a wide enough compass to contain the whole of the destructive capacity of the weapon and so display its full range and power. The committee inquiring into likely targets wanted one "more than three miles in diameter" because anything smaller would be too inadequate a canvas for the picture it was supposed to hold.[11]

The third option was to stage a kind of *dress rehearsal* by detonating a bomb in some remote corner of the world—a desert or empty island, say—to exhibit to international observers brought in for the purpose what the device could do. The idea had been proposed by a group of scientists in what has since been called the Franck Report, but it commanded no more than a moment's attention. It had the same problems as the benign strike: The risk of being embarrassed by a dud was more than most officials in a position to decide were willing to take, and there was a widespread feeling that any demonstration involving advance notice would give the enemy too much useful information.

The fourth option involved a kind of *warning shot*. The thought here was to drop a bomb without notice over a relatively uninhabited stretch of enemy land so that the Japanese high command might see at first hand what was in store if Japan failed to surrender soon. Edward Teller thought that an explosion at night high over Tokyo Bay would serve as a brilliant visual argument,[12] and Admiral Lewis Strauss, soon to become a member (and later the chair) of the Atomic Energy Commission, recommended a strike on a local forest, reasoning that the blast would "lay the trees out in windrows from the center of the explosion in all directions as though they were matchsticks," meanwhile igniting a fearsome fire storm at the epicenter. "It seemed to me," he added, "that a demonstration of this sort would prove to the Japanese that we could destroy any of their cities at will."[13] The physicist Ernest O. Lawrence may have been speaking half in jest when he suggested that a bomb might be used to "blow the top off" Mount Fujiyama,[14] but he was entirely serious when he assured a friend early in the war: "The bomb will never be dropped on people. As soon as we get it, we'll use it only to dictate peace."[15]

Now, hindsight is no rare talent. But it seems evident that the fourth of those options, the warning shot, was much to be preferred over the other three and even more to be preferred over use on living targets. I do not want to argue the case here. I do want to ask, however, why that possibility was so easily dismissed.

The fact of the matter seems to have been that the notion of a demonstration was discussed on only a few occasions once the Manhattan Project neared completion, and most of those discussions were off the record. So a historian trying to reconstruct the drift of those conversations can only flatten an ear against the wall, as it were, and see if any sense can be made of the muffled voices next door. It seems very clear, for example, that the options involving advance notice were brought up so often and so early in official conversations that they came to *mean* demonstration in the minds of several important players. If a James Byrnes, say, soon to be named secretary of state, were asked why one could not detonate a device in unoccupied territory, he might raise the problem posed by prisoners of war, and if the same question were asked of a James Bryant Conant, another science adviser, he might speak of the embarrassment that would follow a dud, thus, in both cases, joining ideas that had no logical relation to each other. Neither prisoners of war nor fear of failure, of course, posed any argument against a surprise demonstration.

There were two occasions, however, on which persons in a position to affect policy discussed the idea of a nonlethal demonstration. Those two conversations together consumed no more than a matter of minutes, so far as one can tell at this remove, and they, too, were off the record. But they seem to represent virtually the entire investment of the government of the United States in "mature consideration" of the subject.

The first discussion took place at a meeting of what was called the Interim Committee, a striking gathering of military, scientific, and government brass under the chairmanship of Secretary of War Henry Stimson. This group, which included James Byrnes and Chief of Staff General George C. Marshall, met on a number of occasions in May 1945 to discuss policy issues raised by the new bomb, and Stimson recalled later that at one of their final meetings the members "carefully considered such alternatives as a detailed advance warning or a demonstration in some uninhabited area."[16] But the minutes of the meeting, as well as the accounts of those present, suggest otherwise. The only exchange on the subject, in fact, took place during a luncheon break, and while we have no way of knowing what was actually said in that conversation, we do know what conclusion emerged from it. One participant, Arthur H. Compton, recalled later:

"Though the possibility of a demonstration that would not destroy human lives was attractive, no one could suggest a way in which it could be made so convincing that it would be likely to stop the war."[17] And the recording secretary of the meeting noted: "Dr. Oppenheimer . . . said he doubted whether there could be devised any sufficiently startling demonstration that would convince the Japanese they ought to throw in the sponge."[18]

Two weeks later four physicists who served as advisers to the Interim Committee met in Los Alamos to consider once again the question of demonstration. They were Arthur Compton, Enrico Fermi, Ernest Lawrence, and Robert Oppenheimer—as distinguished an assembly of scientific talent as could be imagined, the first three of them Nobel laureates—and they concluded, after a discussion of which we have no record: "We can propose no technical demonstration likely to being an end to the war; we see no acceptable alternative to direct military use."[19] That, so far as anyone can tell, was the end of it.

We cannot be sure that a milder report would have made a difference, for the Manhattan Project was gathering momentum as it moved toward the more steeply pitched inclines of May and June, but we can be sure that the idea of a demonstration was at that point spent. The Los Alamos report ended with something of a disclaimer ("We have, however, no claim to special competence . . ."), but its message was clear enough. When asked about the report nine years later in his security hearings, Oppenheimer said, with what may have been a somewhat defensive edge in his voice, "We did not think exploding one of those things as a firecracker over the desert was likely to be very impressive."[20]

Perhaps not. But those fragments are telling for another reason. If you listen to them carefully for a moment or two, you realize that these are the voices of nuclear physicists trying to imagine how a strange and distant people will react to an atomic blast. These are the voices of nuclear physicists dealing with psychological and anthropological questions about Japanese culture, Japanese temperament, Japanese will to resist—topics, we must assume, about which they had no knowledge at all. They did not know yet what the bomb could actually do since its first test was not to take place for another month. But in principle, at least, Oppenheimer and Fermi reflecting on matters relating to the Japanese national character should have had about the same force as Ruth Benedict and Margaret Mead reflecting on matters relating to high-energy physics, the first difference being that Benedict and Mead would not have presumed to do so and the second being that no one in authority would have listened to them if they had.

The first of the two morals I want to draw from the foregoing—this being a parable after all—is that in moments of critical contemplation it is often hard to know where the competencies of soldiers and scientists and all the rest of us begin and end. Many an accidental judgment can emerge from such confusions.

But what if the conclusions of the scientists had been correct? What if some kind of demonstration had been staged in a lightly occupied part of Japan and it *had* been greeted as a firecracker in the desert? What then?

Let me shift gears for a moment and discuss the subject in another way. It is standard wisdom for everyone in the United States old enough to remember the war, and for most of those to whom it is ancient history, that the bombings of Hiroshima and Nagasaki were the only alternative to an all-out invasion of the Japanese mainland involving hundreds of thousands and perhaps millions of casualties on both sides. Unless the Japanese came to understand the need to surrender quickly, we would have been drawn by an almost magnetic force toward those dreaded beaches. This has become an almost automatic pairing of ideas, an article of common lore. If you lament that so many civilians were incinerated or blown to bits in Hiroshima and Nagasaki, then somebody will remind you of the American lives thus saved. Truman was the person most frequently asked to account for the bombings, and his views were emphatic on the subject:

> It was a question of saving hundreds of thousands of American lives. I don't mind telling you that you don't feel normal when you have to plan hundreds of thousands of complete, final deaths of American boys who are alive and joking and having fun while you are doing your planning. You break your heart and your head trying to figure out a way to save one life. The name given to our invasion plan was "Olympic," but I saw nothing godly about the killing of all the people that would be necessary to make that invasion. I could not worry about what history would say about my personal morality. I made the only decision I ever knew how to make. I did what I thought was right.* [21]

Veterans of the war, particularly those who had reason to suppose that they would have been involved in an invasion, have drawn that same connection repeatedly, prominent among them Paul Fussell in the pages of the *New Republic*. Thank God for the bomb, the argument goes, it saved the lives of countless numbers of us. [22] And so, in a sense, it may have.

---

*Merle Miller notes, in *Plain Speaking: An Oral Biography of Harry S. Truman*, that Truman may have had moments of misgiving: "My only insight into Mr. Truman's feeling about the Bomb and its dropping, and it isn't much, came one day in his private library at the Truman Memorial Library. In one corner was every book ever published on the Bomb, and at the end of one was Horatio's speech in the last scene of Hamlet." Mr. Truman had underlined these words:

> . . . let me speak to the yet unknowing world
> How these things came about: So shall you hear
> Of carnal, bloody, and unnatural acts,
> Of accidental judgements, casual slaughters
> Of deaths put on by cunning and forced cause,
> And, in this upshot, purposes mistook
> Fall'n on the inventors' heads. . . .

But the destruction of Hiroshima and Nagasaki had nothing to do with it.

Good sense requires us to assume, even if few people were well enough positioned in early August to see the situation whole, that there simply was not going to be an invasion. Not ever. For what sane power, with the atomic weapon securely in its arsenal, would hurl a million or more of its sturdiest young men on a heavily fortified mainland? To imagine anyone ordering an invasion when the means were at hand to blast Japan into a sea of gravel at virtually no cost in American lives is to imagine a madness beyond anything even the worst of war can induce. The invasion had not yet been called off, granted. But it surely would have been, and long before the November 1 deadline set for it.

The United States did not become a nuclear power on August 6 with the destruction of Hiroshima. It became a nuclear power on July 16, when the first test device was exploded in Alamogordo, New Mexico. Uncertainties remained, of course, many of them. But from that moment on the United States knew how to produce a bomb, knew how to deliver it, and knew it would work. Stimson said shortly after the war that the bombings of Hiroshima and Nagasaki "ended the ghastly specter of a clash of great land armies,"[23] but he could have said, with greater justice, that the ghastly specter ended at Alamogordo. Churchill came close to making exactly that point when he first learned of the New Mexico test: "To quell the Japanese resistance man by man and conquer the country yard by yard might well require the loss of a million American lives and half that number of British. . . . Now all that nightmare picture had vanished."[24]

It *had* vanished. So far as the war with Japan was concerned, the time of inch-by-inch crawling over enemy territory, the time of Guadalcanal and Iwo Jima and Okinawa, was just plain over.

The point is that once we had the bomb and were committed to its use, the terrible weight of invasion no longer hung
over our heads. The Japanese were incapable of mounting
any kind of offensive, as every observer has agreed, and it
was our option when to close with the enemy and thus risk
casualties. So we could have easily afforded to hold for a
moment, to think it over, to introduce what Dwight Eisen-
hower called "that awful thing" to the world on the basis of
something closer to mature consideration. We could have
afforded to detonate a bomb over some less lethal target
and then pause to see what happened. And do it a second
time. Maybe a third. And if none of those demonstrations
had made a difference, we would presumably have had to
strike harder. Hiroshima and Nagasaki would still have been
there a few weeks later for that purpose, silent and un-
touched—"unspoiled" was the term General H. H. Arnold
used[25]—for whatever came next.

Common lore also has it that there were not bombs
enough for such niceties, but that seems not to have been
the case. The United States was ready to deliver a third
bomb toward the end of August, and Groves had already
informed Marshall and Stimson that three or four more
bombs would be available in September, a like number in
October, at least five in November, and seven in December,
with substantial increases to follow in early 1946.[26] Even if
we assume that Groves was being too hopeful about the
productive machinery he had set in motion, as one expert
close to the matter has suggested to me, a formidable number of bombs would have been available by the date originally set for invasion.

That brings us back to the matter of momentum. The
best way to tell the story of those days is to say that the
"decision to drop" had become a force like gravity. It had
taken life. The fact that the bomb existed supplied its own
meaning, its own reason for being. Elting E. Morison, Stimson's biographer, put it well:

Any process started by men toward a special end tends, for reasons logical, biological, aesthetic or whatever they may be, to carry forward, if other things remain equal, to its climax. [This is] the inertia developed in a human system. . . . In a process where such a general tendency has been set to work it is difficult to separate the moment when men were still free to choose from the moment, if such there was, when they were no longer free to choose.[27]

I have said almost nothing about Nagasaki so far because it does not seem to have been the subject of any thought at all. The orders of the bomber command were to attack Japan as soon as the bombs were ready. One was ready on August 9, three days after the leveling of Hiroshima. Boom. When Groves was later asked why the attack on Nagasaki had come so soon after the attack on Hiroshima, leaving so little time for the Japanese to consider what had happened to them, he simply said: "Once you get your opponent reeling, you keep him reeling and never let him recover."[28] And that is the point, really. There is no law of nature that compels a winning side to press its superiority, but it is hard to slow down, hard to relinquish an advantage, hard to rein in the fury. The impulse to charge ahead, to strike at the throat, is so strong a habit of war that it almost ranks as a reflex. Many a casual slaughter can emerge from such moods.

If it is true, as I have suggested, that there were few military or logistic reasons for striking as sharply as we did and that the decision to drop moved in on the crest of an almost irreversible current, then it becomes important to ask what were some of the drifts that became a part of that larger current. An adequate accounting would have to consider a number of military, political, and other matters far beyond the reach of this brief essay, the most important of them by far being the degree to which the huge shadow of the Soviet Union loomed over both official meetings and private thoughts. It is nearly impossible to read the remaining record without assuming that the wish to make a loud announcement to the Russians was a persuasive factor in the minds of many of the principal participants. There were other drifts as well, of course, and I would like to note a few of the sort that sometimes occur to social scientists.

For one thing, an extraordinary amount of money and material—both of them in short supply in a wartime economy—had been invested in the Manhattan Project, and many observers thought that so large a public expense would be all the more willingly borne if it were followed by a striking display of what the money had been spent for.

And, too, extraordinary investments had been made in men and talent. The older of the people involved in the Manhattan Project—soldiers, engineers, scientists—made sacrifices in the form of separated families, interrupted careers, and a variety of other discomforts, and it makes a certain psychological sense that a decisive strike would serve as a kind of vindication for all the trouble. The younger of them, though, had been held out of combat, thus avoiding the fate of so many men of their generation, by accidents of professional training, personal skill, and sheer timing. The project was their theater of war, and it makes even more psychological sense that some of them would want the only shot they fired to be a truly resonant one.

The dropping of such a bomb, moreover, could serve as an ending, something sharp and distinct in a world that had become ever more blurred. The Grand Alliance was breaking up, and with it all hope for a secure postwar world. Roosevelt was dead. The future was full of ambiguity. And, most important, everybody was profoundly tired. In circumstances like that, a resounding strike would serve to clarify things, to give them form, to tidy them up a bit.

There are other matters one might point to, some of them minor, some of them major, all of them strands in the larger weave. There was a feeling, expressed by scientists and government officials alike, that the world needed a rude and decisive shock to awaken it to the realities of the atomic age. There was a feeling, hard to convey in words but easy to sense once one has become immersed in some of the available material, that the bomb had so much power and majesty, was so compelling a force, that one was almost required to give it birth and a chance to mature. There was a feeling, born of war, that for all its ferocity the atomic bomb was nevertheless no more than a minor increment on a scale of horror that already included the fire bombings of Dresden, Tokyo, and other enemy cities. And there was a feeling, also born of war, that living creatures on the other side, even the children, had somehow lost title to the mercies that normally accompany the fact of being human.

The kinds of points I have been making need to be stated either very precisely or in some detail. I have not yet learned to do the former; I do not have space enough here for the latter. So let me just end with the observation that human decisions do not always emerge from reflective counsels in which facts are arrayed in order and logic is the prevailing currency of thought. They emerge from complex fields of force, in which the vanities of leaders and the moods of constituencies and the inertias of bureaucracies play a critical part. That is as important a lesson as one can learn from the events of 1945—and as unnerving a one.

The bombings of Hiroshima and Nagasaki supply a rich case study for people who must live in times like ours. It is not important for us to apportion shares of responsibility to persons who played their parts so long ago, and I have not meant to do so here; these were humane and considerate people for the most part, operating with reflexes that had been tempered by war. We need to attend to such histories as this, however, because they provide the clearest illustrations we have of what human beings can do—this being the final moral to be drawn from our parable—when they find themselves in moments of crisis and have more destructive power at their disposal than they know what to do with.

7

Yucca Mountain: Good Riddance, Bad Rubbish

As this nation enters the second half century of the nuclear age, it confronts the extraordinary challenge of deciding what to do with its spent fuel and other forms of high-level nuclear waste. The most dangerous of these wastes have half-lives of a hundred thousand years or more, and they pose a measurable hazard for a good deal longer than that. To call them spent, in fact, is almost to turn language on its head. The wastes need to be set aside not because their vigor is drained or their fever cooled but exactly because they have become too irradiated for further use.

Three broad options are available for dealing with those materials.

The first is to reprocess them chemically in such a way that their uranium and plutonium can be recovered and used again as fuel. This procedure has the obvious appeal of treating them as a resource that can be recycled indefinitely, but it creates a number of other disposal problems in doing so and thus cannot be counted on as a long-term solution.

The second is to try to dispense with the wastes altogether by such measures as launching them into outer space, burying them under sediments on the ocean floor, depositing them on distant pacific atolls or on the frozen plains of Antarctica, or sealing them away in deep geological formations for the many millennia it will take them to cool.

The third option—not so much a long-term solution as a short-term policy—is to store them near the reactor that produced them or to transfer them to storage facilities on or near the earth's surface in the expectation that a better disposal strategy will be developed over time. (This might be called the Charlie Dressen strategy in honor of the onetime manager of the Brooklyn Dodgers who once said to his team as they were about to take the field in the late innings of a game in which they were desperately behind: "OK, guys, go out there and hold them while I think of something.")

Although some nuclear powers like France and Great Britain rely on reprocessing for a good part of their fuel needs, virtually all nations with the capacity to generate nuclear power now see deep geological burial as the eventual solution to the problem of waste disposal. But they vary considerably in the urgency with which they approach that eventuality. In most of the world authorities are content to let the wastes cool indefinitely on the surface (along with the political tempers the wastes always seem to arouse) and, in that relaxed frame of mind, have scarcely begun the search for permanent disposal sites.

The United States, however, is impatient to entomb those wastes once and for all, even though it is widely acknowledged that there are no compelling technical reasons for doing so anytime soon. The need to tidy things up in this way may run deeper in the American grain than is the case elsewhere—good riddance to bad rubbish—but there are powerful political reasons, too: The nuclear industry and the government agencies sharing its concerns clearly hope that a crisp and decisive solution to the waste problem will help breathe new life into what is now a declining enterprise.

Underground burial, whatever its technical merits, reflects a kind of natural logic. The uranium at the heart of those wastes was once an ore brought up from deep beneath the ground, and even though humankind has fired that ore into something truly awesome, it seems to make intuitive sense to put it back. Ashes to ashes, dust to dust. Too, we are creatures of the surface in much the same way that aquatic animals are creatures of the deep, and we find it easy to suppose that we have disposed of something, rid ourselves of something, if it is lofted above or sunk below the plane on which we live.

The Nuclear Waste Policy Act of 1982 has been this nation's official response to the disposal problem. The act set up a kind of unwelcome competition among a number of states to see which of them would serve as host for the first (and for a few years, at least, the only) high-level nuclear waste repository. The bill called for exhaustive scientific study of a number of potential sites, but the real hope, as one senior Senate staffer put it, was to discover a "technically appropriate subsurface with a politically compliant governor on top."[1] The nominated governors, though, proved anything but complaint, and the political strands of what Morris Udall called "that delicate fabric of agreements"[2] worked their way loose long before the most elementary questions about subsurfaces could even be raised. In 1986, before one exploratory shaft had been sunk or more than the most desultory technical work done anywhere, the number of sites selected for study ("characterization" it was to be called) was narrowed to three: a thick deposit of salt under the farmlands of Deaf Smith County in western Texas, a basalt formation under the Hanford Nuclear Reservation in south-central Washington, and a deep layer of volcanic tuff under a desert ridge in southern Nevada known as Yucca Mountain. In 1987, one year later, Congress simply announced in an amendment to the original bill that Yucca Mountain was winner of the competition by default, the understanding being, presumably, that if the site proves wanting geologically, the process will begin all over again somewhere else. So Yucca Mountain is it, although things look murkier than ever as of this writing. The Department of Energy (DOE) has delayed opening of the facility until 2010, and even that distant date seems wildly unrealistic.

It is obvious that the decision to concentrate on Yucca Mountain did not issue from any serious kind of comparative technical research. "What you are watching is an exercise in pure politics," said one member of the House of Representatives at the time of the 1987 amendment. "I am participating in a nonscientific process—sticking it to Nevada."[3] A future historian, moreover, looking in at our time, might very well go one step farther and conclude that the decision to rely on deep geological entombment for high-level nuclear wastes did not issue from a thorough scientific weighing of competing waste technologies either. A good deal of thought was given to alternatives at one point in the process,[4] but the only ones entertained at any length involved forms of "permanent disposal" because President Jimmy Carter distrusted reprocessing and had declared as a matter of policy that "resolving civilian waste management problems shall not be deferred to other generations."[5] A generous impulse, perhaps, but one without much in the way of scientific authority.

While we are peeling away layers of the past, we might add that the government's decision to invest in nuclear energy in the first place did not issue from any effort to evaluate competing energy technologies. The nuclear age came in on the crest of so strong a wave that it seemed almost to be ordained, and it was essentially the same wave that carried the first nuclear bombs to Hiroshima and Nagasaki. The development of a civilian nuclear program was a natural continuation of the wartime Manhattan Project, made more urgent by the cold war and by the hope that a peaceful atom might atone for what the wartime atom had done. David E. Lilienthal, the first chairman of the Atomic Energy Commission, spoke of the "conviction" he shared with his fellow nuclear enthusiasts "that somehow or other the discovery that had produced so terrible a weapon simply *had* to have an important peacetime use. . . . We were grimly determined to prove that this discovery was not just a weapon."[6]

Yucca Mountain is as barren a part of the United States as can be found. It is one hundred miles north and west of Las Vegas and fifty miles east of Death Valley. It sits on the western rim of (and, in fact, is partly in) the Nevada Nuclear Test Site, and it sits on the southern rim of (and is partly in) the Nellis Air Force Range. Fate made Yucca Mountain a dry, remote, gritty place. It slopes up from the rangelands of southern Nevada, covered with sagebrush and creosote, and it is a thing of immense silence and great beauty. Human beings, however, have been pounding the surrounding lands for more than forty years. Hundreds of nuclear devices have been detonated at the nearby test site, both underground and on the surface, and immediately to the north the gunnery range at Nellis has been bombarded not only by tens of thousands of bombs weighing up to five hundred pounds but by millions of rounds of strafing fire.

The test site and the Air Force range, together with lands managed by the Department of the Interior, occupy a considerable portion of southern Nevada. If one begins at Las Vegas in the south and circles clockwise from settlement to settlement around the edge of the enclosed federal lands—

a perimeter of hundreds of miles—one passes through a variety of places: the homes of small groups of southern Paiute and western Shoshone; towns like Pahrump, in the midst of a sharp real estate boom, and towns like Goldfield, once a lively mining town of twenty thousand but now home to barely four hundred; or towns like Caliente, once an important depot for coast-to-coast trains but now dominated by a railroad right-of-way along which few trains pass and none stop. The traveler passes through government installations and Mormon farms, brothels and trading posts, truck stops and small clusters of house trailers, and, in between, huge empty spaces.

As one circles the northern rim of the government lands, one crosses an important but unmarked boundary. People who live west of the test site—in Indian Springs, Pahrump, Amargosa Valley, Beatty, Goldfield, Tonopah—are much more likely to approve of plans for the repository not only because they live nearby and thus may be in a better position to profit from it but also because they were upwind during the period of atmospheric testing in the 1950s and early 1960s and have a more benign view of the dangers of radiation. People living east of the test site, on the other hand, and thus downwind—in Pioche, Panaca, Caliente, Alamo, Mesquite, Moapa—are far more apt to view the repository with suspicion. They are too far away to count it a source of income, for one thing, and many of them are convinced that their home territories were visited by drifting clouds of radioactivity during the times of atmospheric testing. So they have learned to be wary not only of nuclear power but of government policies and promises.

Shoshone and Paiute natives, meantime, see that whole tract as part of an ancient claim and view its use by federal agencies as "willful trespass." They have been using Yucca Mountain for at least twelve thousand years, so the notion that it can be "owned" by a government that set foot on it for the first time but a century ago and managed by a department established but a decade ago has an odd ring to them. The fact that depositing nuclear waste into the ground might contaminate underground water supplies as well as do other environmental mischief is a major concern for Indian and Anglo alike. But native people are much more likely than Anglos to think of underground spaces as a living part of the human habitat. The very idea of injecting the most virulent poisons ever known into the body of a mountain seems to them an insult to the earth, an affront to ancestors, and a violation of natural good sense.

High-level nuclear wastes, remember, can be dangerous for many thousands of years, and in recognition of that obdurate reality the Environmental Protection Agency has insisted on guarantees that they will stay isolated from "the accessible environment" for a full ten thousand years—held secure in canisters for a few hundred of those years and then, as the containers begin to degrade, by the geological formations in which they are entombed. That requirement is now under review, but the problem it was meant to solve remains the same: Somehow a way needs to be found to protect not only ourselves from those furiously radioactive materials but the people of a distant future whose way of life and cast of mind we can know nothing about.

The nation needs to find answers to two essential questions: Can the geological formations be counted on to remain stable for ten millennia? And can human beings be counted on not to interfere?

A very considerable amount of research has been done (or is now in the planning stages) on the first of these questions—studies in geology, hydrology, seismology, climatology, and so on. But practically no research has been done (or is now being planned) on the second question. Nor is it at all obvious how one would proceed even if endless sums had been set aside for the purpose.

The 1982 Nuclear Waste Policy Act gave each nominated state the right to conduct evaluations of target sites within its borders independently of any research undertaken by the Department of Energy, and it authorized federal grants to help them do so. In 1983 the state of Nevada, still imagining itself one of a number of reluctant contenders, set up an ambitious program of research, drawing upon the methods and models of the social sciences to consider what effects the opening of such a facility might have on the everyday life of Nevada. At issue here were not geotechnical studies of the site itself—that would be the work of other research groups—but socioeconomic studies of its human surroundings.

The first set of studies conducted by Nevada were an effort to learn about "standard effects," the research question being: What is likely to happen to the economy and culture of Nevada if an operation the size of the repository opens on the eastern flank of Yucca Mountain but the risks posed by radiation are not for the moment taken into account?

These questions are relatively easy to frame and easy to ask, being of a kind posed in any socioeconomic impact study. How much is it likely to cost to build and maintain the facility? How many of those dollars can be expected to remain in Nevada? How large a labor force should be required for the operation? What portion of that force is likely to be drawn from the local labor pool? What revenues and what expenditures should surrounding neighborhoods expect? And so on, as the analysis turns from tax bases to housing markets, from land uses to water tables, from air qualities to health needs, and so on.

This is exacting technical work, and it takes both skill and experience to do it well. But it nonetheless calls upon familiar mental reflexes and familiar research procedures, and it does not require any stretching of established perspectives. The task is to come up with reasonable forecasts on the basis of trends already in motion or of schedules already announced and then enter them into computer models of one kind or another.

A second set of studies, however, focusing on what came to be called "special effects," draws upon a different set of mental reflexes. The question at issue here is: What impacts is it reasonable to expect from the opening of such a repository as a consequence of the fact that very special risks are involved? This, clearly, is unfamiliar conceptual terrain for the social sciences, if only because we are talking about a period twice as long as the whole of recorded human history. To take on the challenge of imagining (never mind measuring) something so immense is like peering into a universe of darkness armed only with a pocket flashlight. Ten thousand years! What vocabulary can we draw on to speak sensibly of such a thing? What compass can we use to find our way in such a vastness?

A choice needs to be made in such a situation as that. Either one can look for a compelling way to convey the immensity of that darkness, the volume of that void (in which event one might be better advised to call on the skills of a poet than to engage a research consulting firm), or one can make the most of an awkward position by studying the realities illuminated by the one thin beam of light one has.

And that, really, is what the available research funds have been spent on. The situation, as Kristin Shrader-Frechette points out, is uncomfortably like that of the famous drunk who looks for a missing set of keys under a streetlight not because he has any reason to think he lost them there but because it is the only light available.[7] It is hard to see how the research team could have acted otherwise, considering that specialists called to do a job are bound to bring what resources they have to it. But it is a risky process all the same because no matter how energetically one qualifies and explains, no matter how often one speaks of "uncertainties," one can hardly help giving the impression that the terrain being illuminated by that flashlight is larger than it is, that one's comprehension of the problem is surer than it is. The nation will have invested millions of dollars engaged in the equivalent of inspecting a few inches of the Burma Road, and the logic of that effort, no matter how sharply one insists otherwise, can only be that the rest of the thousand-mile stretch of road must be at least something like the strip under study. Why else bother?

What can one see by such a light? One can draw population samples to learn how people feel about nuclear power in general and about nuclear wastes in particular. One can ask individuals who have a special impact on the economy of Nevada—business representatives and convention planners, for example—what they are likely to do if the repository goes on-line. One can ask local persons whose lives might be affected by the opening of the facility how they think they would react if that were to happen. One can try to get a feel for the social and cultural pulse of the region by positioning observers in affected communities. One can ask people how much compensation they would require in order to accept the siting of a repository within a certain distance of their homes. One can ask persons from outside Nevada how their images of the state would change if the waste facility opened and, by doing so, gain valuable insights into the effects of the repository on tourism and in-migration. All those approaches have been tried, and most of the ensuing studies are as good as the state of our art permits.

The accumulative results of these studies are both clear and (from the point of view of Nevada at least) alarming. *If* the repository goes on-line and *if* people continue to feel toward it as they do now—the second of those "ifs" a big one, as every social scientist knows—the effects on the Nevada economy will be devastating. Tourists will be less likely to visit Nevada, and their images of it will become a good deal more negative. Conventions will move elsewhere, and businesses will relocate. The numbers of people who migrate into the state to assume new jobs or raise families or retire will be greatly reduced. And the anxieties of those Nevadans who do nothing at all are likely to increase, since one of the clearest findings to emerge from all these studies is that the amount of apprehension people have about things nuclear is very great indeed.

In one sense, then, the Nevada authorities have the answer they need. Should Yucca Mountain become the nation's nuclear waste dump, the costs to the state, by all present appearances, will outweigh the benefits by an enormous margin. Things may change, of course. It is well known that people often behave differently from the way they tell visiting interviewers they intend to, so one must read the data cautiously. Still, this is the best sense that can be made of an important set of findings, and it would be altogether irresponsible to discount them casually. So much for that.

Yet no matter how much confidence one has in the research done to date, there is no mistaking the fact that it focuses exclusively on the consequences one might expect from the opening of the facility and maybe from its first years of operation. Until recently the Department of Energy has been working on the assumption that site characterization would begin in 1988, that the Nuclear Regulatory Commission would begin its review of the chosen site in 1994 and issue a construction permit in 1998, that the repository would accept wastes from 2003 to 2028, that a caretaker phase would then follow for twenty years (during which time the wastes could be retrieved if desired or necessary), and, finally, that the facility would be decommissioned, decontaminated, and sealed forever between 2053 and 2060. The starting date of the project has now been postponed, but its operating career, once under way, will be of that duration. That may feel like a daunting stretch of time, but as soon as we are more comfortable with the still-unfamiliar numbers that we will need to name the years of the coming century, we will be dealing with a period of time more or less within the compass of the familiar: seventy-two years, an almost perfect biblical life-span. Our flashlight can probably be counted on to cast a beam at least some part of that distance.

The ten-thousand-year future we are supposed to be contemplating, however, will hardly have begun by then, so a new and far more important question emerges: What will happen if something goes wrong not in the *operational life of the repository* but in the *radioactive life of the wastes*? What if there is a leak into the biosphere at any moment in the ten millennia the repository is required by law to remain secure? In posing a question like that one is asking something very special of the social science imagination. On the old DOE calendar, the period of years we are being asked to think about stretches from 1998 to 11,998; on the more recent calendar, from 2010 until 12,010. Now if one were to write the numbers 11,998 and 12,010 on every blackboard in America, how many people would guess that they referred to dates? Figures like those lie outside our normal reckonings of time. They lie outside the span we usually count as human history. And they are certainly outside the reach of even the most hysterical efforts at prediction.

So what can contemporary researchers, adept in the ways of the social sciences but anchored to their own time and place, do about all that? Nothing, perhaps, except to allow over and over again that it is mighty hard to see ten thousand years into the future. The summary reports issuing from Nevada sound that warning as often as one could ask. Indeed, some form of the word "uncertainty" appears thirty-two times in the first several pages of one of them, along with a reference to "future conditions that will be very difficult to fully anticipate" and a grave acknowledgment that "these hazards are not all knowable." The report speaks of "external perturbations and surprises" and "unanticipated events"; it concedes that "the range of uncertainty is great" and that "any methodology that claims precision in the anticipation of repository consequences must be viewed with appropriate caution."

Comments like these accent such reports from beginning to end. But they are like the warnings found on packs of cigarettes. They are cautionary notes, parenthetic remarks, annotations. They are not worked into the flow of the argument at all. And in the end the effect of all that talk about "uncertainties" and "perturbations" and "surprises" is oddly comforting, as if the empirical territories covered by the report were broad and secure, even if the outer edges were a bit soft and tinged with ambiguity.

The words matter. Instead of saying, "The reality is that these hazards are not all knowable," why not say, "The reality is that these realities are wholly beyond our ken"? Instead of talking about "future conditions that will be very difficult to fully anticipate," why not talk about "conditions that will be impossible to anticipate"? And instead of saying, "Any methodology that claims precision in the anticipation of repository consequences must be viewed with appropriate caution," how about declaring flatly that "any methodology that claims precision in that regard must be regarded as ridiculous"? By any useful standard, the corrected phrases are more accurate both philosophically and technically than the versions they replace.

And what is the logic of choosing a term like "surprise" to refer to events that may take place five or ten thousand years from now? The expression may have an established meaning in technical conversations, but to use it carelessly in a context like this has telling implications. "Surprise" seems to speak of something out of the ordinary, something that bolts from the blue and imposes itself upon a pattern of life events that one would otherwise expect to have remained fixed and immutable. As if absence of change were nature's way. As if absence of change were the way of human history.

A good deal of attention has been given by DOE to the risks that the wastes will be disturbed by some natural change in the site itself—seismic, geologic, climatic, volcanic, hydrologic, tectonic, something else—during the ten thousand years after the repository has been sealed and decommissioned. But scarcely any attention has been given to the possibility that human beings might wander into the site and find a way to release its awesome burden. The Department of Energy has for the most part assumed that the risks of human interference in the workings of a repository, whether intentional or unintentional, are so remote that they need not be taken into account in any but the most glancing way. Human behavior is being set aside, really, because it is so hard to come to terms with—so intractable, so noisy, so difficult to discuss (as a DOE report once put it) "in quantitative or probabilistic terms."[8] It is difficult to predict what human beings will do a year hence, hard even to guess what they will do a decade hence, but preposterous to think that one can even begun to know what they will do a century or a millennium hence. So? So to hell with it.

The Department of Energy has focused on two major possibilities, although neither of them seems to have been ranked so far as "sufficiently credible to warrant further consideration."[9] The first is that someone will drill down into the repository from the surface and breach a waste package, allowing radioactivity to escape into the environment. The only commodity DOE experts now count as worth drilling for is groundwater, but they plan to review the possibilities that mineral or energy resources may one day prove valuable enough to attract activity. The second is that somebody will rearrange the flows of water on the surface—constructing dams, for instance, or engaging in massive irrigation projects—or in some other way disturb underground water supplies and increase the possibility that they will be contaminated by those lurking wastes.

DOE experts have been almost wholly unimpressed by the possibility that people in the future will have other reasons for boring into the site or for wanting to peel away the protective layers of rock above it with new kinds of earth-moving equipment already visible on the technological horizon. But it is hard to take much comfort from their calculations on this score since those calculations seem to be based for the most part on the assumption that the human future will be characterized by twentieth-century political structures, twentieth-century living arrangements, twentieth-century thought processes, and, most alarming of all, twentieth-century technologies. To announce solemnly, as DOE does in its Yucca Mountain Site Characterization Plan of 1988, that it plans to do research "to determine the anticipated drillhole density, borehole diameter, and depths of the drillholes over the next 10,000 years in the vicinity of Yucca Mountain"[10] is to run the risk of sounding absurd. The very use of the term "drilling" is enough to betray the limits of DOE's imaginative reach since the history of technology should lead us simply to assume that humankind will have found other ways to penetrate rock a hundred—never mind a thousand—years from now.

Most of the intrusions the Energy Department has considered, even the ones it has dismissed as "not credible," are assumed to be unintentional. Indeed, the terms "human interference" and "human intrusion" are defined in the glossary of the 1988 Site Characterization Plan as "the inadvertent effects of future human activities" on buried waste material. It is understandable, then, that technical discussions at DOE and elsewhere would turn on matters of communication. Can the site be marked so unmistakably that no one blunders into it unawares and lets radioactivity escape? The Site Characterization Plan notes that "a warning system composed of surface markers and monuments will be placed at the site as a means of informing future generations of the risks associated with the repository and its contents."[11] But what monuments can be counted on to last? What warnings can be counted on to be both decipherable and impressive several thousand years from now?

That is no trivial matter either. We have some idea what monuments have survived the erosions of time because we have an archaeological record to draw on. The earliest Sumerian cuneiform tablets are five thousand old, and the earliest pyramids are about the same age. Stonehenge is forty-five hundred years old or so, and the Great Wall of China twenty-five hundred. But history is an imperfect guide here at best because we have no way of knowing what markers have failed to survive. Moreover, it is increasingly clear that new forms of environmental degradation—acid rain is but one of a number of examples—create perils altogether unlike those endured for five thousand years by the patient, uncomplaining Sphinx of Gizeh. And what symbols or words shall we call on to make the point? Languages have half-lives far shorter than nuclear wastes, or so our experience to date would suggest, and even if we suppose that English survives (whatever that really means), the expressions we select from our twentieth-century vocabulary to convey the awe in which we hold those wastes are almost sure to have a different meaning and a different emphasis in the distant future. If Geoffrey Chaucer—ostensible father of the English we speak—were asked to propose lines for such a monument, he might well choose these from the closing of TROILUS AND CRISEYDE:

> *So prey I God that non myswrite the,*
> *Ne the mysmetre for defaute of tonge.*
> *And red wher-so thou be, or elles song,*
> *That thou be understonde. . . .*

Meaning, in effect, "I hope to God that nobody misunderstands what I have written here." And if that is what six hundred years can do, what about six thousand? (The thought almost calls for a science fiction story. "A stranger dressed in furs moves slowly up the desert ridge," it begins, "as if in search of something. But what? God? Love? Water? A place to burrow underground? She comes across a block of stone, pitted by the storms of nature and the delinquencies of humankind, and runs a curious finger over the markings carved into its flank: 'Ne the mysmetre . . .' ")

The chances that people will be allowed to forget actually have to be counted as remote. Knowledge is not that easily lost, for one thing, and if we can find ways to assure that the message will be reviewed and revised every half century or so, we should have more confidence in our ability to communicate with generations yet to come. But it is important to remember that language is far more perishable than the stone on which it is often carved and that other efforts to inform the future—Sumerian tablets, hieroglyphic scripts, Dead Sea Scrolls—have been a failure.

Darius the Great was so anxious to leave a message for those who were to follow him that he had it carved high on a cliff in three versions of the cuneiform, the only languages he was aware of, and for good measure, he added a fearful curse to anyone who might deface it. "Saith Darius the king: if thou shalt behold this tablet or these sculptures, and shalt destroy them . . . then may Ahura Mazda slay thee, and may thy race come to nought." Did travelers tremble? Apparently not. Cuneiform was no longer in use a century or two later, and in fact the curse remained unintelligible even to scholars until the middle of the nineteenth century.

We are used to the idea that shifts in the natural order—the changing of climates, the evolving of species, the comings and goings of ice ages—are slow and measured, providing a steady base line against which all the restless flutterings of humankind can be seen in perspective. But the rate of environmental change—gradual enough when nature sets the pace—is becoming so sensitive to human intrusion that the old assumptions need to be reconsidered. The story of the next hundred, thousand, ten thousand years is likely to be the story of what human beings do even more than what climates and water tables and geological formations do. Indeed, the impacts of human behavior on the natural world are likely to be so profound that geology and seismology and hydrology might soon need to be counted social sciences as well as physical sciences. The ability to induce changes in climate, to provoke seismic activity, to reshape land contours millions of years in the making, to rechannel underground flows of water—by design or by accident in all these cases—are likely to be in the human repertory before long, and for that matter, the constitution of our species may soon depend more upon genetic engineering and developments in artificial intelligence than on the slower rhythms of natural selection. And I am speaking now only of things that come casually to a mind tuned to the realities of our own age.

If those things are so, how can one even begin to focus intelligently on the rate of technological change? We often look behind us in history to try to get some sense for the pulse and cadence of passing time. "Without a long running start in history," Lewis Mumford says, "we shall not have the momentum needed to take a sufficiently bold leap into the future."[12] Ten thousand years ago, we might note, the plains just north of Nevada had only recently emerged from under a sheath of ice a mile thick. Ten thousand years ago Stone Age hunters elsewhere, speaking a language that no one now could make out, were learning for the first time to plant seeds in the ground and to harvest the result. Can we use that span to measure how much change we might expect over the next ten thousand years? Clearly not, since the rate of technological innovation promises to be infinitely more rapid in years to come than it has been in years past. The distance we have come from the time of that tentative farmer, scratching the ground with a stick, is nothing compared with the distance—the potential distance at least—separating us from those who will follow.

And human habits, every bit as volatile and as elusive, are likely to change in dramatic ways as well. What are the odds that people will have so grown in number and will have devised so many new ways to cope with the elements that they will move to places now thought to be remote and uninhabitable? Pacific atolls, for example, or polar ice caps? What are the odds, for that matter, that people will have so befouled the surfaces of the earth that they will seek a new habitat underground? What are the odds that a mineral for which no one now can imagine any use will come to be seen as valuable enough to be worth the risking of lives? (Uranium, to offer one somewhat ironic example, had no known uses as recently as a hundred years ago.)

It would be easy to add scenarios to the short list above, but the main point I want to make here as I bring these comments to an end is something else. Marcus Aurelius wrote eighteen hundred years ago: "You can see for yourself what has gone before. . . . So you can see what will happen, for it will all be formed the same. It is impossible to break the rhythm of the past. So it is the same to look at human life across forty years as across ten thousand. What more could you see?[13]" But no sensible person in our time would dare say the same. The contemporary imagination simply cannot be expected to produce anything like a sound forecast of future actualities. Our intellectual resources are shaped by the realities of our own time, tempered by the experiences of our own age. And when the future we are trying to make out does arrive, the thought processes we will have used to imagine it will themselves be antiques, relics of an epoch long past. Ask Agamemnon to visualize a device the size of a hogshead that in one brilliant flash could vaporize not only the whole of Troy but all the encircling armies of Greece. Ask an ancient oarsman, chained to the benches of a wooden trireme, to visualize an underwater vessel that glides soundlessly at fifty times the speed of the fastest galley and does not need to surface for months at a time. It is a profound misunderstanding of the nature of human intelligence to think that the mind of one epoch can even begin to read the mind of another, especially across so vast a span of years. The two instruments are strung in very different ways.

Note, for example, that when specialists speak of "isolating" nuclear wastes "from the biosphere" or "from the accessible environment," they are using expressions that are themselves a reflection of our own technological age. The outer edges of the biosphere are set not by the physical universe but by the range of biological activity within it, and that portion of the biosphere represented by the venturings of humankind has expanded tremendously in relatively recent times—out into (and under) the sea, for example, and up into (and beyond) the atmosphere. One might want to question the logic by which water and mineral resources that are part of our lives on earth are thought to be "out of the environment," and, for that matter, one might ask how a region of earth we can reach even now with a simple drill can be properly described as "inaccessible." But the point is that the skies above and the depths below all are part of the natural envelope in which our species lives, and if for the time being it is technically correct to describe an underground chamber one thousand feet below the surface of Nevada as "outside the biosphere" or "outside the environment," it is well within that natural envelope. Those Paiute and Shoshone natives had it right all along.

Moreover, the very fact that those awesome wastes have been sealed away in underground vaults is almost sure to change the shape of the future we are being asked to consider—and in ways that will be, by definition, beyond our ability to envision. What we know about the perversities and the curiosities and the obsessions of our own kind should make us very sensitive to the likelihood that the sheer presence of the wastes will concentrate human energies in new ways and induce new forms of human inventiveness. In that sense, a repository like the one proposed at Yucca Mountain is very apt to change the landscape of human sensibility as well as the landscape of fact. The danger is not that the warning system will fail to alert people but that it will do so all too well.[14] Some people may come to believe that a powerful weapon lies buried out there in the middle of enemy territory, waiting only to be activated. What ingenuities might that provoke? Some may come to believe that the remains of an ancient culture lie buried out there in the middle of a new one, set in the deepest tombs the age could dig and protected by a mysterious curse. What curiosities might that excite? Some may come to believe that a thing of supernatural force and energy lies buried out there in the middle of a remote desert, crowned by monuments so large and exuberant that they cry out for attention. What religious awe might that inspire? We do not know how to answer those questions or even to phrase them intelligently. And precisely because that is so, we must accord them a special measure of respect and count our inability to come to terms with them as reasons enough to move ahead in this matter with extreme caution. "Human beings have gotten pretty good at looking into deep space," says a thoughtful consultant to DOE, "but we are really no good at looking into deep time."[15]

Thus the time may have come to abandon the cool, measured language of technical reports—all that talk of "perturbations" and "surprises" and "unanticipated events"—and simply blurt out: "Holy shit! Ten thousand years! That's incredible!" To speak in this way is not just to utter a casual obscenity or to indulge in a passing exclamation of wonder-

ment either. For the notion that one can actually see something across a span of ten thousand years really *is* incredible,
and if "holy shit" is not the right way to refer to human
wastes so terrible that they need to be sealed away for ten
millennia, what would be?

The most mature and accurate scientific report we can
issue, it seems to me, would conclude: We do not know,
we cannot know, and we dare not act as though we do
know. To speak thus is not to introduce a note of drama
into what can otherwise seem a dry and technical business
but to assess the matter in as rational and unemotional a
way as language permits. Things will change drastically over
the next few hundred years—never mind the next few thousand—and in ways that we cannot, by definition, foresee.
To think otherwise is unrealistic, unscientific, and more than
a little crazy.

What, then, should the nation do? When one is faced with
such high levels of uncertainty, the wisest course would
seem to preserve as much flexibility as possible and to turn to
irreversible measures only if there are no viable alternatives.
Deep geological entombment is clearly one of the least re-
versible options that can be imagined; indeed, that has long
been regarded as its principal virtue.

Federal policy, as I noted earlier, has been to assure that
"waste management problems shall not be deferred to future
generations," and many environmental groups have shared
the same view. Geological burial—at first glance, anyway—
looks like an ideal way to do that since, after all, it "removes"
the wastes "from the environment" and solves the problem
once and for all. But in many ways entombment does just
the opposite. It deliberately poisons a portion of the natural
world for as many as half a million years, and in doing so,
it not only leaves future generations with thousands of tons
of the most dangerous rubbish imaginable on their hands

but makes it as difficult as the state of our technology permits for them to deal with it. We cannot promise our own children—never mind those who follow hundreds or thousands of years hence—that they will be safe from the wastes. And so long as that is so, we are not taking the *problem* out of their hands so much as we are taking the *solution* out of their hands.

So perhaps the government should relax its insistence on immediate and irreversible burial and turn to forms of storage that allow both continuous monitoring and retrieval. That may sound like the Charlie Dressen solution. But I would claim that it is the wisest stratagem our age can devise because, in the face of all the doubts and uncertainties that attend nuclear waste management, it maximizes flexibility and keeps options open.

Epilogue:
On Trauma

The scenes described in the preceding chapters are different in many ways, but the reactions of the people who live in them to the troubles they experienced are so alike that one can speak of a syndrome—"a group of symptoms," the dictionary on my desk puts it, "that together are characteristic of a specific condition." That was the resemblance the chief of the Grassy Narrows Ojibwa caught when he likened his people to the survivors of Buffalo Creek, and it was the resemblance the trooper from South Florida caught when the Haitian farm workers of Immokalee reminded him of his fellow combat veterans in Vietnam. Over the past decade or so, moreover, a number of reports describing the travails of other afflicted communities have entered the literature, and the portraits they draw are largely the same. (Some of them have wondrous, haunted names like Times Beach and Love Canal and Bloody Run to join a roster that already includes

Grassy Narrows, Three Mile Island, and East Swallow. It seems like far too much to ask of whatever muse presides over irony, but two of the darkest and most virulent toxic waste sites to make the news in recent times were found in Devil's Swamp, Louisiana, and Hemlock, Michigan.[1])

As the East Swallow litigation reached a point of decision, for example, I asked several researchers who had studied other cases of toxic contamination to read a draft of my report and to compare the communities they knew with the one I was describing.[2] I was looking for an efficient and compelling way to say in court what I already knew to be true: that the reactions of the people of East Swallow were exactly what one would expect in such circumstances and were not, by any stretch of even the most disputatious imagination, something local or idiosyncratic. Everyone I consulted agreed that the similarities were "striking" and "resonant," even "haunting." Michael Edelstein, a seasoned observer, thought that patterns of behavior found in East Swallow were "exactly what I saw" in the "contaminated communities" he had visited, and Adeline Levine, who spent years studying Love Canal, commented: "My general impression is that the East Swallow residents express feelings and reactions very similar, and often identical, to those of the people I have known, interviewed, and observed at Love Canal. There were times when I was reading some of the quotations you provided that I could almost hear the voices of Love Canal people."

Those are the voices one hears in a wide range of other places visited by this new species of trouble, and the pain reflected in them is a form of trauma.

I

I have been using the term "trauma" throughout these pages to refer not only to the psychological condition of the people one encounters in those scenes but also to the social texture of the scenes themselves, and that is departure enough from normal usage for me to consider for a moment how "trauma" can serve as a broad social concept as well as a more narrowly clinical one.

Trauma is generally taken to mean a blow to the tissues of the body—or, more frequently now, to the structures of the mind—that results in injury or some other disturbance. Something alien breaks in on you, smashing through whatever barriers your mind has set up as a line of defense. It invades you, possesses you, takes you over, becomes a dominating feature of your interior landscape, and in the process threatens to drain you and leave you empty. The classical symptoms of trauma range from feelings of restlessness and agitation at one end of the emotional scale to feelings of numbness and bleakness at the other. Traumatized people often scan the surrounding world anxiously for signs of danger, breaking into explosive rages and reacting with a start to ordinary sights and sounds, but at the same time all that nervous activity takes place against a numbed gray background of depression, feelings of helplessness, and a general closing off of the spirit as the mind tries to insulate itself from further harm. Above all, trauma involves a continual reliving of some wounding experience in daydreams and nightmares, flashbacks and hallucinations, and in a compulsive seeking out of similar circumstances. Paul Valéry wrote: "Our memory repeats to us what we haven't understood." That's almost it. Say instead: "Our memory repeats to us what we haven't yet come to terms with, what still haunts us."[3]

"Trauma," however, is used in so many different ways and has found a place in so many different vocabularies that we need to resolve two terminological matters before proceeding.

First, in classical medical usage "trauma" refers not to the *injury* inflicted but to the *blow* that inflicted it, not to the *state of mind* that ensues but to the *event* that provoked it. The term "posttraumatic stress disorder" (a peculiar gathering of syllables, if you listen carefully) is an accommodation to that medical convention. The disorder, that is, is named for the stimulus that brought it into being—a logic very like the one that would be at work if mumps were known as "postexposure glandular disorder."

In both clinical and common usage, however, that distinction is becoming blurred. The dictionary on my desk (to return to that excellent source) defines trauma both as "a stress or blow that may produce disordered feelings or behavior" and as "the state or condition produced by such a stress or blow." In a sense, then, the location of the term, its center of gravity, has been shifting from the first meaning to the second, and I am not only taking advantage of that shift here but encouraging it for general use.

There are good reasons for doing so. The historian who wants to know where a story starts, like the therapist who needs to identify a precipitating cause in order to deal with the injury it does, will naturally be interested in beginnings. But those are no more than details to everyone else (and not even very important ones at that), because it is *how people react to them* rather than *what they are* that give events whatever traumatic quality they can be said to have. The most violent wrenchings in the world, that is to say, have no clinical standing unless they harm the workings of a mind or body, so it is the *damage done* that defines and gives shape to the initial events, the *damage done* that gives it its name. It scarcely makes sense to locate the term anywhere else.

Second, in order to serve as a generally useful concept, "trauma" has to be understood as resulting from a *constellation of life experiences* as well as from a discrete happening, from a *persisting condition* as well as from an acute event. Now I know that in dragging across this already well-traveled and well-charted conceptual ground, I am scuffing up a widely observed line differentiating "trauma" from "stress."

"Trauma," in this familiar distinction, refers to a violent event that injures in one sharp stab, while "stress" refers to a series of events or even to a chronic condition that erodes the spirit more gradually. But that line, I submit, was drawn in the wrong place to begin with, at least for such purposes as these. A difficult marriage is stressful, yes. So is a draining job. But Auschwitz? A prolonged period of terror or brutality? No, it only makes sense to insist that trauma can issue from a sustained exposure to battle as well as from a moment of numbing shock, from a continuing pattern of abuse as well as from a single searing assault, from a period of severe attenuation and erosion as well as from a sudden flash of fear. The effects are the same, and that, after all, should be our focus.

Moreover, as I noted earlier, trauma has the quality of converting that one sharp stab into an enduring state of mind. A chronicler of passing events may report that the episode itself lasted no more than an instant—a gunshot, say—but the traumatized mind holds on to that moment, preventing it from slipping back into its proper chronological place in the past, and relives it over and over again in the compulsive musings of the day and the seething dreams of night. The moment becomes a season; the event becomes a condition.

II

With these clarifications, "trauma" becomes a concept social scientists as well as clinicians can work with. I want to use my broadened vocabulary, in fact, to suggest that one can speak of traumatized communities as something distinct from assemblies of traumatized persons. Sometimes the tissues of community can be damaged in much the same way as the tissues of mind and body, as I shall suggest shortly, but even when that does not happen, traumatic wounds inflicted on individuals can combine to create a mood, an ethos—a group culture, almost—that is different from (and more than) the sum of the private wounds that make it up. Trauma, that is, has a social dimension.

Let me begin by suggesting that trauma can create community. In some ways that is a very odd thing to claim. To describe people as traumatized is to say that they have withdrawn into a kind of protective envelope, a place of mute, aching loneliness, in which the traumatic experience is treated as a solitary burden that needs to be expunged by acts of denial and resistance. What could be less "social" than that?

But traumatic conditions are not like the other troubles to which flesh is heir. They move to the center of one's being and, in doing so, give victims the feeling that they have been set apart and made special. One Buffalo Creek survivor said: "The black water came down the bottom we lived in. I couldn't stand any more. It was like something was wiped over me and made me different." That woman was talking of a feeling shared by millions of others. She viewed herself as having an altered relationship to the rest of humankind, to history, to the processes of nature. She viewed herself as marked, maybe cursed, maybe even dead. "I feel dead now," one of her neighbors said. "I have no energy. I feel numb, like I died long ago."

For some survivors, at least, this sense of difference can become a kind of calling, a status, where people are drawn to others similarly marked. The wariness and numbness and slowness of feeling shared by traumatized people everywhere may mean that relating to others comes hard and at a heavy price, so I am not speaking here of the easy comradeship one often finds among those who live through telling experiences together. Still, trauma shared can serve as a source of communality in the same way that common languages and common cultural backgrounds can. There is a spiritual kinship there, a sense of identity, even when feel-

ings of affection are deadened and the ability to care
numbed. A compelling example is provided by the young
married couple, described by Shoshana Felman, who survived the Holocaust miraculously and remained together
afterward not because they got along (they did not) but
because "he knew who I was—he was the only person who
knew . . . and I knew who he was."[4] At a recent reunion of
Americans who had been held hostage in Iran, one explained
to a reporter: "It is easy to be together. We don't have to
explain things. We carry the same pain."

So trauma has both centripetal and centrifugal tendencies.
It draws one away from the center of group space while at
the same time drawing one back. The human chemistry at
work here is an odd one, but it has been noted many times
before: Estrangement becomes the basis for communality,
as if persons without homes or citizenship or any other
niche in the larger order of things were invited to gather in
a quarter set aside for the disfranchised, a ghetto for the
unattached.

Indeed, it can happen that otherwise unconnected persons
who share a traumatic experience seek one another out and
develop a form of fellowship on the strength of that common tie. Veterans haunted by dark memories of Vietnam,
for example, or adults who cannot come to terms with childhood abuse sometimes gather into groups for reasons not
unlike the Holocaust couple cited earlier: They know one
another in ways that the most intimate of friends never will,
and for that reason they can supply a human context and a
kind of emotional solvent in which the work of recovery
can begin. It is a gathering of the wounded.

III

For the most part, though, trauma damages the texture of
community. I want to suggest, in fact, that there are at least

two senses in which one can say that a community—as distinct from the people who constitute it—has become traumatized.

When I first wrote about the Buffalo Creek catastrophe, I tried to make a distinction between what I then called "individual trauma" and "collective trauma." To quote myself:

> By *individual trauma* I mean a blow to the psyche that breaks through one's defenses so suddenly and with such brutal force that one cannot react to it effectively. . . . [The] Buffalo Creek survivors experienced precisely that. They suffered deep shock as a result of their exposure to death and devastation, and, as so often happens in catastrophes of this magnitude, they withdrew into themselves, feeling numbed, afraid, vulnerable, and very alone.

> By *collective trauma*, on the other hand, I mean a blow to the basic tissues of social life that damages the bonds attaching people together and impairs the prevailing sense of communality. The collective trauma works its way slowly and even insidiously into the awareness of those who suffer from it, so it does not have the quality of suddenness normally associated with "trauma." But it is a form of shock all the same, a gradual realization that the community no longer exists as an effective source of support and that an important part of the self has disappeared. . . . "I" continue to exist, though damaged and maybe even permanently changed. "You" continue to exist, though distant and hard to relate to. But "we" no longer exist as a connected pair or as linked cells in a larger communal body. . . .

To say that Buffalo Creek as a social organism was traumatized—at least when one reflects on the matter—is to run the risk of sounding obvious. Buffalo Creek is part of a cultural setting in which the sense of community is so palpable that it is easy to think of it as tissue capable of being injured.

Now one has to realize when talking like this that one is in danger of drifting into a realm of metaphor. Communities do not have hearts or sinews or ganglia; they do not suffer or rationalize or experience joy. But the analogy does help suggest that a cluster of people acting in concert and moving to the same collective rhythms can allocate their personal resources in such a way that the whole comes to have more humanity than its constituent parts. In effect, people put their own individual resources at the disposal of the group— placing them in the communal store, as it were—and then draw on that reserve supply for the demands of everyday life. And if the whole community more or less disappears, as happened on Buffalo Creek, people find that they cannot take advantage of the energies they once invested in the communal store. They find that they are almost empty of feeling, empty of affection, empty of confidence and assurance. It is as if the individual cells had supplied raw energy to the whole body but did not have the means to convert that energy back into a usable personal form once the body was no longer there to process it.[5]

In places like Buffalo Creek, then, the community in general can almost be described as the locus for activities that are normally thought to be the property of individual persons. It is the *community* that offers a cushion for pain, the *community* that offers a context for intimacy, the *community* that serves as the repository for binding traditions. And when the community is profoundly affected, one can speak of a damaged social organism in almost the same way that one would speak of a damaged body. The Buffalo Creek incident provided a telling test case of that idea, by the way, since a number of residents who were clearly traumatized by what had happened proved to have been a long way from home when the disaster struck and thus never experienced the raging waters and all of the death and devastation at first hand. They were injured by the loss of a sustaining community.

This does not mean that Buffalo Creek had become a desert, an empty space as a consequence of the flood. The people of the hollow still had memory, kinship, contiguity in common, so there were materials to build with. But for the moment, at least, they were torn loose from their cultural moorings—alone, adrift, floating like particles in a dead electromagnetic field.

Now tightly knit communities like Buffalo Creek are rare in this country and becoming more so. Grassy Narrows may be the only other community described in this book so torn by disaster that one can liken it to injured tissue. But trauma can work its way into the fabric of community life in other ways as well.

IV

Among the most common findings of research on natural disasters, as I also noted in my report on Buffalo Creek, is that a sudden and logically inexplicable wave of good feeling washes over survivors not long after the event itself. For one dread moment they thought that the world had come to an end, that they had been "left naked and alone in a terrifying wilderness of ruins," as Anthony F. C. Wallace put it. But, according to Wallace, a "stage of euphoria" quickly follows in most natural disasters as people come to realize that the general community is not dead after all.[6] The energy with which rescuers work and the warmth with which neighbors respond act to reassure victims that there is still life among the wreckage, and they react with an outpouring of communal feeling, an urgent need to make contact with and even touch others by way of renewing old pledges of fellowship. They are celebrating the recovery of the community they momentarily thought dead, and, in a way, they are celebrating their own rebirth. One well-known study spoke of a "city of comrades," another of a "democracy of distress," and a third of a "community of sufferers."[7] Martha Wolfenstein, reviewing the literature on disasters in general, called the phenomenon a "post-disaster utopia,"[8] while Allen H. Barton, having surveyed much the same literature, talked about an "altruistic community."[9] "Therapeutic communities" Charles E. Fritz called them in a classic essay on disasters.[10] It is as if survivors, digging out from under the masses of debris, discover that the communal body is not only intact but mobilizing its remaining resources to dress the wound on its flank.

Nothing of the sort happened on Buffalo Creek. Nothing of the sort happened in *any* of the disaster situations described in these pages, in fact, nor has it happened in any of the other incidents I have been citing as examples of the new species of trouble.

For one thing, these disasters (or near disasters) often seem to force open whatever fault lines once ran silently through the structure of the larger community, dividing it into divisive fragments. In a number of places where such emergencies have taken place, the people of the community have split into factions to such an extent that one wise student of such matters calls them "corrosive communities" to contrast them with the "therapeutic communities" so often noted in an earlier literature.[11] The fault lines usually open to divide the people affected by the event from the people spared, exactly the opposite of what happens in a "city of comrades." Those not touched try to distance themselves from those touched, almost as if they are escaping something spoiled, something contaminated, something polluted. "Corrosive" is a good word, too, because the disasters that provoke this reaction tend for the most part to involve some form of toxicity. This is what happened at Three Mile Island and at East Swallow, and it was a prominent feature of the social landscape of Love Canal and elsewhere.[12] The net effect is to set the afflicted apart.

In such circumstances, traumatic experiences work their

way so thoroughly into the grain of the affected community that they come to supply its prevailing mood and temper, dominate its imagery and its sense of self, govern the way its members relate to one another. The point to be made here is not that calamity serves to strengthen the bonds linking people together—it does not, most of the time—but that the shared experience becomes almost like a common culture, a source of kinship. Something of that sort happened in each of the places I have described here, and it is in that sense that they can be fairly described as traumatized. (I do not have time to go into it now, but I would add that something of the sort can also happen to whole regions, even whole countries. I lectured to students on trauma and related matters in Romania not long after the end of one of the most abusive and arbitrarily despotic regimes on human record, and the flashes of recognition that erupted from those warm and generous audiences when I spoke in terms not unlike the ones I am using here—outbursts might be a better term—spoke volumes about the damage that can be done to a whole people by sustained dread and dislocation.)

So communal trauma, let's say, can take two forms, either alone or in combination: damage to the tissues that hold human groups intact and the creation of social climates, communal moods, that come to dominate a group's spirit.

V

I introduced two themes in the Prologue that have surfaced and resurfaced throughout the rest of the book like threads in a fabric.

In the first place, disasters that are thought to have been brought about by other human beings (as was the case in each one of the events described here, as well as in Romania) not only hurt in special ways but bring in their wake feelings of injury and vulnerability from which it is difficult to recover. I discussed this process most thoroughly in my report on East Swallow, but it is a common one.

A scattering of people, unaware for the most part of the risks they were running, are damaged by the activities of some kind of corporate group. The corporation is sometimes huge (Buffalo Creek, East Swallow, Three Mile Island), and it is sometimes no more than a family business (Immokalee). But most of the time—so often, in fact, that we can almost think of it as a natural reflex—the company draws into its own interior spaces and posts lawyers around its borders like a ring of pickets. Nothing unexpected in that, surely. Anyone who reads newspapers knows how that reflex works.

It can be profoundly painful when the people in charge of a company at the time of a severe mishap deny responsibility, offer no apology, express no regrets, and crouch out of sight behind that wall of lawyers and legalisms. A miner from Buffalo Creek, stripped of everything by the flood, said: "I've often thought some of this stuff [the lawsuit] could have been avoided if somebody would have come around and said, 'Here's a blanket and here's a dress for your wife,' or 'Here's a sandwich, could I get you a cup of coffee?' But they never showed up. Nobody showed up to give us a place to stay. . . . The Pittston Company never offered me a pair of pants to put on, no shirt." And the woman from East Swallow quoted earlier, whose losses were of a different kind and did not need a dress or a cup of coffee, thought: "In all of these years that the spill has been going on, not once has anyone [from the gas company] said, 'Hey, we spilled gasoline under your street and, gee, we're sorry and we'd like to help you clean it up.' Nobody has ever said that. It's been a matter of seeing how much they can cover up and how much they can get away with. . . . I just don't think that's right." What these people were asking for is so elementary a feature of social life that its absence becomes inhuman. This is not the way of neighbors, of fellow townspeople, of compatriots. It is the way of hostile strangers who treat one as if one belonged to a different order of humanity, even a different species altogether, and that makes it all the more cruel.

The mortar bonding human communities together is made up at least in part of trust and respect and decency and, in moments of crisis, of charity and concern. It is profoundly disturbing to people when these expectations are not met, no matter how well protected they thought they were by that outer crust of cynicism our century seems to have developed in us all. They have already been made vulnerable by a sharp trick of fate, and now they must face the future without those layers of emotional insulation that only a trusted communal surround can provide. That's hard. But the real problem in the long run is that the inhumanity people experience comes to be seen as a natural feature of human life rather than as the bad manners of a particular corporation. They think their eyes are being opened to a larger and profoundly unsettling truth: that human institutions cannot be relied on.

In the second place, disasters that involve toxic contamination of one kind or another are of a special kind for all the reasons I reviewed in Chapter 4. I do not need to return to these matters now, but I would like to add without doing so in the detail it deserves that we may need to go beyond the strict chemical meaning of "toxic" to draw a wider and more meaningful boundary about this new species of trouble. Buffalo Creek is a good example of a disaster in which toxins figured prominently enough to qualify for inclusion, but in which the feeling that something dark and baneful has worked its way into the grain of everyday social life goes beyond the chemical property of the contaminant itself. Streaks of oily muck seeped through floorboards and windowsills for years after the flood itself, and no one in Buffalo Creek will ever forget that the bodies picked out of the noxious wreckage, like everything else in that forsaken hollow, were covered with a thick coat of black sludge. We will eventually need to figure out, moreover, what to make of the fact that many of us shrink from the homeless almost as if they were toxic. The homeless man Jonathan Kozol called Richard Lazarus, speaking of the plastic gloves shelter guards sometimes wear, understood: "It reminds me of the workers in the nuclear reactors," he said. "They have to wear protective clothing if they come into contact with waste."[13]

Disasters that share these features, as I have been suggesting throughout, are becoming one of the social and psychological signatures of our time, both because the catastrophes we encounter are increasingly the product of human hands and because more and more of them involve toxins of one kind or another as a consequence of the way we choose to live. The age can probably be said to have begun with the Holocaust (about which I am too much in awe to say much) and the bombings of Hiroshima and Nagasaki (which I have approached gingerly), but if historians later conclude that these events were not the genetic ancestors of the disasters discussed here, they are certainly its reigning symbols.

VI

Persons who survive severe disasters, as I noted earlier, often come to feel estranged from the rest of humanity and gather into groups with others of like mind, drawn together by a shared set of perspectives and rhythms and moods that derive from the sense of being apart.

Among those shared perspectives, often, is an understanding that the laws by which the natural world has always been governed as well as the decencies by which the human world has always been governed are now suspended—or were never active to begin with. They look out at the world through different lenses. And in that sense they may be said to have experienced not only (a) a *changed sense of self* and (b) a *changed way of relating to others* but (c) a *changed world view* altogether.

That new ethos can involve a feeling that the persons and institutions in charge of complex technologies cannot be relied upon, that the technologies themselves are based on theories and calculations of no merit, and that the environment in which all this takes place—both social and natural—has proved to be brittle and full of caprice. It is a view of life born of the sense that the universe is regulated not by order and continuity but by chance and a kind of natural malice that lurks everywhere. It is a new and special truth. One death camp survivor put the matter in chilling perspective, speaking fifty years after his internment: "[I]t's more a view of the world, a total world view . . . of extreme pessimism . . . of really knowing the truth about people, human nature, about death, of really knowing the truth in a way that other people don't know it."[14]

A good and strong woman from Buffalo Creek knew that feeling well:

> This disaster that happened to us, I believe it opened up a lot of people's eyes. . . . I believe there will be wars, and there will be a bomblike thing that will just destroy this place to pieces. Somebody, some fool, is going to blow it all to pieces. Sure as I'm sitting here and you're sitting there, it'll happen. . . . So the flood has more or less opened up my imagination. It's got me thinking more and more about the way of life we're having to live, the way our kids is going to have to live, and things like that. I wasn't thinking about those things before the flood. It just seemed like it woke up a new vision, I guess you'd call it, of what is and what used to be. Sometimes I'll go to bed and think about it, you know, the end of time, destruction, what's going on in wars. It's like growing up, I guess. Before I wasn't thinking about nothing

but making sure the house was kept clean, making sure my husband had things he needed for his dinner bucket, making sure the kids had the right clothes on, making sure they was clean, making sure I went to this place at the right time and that place at the right time.

Human beings are surrounded by layers of trust, radiating out in concentric circles like the ripples in a pond. The experience of trauma, at its worst, can mean not only a loss of confidence in the self but a loss of confidence in the scaffolding of family and community, in the structures of human government, in the larger logics by which humankind lives, and in the ways of nature itself.

Notes

1: THE OJIBWA OF GRASSY NARROWS

1. Anastasia M. Shkilnyk, *A Poison Stronger than Love: The Destruction of an Ojibwa Community* (New Haven: Yale University Press, 1985), p. 4.

2. "Reserve" in Canadian usage has the same meaning as "reservation" in the United States: a tract of public land set aside for the use of Native American tribes.

3. Hugh Brody, *Maps and Dreams* (New York: Pantheon, 1981), p. 110.

4. Rev. Peter Jones, *History of the Ojebway People* (London: A. W. Bennett, 1861), p. 167.

5. For a wonderful account, see Craig MacAndrew and Robert B. Edgerton, *Drunken Compartment: A Social Explanation* (Chicago: Aldine, 1969).

6. By Hiroyuki Miyamatsu and Anastasia Shkilnyk, reported in Shkilnyk, op. cit.

7. The quote is from Shkilnyk's book. Unless otherwise indicated, in fact, the information on Grassy Narrows reported and the quotations used are from that source.

8. See, for example, A. Irving Hallowell, *Culture and Experience* (Philadelphia: University of Pennsylvania Press, 1955), pp. 120, 136.

9. Chief Simon Fobister, address to joint delegation, governments of Canada and Ontario, December 15, 1978. Mimeo.

10. From transcript of Canadian Broadcasting Corporation broadcasts, *Ideas*, "Under Attack: In Grassy Narrows," February 1–22, 1983. Other quotations from that source will be indicated CBC.

11. Most of the available figures are reviewed in Shkilnyk, op. cit., and in Peter J. Usher, Jill E. Torrie, Patricia Anderson, Hugh Brody, and Jennifer Keck, "Mercury Contamination of an Indian Fishery in Subarctic Canada," unpublished paper, 1990; Peter J. Usher, "Socio-Economic Effects of Elevated Mercury Levels in Fish in Subarctic Native Communities," *Proceedings of the Conference on Contaminants in the Marine Environment of Nunavik* (Quebec: Laval University Press, 1991); and Peter J. Usher, Patricia Anderson, Hugh Brody, Jennifer Keck, and Jill E. Torrie, "The Economic and Social Impact of Mercury Pollution on the Whitedog and Grassy Narrows Indian Reserves, Ontario," an unpublished report prepared for the Whitedog and Grassy Narrows Indian Bands, 1979.

12. For a general sense of old Ojibwa life, see Hallowell, op. cit.; Harold Hickerson, *The Chippewa and Their Neighbors: A Study in Ethnohistory* (New York: Holt, Rinehart, and Winston, 1970); Basil Johnston, *Ojibway Heritage* (Toronto: McClelland & Steward, 1976); Ruth Landes, *Ojibwa Sociology* (New York: AMS Press, 1969 [1937]), and *The Ojibwa Woman* (New York: AMS Press, 1969 [1938]); Christopher Vecsey, *Traditional Ojibwa Religion and Its Historical Changes* (Philadelphia: American Philosophical Society, 1983) and "Grassy Narrows Reserve: Mercury Pollution, Social Disruption, and Natural Resources: A Question of Autonomy," *American Indian Quarterly*, 11:287–314 (1987).

13. R. W. Dunning, *Social and Economic Change among the Northern Ojibwa* (Toronto: University of Toronto Press, 1959), p. 7.

14. Interview, Christopher Vecsey and Andy Keewatin, January 7, 1979.

15. This version is from Edwin James, ed., *A Narrative of the Captivity and Adventures of John Tanner (U.S. Interpreter at the Sault de Ste. Marie) during Thirty Years Residence among the Indians in the Interior of the United States* (Minneapolis: Ross & Haines, 1956 [1830]), p. 162. A similar version can be found in Vernice Aldrich, "Father George Antoine Belcourt, Red River Missionary," *North Dakota Historical Quarterly*, 2:30–53 (1927), p. 37. Belcourt was active in the 1830s and 1840s.

16. Interview, Christopher Vecsey and Simon Fobister, January 6, 1979.

17. Usher, et al., "Mercury Contamination . . . ," p. 5.

18. Ibid. p. 7.

19. Shkilnyk, op. cit., p. 110.

20. Colin Trumbull, *The Mountain People* (New York: Simon & Schuster, 1972), p. 259.

2: THE HAITIANS OF IMMOKALEE

1. David Griffith and Jeronimo Camposeco, "Immokalee, Florida: Preliminary Ethnographic Findings," unpublished paper, 1990.

2. *Miami Herald*, March 22, 1981.

3. Deposition of Fred H. Edenfield, November 12, 1984, as part of *Clotaire Alfred et al. v. Crawford, Crawford, Edenfield, and Edenfield.*

4. Ibid.

5. *Miami Herald,* March 22, 1981.

6. On this and related matters, see Bruce Allen Bernstein, "Migration, Health, and Nutrition: Haitians in Immokalee, A South Florida Farm Worker Town," Ph.D. dissertation, University of Connecticut, 1986; Robert Debs Heinl and Nancy Gordon Heinl, *Written in Blood: The Story of Haitian People, 1492–1971* (Boston: Houghton Mifflin, 1978); Simon M. Fass, *Political Economy in Haiti: The Drama of Survival* (New Brunswick, N.J.: Transaction, 1988); Brian Weinstein and Aaron Segal, *Haiti: Political Features, Cultural Successes* (New York: Praeger, 1984); Sidney W. Mintz, *Caribbean Transformation* (Baltimore: Johns Hopkins, 1974).

7. On this and related matters, see Michel S. Laguerre, *American Odyssey: Haitians in New York City* (Ithaca, N.Y.: Cornell, 1984); Aaron Segal, "Demographic Factors in Haitian Development," and Alex Stepick, "The Roots of Haitian Migration," in *Haiti: Today and Tomorrow,* ed. Charles R. Foster and Albert Valdman, (Lanham, Md.: University Press of America, 1984).

8. Estimates vary considerably. See Bernstein, op. cit.; Weinstein and Segal, op. cit.; Alex Stepick, "The New American Exodus: The Flight from Terror and Poverty," *Caribbean Review,* 11 (1):14–17, 55–57 (1982); and Thomas D. Boswell, "The New Haitian Diaspora: Florida's Most Recent Residents," *Caribbean Review,* 11 (1):18–21 (1982).

9. Laguerre, op. cit., p. 42.

10. James Allman and Karen Richman, "Migration Decision Making and Policy: The Case of Haitian Internal Migration, 1971–1984." Paper presented at the meetings of the Population Association of America, Boston, March 28–30, 1985, p. 7.

11. Bernstein, op. cit.

12. Allman and Richman, op. cit., pp. 9–10.

13. Harold Courlander, *The Drum and the Hoe: Life and Lore of the Haitian People* (Berkeley: University of California Press, 1960), p. 336.

14. Weinstein and Segal, op. cit.

15. Segal, in *Haiti: Today and Tomorrow,* op. cit.

16. See, for example, Allman and Richman, op. cit., and Segal, ibid.

17. "Project Immokalee," *Naples Daily News,* five-part series, May 21–25, 1989.

18. Griffith and Camposeco, op. cit., p. 9.

19. *New York Times,* July 27, 1987.

20. Amy Wilentz, *The Rainy Season: Haiti since Duvalier* (New York: Simon & Schuster, 1989), p. 140.

21. In a deposition, Fred Edenfield was asked: "Do you think you should have gotten your money before the farm workers?" "It was a just claim," he answered in part. "You thought it was a higher priority claim?" "Sure."

Notes

3: The View from East Swallow

1. Kai Erikson, *Everything in Its Path* (New York: Simon & Schuster, 1976); Harry Estill Moore, *Tornadoes over Texas* (Austin: University of Texas Press, 1958); and Marc Fried, "Grieving for a Lost Home," in *The Urban Condition*, ed. Leonard J. Duhl (New York: Basic Books, 1963).

2. Michael Edelstein, *Contaminated Communities: The Social and Psychological Impacts of Residential Toxic Exposure* (Boulder, Colo.: Westview Press, 1988).

4: Three Mile Island: A New Species of Trouble

1. Cynthia B. Flynn, Three Mile Island Telephone Survey: Preliminary Report on Procedures and Findings (NUREG/CR-1093, U.S. Nuclear Regulatory Commission). Donald J. Zeigler, Stanley D. Brunn, and James H. Johnson, Jr., "Evacuation from a Nuclear Technological Disaster," *Geographical Review*, 71:1–16 (1981).

2. Zeigler, Brunn, and Johnson, op. cit.

3. Charles Perrow, *Normal Accidents* (New York: Basic, 1984).

4. This would give us a four-cell table of roughly the following sort

	Technological	Natural
Non-Toxic	a	b
Toxic	c	d

The first cell would contain technological mishaps like explosions and collisions; the second would contain the usual gatherings of floods, earthquakes, storms, and so on; the third would contain events like the ones described in this essay—Chernobyl and Bhopal, Love Canal and Three Mile Island, Grassy Narrows and East Swallow—and the fourth would contain natural forms of toxic poisoning like radon. We will need a more complex diagram eventually—some kind of scatter plot, probably—since some events need to be represented as closer to the lines separating technological from natural and toxic from nontoxic than others. But that is another problem for another time.

5. See Paul Slovic, Sarah Lichtenstein, and Baruch Fischoff, "Images of Disaster: Perception and Acceptance of Risks from Nuclear Power," in *Energy Risk Management*, ed. G. Goodman and W. Rowe (New York: Academic, 1979). Slovic, Fischoff, and Lichtenstein, "Rating the Risks," *Environment*, 21:14–38 (1979). Slovic, Fischoff, and Lichtenstein, "Facts and Fears: Understanding Perceived Risk," in *Societal Risk Assessment*, ed. R. C. Schwing and W. A. Albers, Jr. (New York: Plenum, 1980). Slovic and Fischoff, "How

Safe Is Safe Enough? Determinants of Perceived and Acceptable Risk," in *Too Hot to Handle?*, ed. C. A. Walker, L. C. Gould, and E. J. Woodhouse (New Haven: Yale University Press, 1983). And so on . . .

6. Social Data Analysts, "Attitudes toward Evacuation: Reactions of Long Island Residents to a Possible Accident at the Shoreham Nuclear Power Station," report prepared for Suffolk County, New York, 1982. James H. Johnson, Jr., and Donald J. Zeigler, "Further Analysis and Interpretation of the Shoreham Evacuation Survey," Vol. III, Suffolk County Radiological Emergency Response Plan, November 1982. Donald J. Zeigler, James H. Johnson, Jr., and Stanley D. Brunn, *Technological Hazards* (Washington, D.C.: Association of American Geographers, 1983).

7. Howard Kunreuther, William H. DesVouges, and Paul Slovic, "Nevada's Predicament: Public Perceptions of Risk from the Proposed Nuclear Waste Repository," *Environment* 30:17–20, 30–33 (October 1988).

8. Alvin M. Weinberg, "The Maturity and Future of Nuclear Energy," *American Scientist*, 64:16–21 (1976).

9. See Phil Brown and Edwin J. Mikkelson, *No Safe Place: Toxic Waste, Leukemia, and Community Action*, (Berkeley: University of California Press, 1990). Michael Edelstein, *Contaminated Communities: The Social and Psychological Impacts of Residential Toxic Exposure*, (Boulder, Colo.: Westview Press, 1988). Peter Houts, *The Three Mile Island Crisis*, (University Park, Pa.: Pennsylvania State University Press, 1989). J. Stephen Kroll-Smith and Stephen Robert Couch, *The Real Disaster Is above Ground* (Lexington, Ky.: University of Kentucky Press, 1990). Adeline Gordon Levine, *Love Canal: Science, Politics and People*, (Lexington, Mass.: Lexington Books, 1982). H. Karl Reko, *Not An Act of God: The Story of Times Beach* (St. Louis, Mo.: Ecumenical Dioxin Response Task, 1984). Anastasia M. Shkilnyk, *A Poison Stronger than Love: The Destruction of an Ojibway Community* (New Haven: Yale University Press, 1985).

10. Aristotle, *The Poetics*, tr. W. Hamilton Fyve (Cambridge, Mass.: Harvard University Press, 1932), pp. 29–31.

11. Frederic J. Brown, *Chemical Warfare: A Study in Restraints* (Princeton: Princeton University Press, 1968), p. 18.

12. Mary Douglas and Aaron Wildavsky, *Risk and Culture* (Berkeley: University of California Press, 1982), p. 7.

13. Henry Fairlie, "Fear of Living," *New Republic*, 200:14–19 (January 23, 1989), p. 15.

14. Kai Erikson, *Everything in Its Path* (New York: Simon & Schuster, 1976), p. 236.

15. Daniel Defoe, *Robinson Crusoe and the Further Adventures* (London and Glasgow: Collins, 1953), p. 163. I borrowed this shamelessly from Douglas and Wildavsky, where it appears on p. 26.

16. Bruce P. Dohrenwend, "Psychological Implications of Nuclear Accidents: The Case of Three Mile Island," *Bulletin of the New York Academy of Medicine*, 59:1060–76 (December 1983).

17. "Talk of the Town," *The New Yorker* (February 18, 1985). I borrowed this, equally shamelessly, from Paul Slovic.

18. The volume by Phil Brown and Edwin J. Mikkelson, cited in note 9

above, was entitled *No Safe Place* because the families they studied in Woburn, Massachusetts, had come to feel that danger lurked everywhere across the American landscape.

19. For Love Canal, see Levine, note 9; for Three Mile Island, Houts; for Centralia, Kroll-Smith and Couch; for East Swallow, Erikson; for Grassy Narrows, Shkilnyk; for Legler, Edelstein; for Times Beach, Reko; for Woburn, Brown and Mikkelson.

5: BEING HOMELESS

1. In James D. Wright, *Address Unknown: The Homeless in America* (Hawthorne, N.Y.: Aldine de Gruyter, 1989), pp. 4, 7–8, 16.

2. Charles Dickens, *Bleak House* (New York: Bantam, 1956), pp. 595–96, ch. 47.

3. Terrence Des Pres, *The Survivor* (New York: Oxford University Press, 1976).

4. See, for example, Howard M. Bahr, ed., *Disaffiliated Man* (Toronto: University of Toronto Press, 1970); Howard M. Bahr and Theodore Caplow, *Old Men: Drunk and Sober* (New York: New York University Press, 1974); Donald B. Bogue, *Skid Row in American Cities* (Chicago: University of Chicago Press, 1963); James A. Spradley, *You Owe Yourself a Drunk* (Boston: Little, Brown, 1970); Samuel E. Wallace, *Skid Row as a Way of Life* (Bedminster, N.J.: Bedminster Press, 1965); Jacqueline O. Wiseman, *Stations of the Lost* (Englewood Cliffs, N.J.: Prentice-Hall, 1970).

5. Kim Hopper and Jill Hamberg, *The Making of America's Homeless: From Skid Row to New Poor* (New York: Community Service Society of New York, 1984).

6. Peter H. Rossi, *Down and Out in America* (Chicago: University of Chicago Press, 1989). Wright, op. cit. See also Martha R. Burt, *Over the Edge: The Growth of Homelessness in the 1980s* (New York: Russell Sage, 1992).

7. These are Rossi's figures. Burt's figures are: single men, 73 percent; single women, 9 percent; married adults without children, 4 percent; and most of the rest families with children. Her estimate of the size of the homeless population on any given evening is five hundred thousand to six hundred thousand.

8. I am again relying on Rossi here. Burt's figures vary somewhat but not appreciably.

9. Jonathan Kozol, *Rachel and Her Children* (New York: Crown, 1988). David A. Snow and Leon Anderson, *Down on Their Luck: A Study of Homeless Street People* (Berkeley: University of California Press, 1993). Barry Jay Seltser and Donald E. Miller, *Homeless Families: The Struggle for Dignity* (Urbana: University of Illinois Press, in press).

10. Kozol, op cit., p. 179.

6: HIROSHIMA: OF ACCIDENTAL JUDGMENTS AND CASUAL SLAUGHTERS

1. Committee for the Compilation of Materials on Damage Caused by the Atomic Bombs in Hiroshima and Nagasaki, *Hiroshima and Nagasaki*, tr. Eisei Ishikawa and David L. Swain (New York: Basic Books, 1981).

2. Leslie R. Groves, *Now It Can Be Told* (New York: Harper, 1962), p. 265.

3. Len Giovannitti and Fred Freed, *The Decision to Drop the Bomb* (New York: Coward-McCann, 1965), frontspiece.

4. Martin J. Sherwin, *A World Destroyed* (New York: Knopf, 1975), Appendix C, p. 284.

5. Ibid., p. 140.

6. Henry L. Stimson and McGeorge Bundy, *On Active Service in Peace and War* (New York: Harper, 1947), p. 613.

7. Harry S. Truman, *Year of Decisions* (New York: Doubleday, 1955), p. 419.

8. Groves, op. cit., p. 265.

9. Winston S. Churchill, *Triumph and Tragedy*, Vol. 6, *The Second World War* (Boston: Houghton Mifflin, 1953), p. 639.

10. Sherwin, op. cit., p. 144.

11. Memorandum to Groves from Target Committee, summary of meetings of May 10 and May 11, 1945.

12. Edward Teller, *The Legacy of Hiroshima* (New York: Doubleday, 1962), p. 14.

13. Giovannitti and Freed, op. cit., p. 145.

14. Peter Wyden, *Day One* (New York: Simon & Schuster, 1984), p. 155.

15. Nuel Pharr Davis, *Lawrence and Oppenheimer* (New York: Simon & Schuster, 1968), p. 142.

16. Henry L. Stimson, "The Decision to Use the Bomb," *Harper's Magazine* (February 1947).

17. Arthur H. Compton, *Atomic Quest* (New York: Oxford University Press, 1956), p. 239.

18. Giovannitti and Freed, op. cit., p. 103.

19. Sherwin, op. cit., Report of the Scientific Panel, Appendix M, p. 305.

20. In the Matter of J. Robert Oppenheimer: Transcript of Hearing before the Personnel Security Board, April 12, 1954, through May 6, 1954 (Washington, D.C.: Government Printing Office, 1954).

21. Lansing Lamont, *Day of Trinity* (New York: Signet, 1965), p. 230.

22. Paul Fussell, "Thank God for the Atomic Bomb," *New Republic* (August 26, 1981).

23. Stimson and Bundy, op cit., p. 633.

24. Churchill, op. cit., p. 638.

25. H. H. Arnold, *Global Mission* (New York: Harper, 1949), p. 492.

26. Memorandum, Groves to Chief of Staff, July 30, 1945. (The second and third pages of the three-page report are headed "memo to Secretary of War.")

27. Elting E. Morison, *Turmoil and Tradition: A Study of the Life and Times of Henry L. Stimson* (Boston: Houghton Mifflin, 1960), pp. 620–21.

28. Lamont, op. cit., p. 233.

Notes

7: YUCCA MOUNTAIN:
GOOD RIDDANCE, BAD RUBBISH

1. Luther J. Carter, *Nuclear Imperatives and Public Trust: Dealing with Radioactive Waste* (Washington, D.C.: Resources for the Future, 1987), p. 202.

2. Ibid., p. 225.

3. Foster Church, untitled review article, *Governing* (April 1990).

4. See Report to the President by the Interagency Review Group on Nuclear Waste Management, USDOE, 1979 (TID-29442); and U.S. Department of Energy (DOE), "Management of Commercially Generated Radioactive Waste," Vol. I, October 1980 (DOE/EIS-0046F).

5. DOE, Interagency Review Group Report, ibid., I.21.

6. David E. Lilienthal, *Change, Hope, and the Bomb* (Princeton: Princeton University Press, 1963), pp. 109–10.

7. Kristin Shrader-Frechette, "Expert Judgment in Assessing RADWASTE Risks: What Nevadans Should Know about Yucca Mountain." Unpublished study submitted to the Nuclear Waste Project Office, State of Nevada, June 1992, p. 154.

8. DOE, Site Characterization Plan: Yucca Mountain Site, Nevada Research and Development Area (SCP), December 1988 (DOE/RW-0199), 8.3.1.9–3.

9. See Jacque Emel, Roger Kasperson, Robert Gable, and Otwin Renn, *Post-closure Risks at the Proposed Yucca Mountain Repository: A Review of Methodological and Technical Issues.* Report submitted to the Nuclear Waste Project Office, State of Nevada, 1988 (NWPO-SE-011-88).

10. DOE, SCP, op. cit., 8.3.1.9–48.

11. Ibid., 8.3.1.9–15.

12. Lewis Mumford, *The City in History* (New York: Harvest/HBJ, 1961), p. 3.

13. Marcus Aurelius, *Meditations*, vii. 9.

14. Indeed, one group of consultants to DOE became so concerned that a proposed monument (of a different nuclear waste facility) might attract rather than repel human attention that it wondered whether DOE "should consider the possibility of not marking the site," since "there is at least some reason to believe that markings of any kind will be attractive to a future society and draw special attention to the region." See Stephen C. Hora, Detlof von Winterfelt, and Kathleen M. Trauth, *Expert Judgment on Inadvertent Human Intrusion into the Waste Isolation Pilot Plant.* Sandia National Laboratories, December 1991 (SAND 90-3063. UC-721), p. C-69.

15. Martin Pasqualetti, quoted in *Sierra* (September–October 1992), p. 55.

EPILOGUE: ON TRAUMA

1. See Michael Brown, *Laying Waste: The Poisoning of America by Toxic Chemicals* (New York: Pantheon, 1979).

2. The persons consulted were Adeline Gordon Levine, author of *Love*

Canal: Science, Politics and People (Lexington, Mass.: Lexington Books, 1982); H. Karl Reko, author of *Not an Act of God: The Story of Times Beach* (St. Louis, Mo.: Ecumenical Dioxin Response Task Force, 1984); Michael Edelstein, author of *Contaminated Communities: The Social and Psychological Impacts of Residential Toxic Exposure* (Boulder, Colo.: Westview Press, 1988); Phil Brown, coauthor with Edwin J. Mikkelson of *No Safe Place: Toxic Waste, Leukemia, and Community Action* (Berkeley: University of California Press, 1990); and J. Stephen Kroll-Smith and Stephen Robert Couch, authors of *The Real Disaster Is above Ground* (Lexington, Ky.: University of Kentucky 1990).

3. Paul Valéry, "Commentaire de *Charmers*," *Oeuvres* (Paris: Gallimard, 1957), Vol. I, p. 1510. Translated by Shoshana Felman and found in her paper "In an Era of Testimony: Claude Lanzmann's *Shoah*," *Yale French Studies*, (1990), p. 76.

4. Shoshana Felman, "Education and Crisis, or the Vicissitudes of Teaching," *American Imago*, 48:13–73 (1991), p. 54.

5. Kai Erikson, *Everything in Its Path* (New York: Simon & Schuster, 1976), pp. 153–54.

6. Anthony F. C. Wallace, *Tornado in Worcester* (Disaster Study Number Three, Committee on Disaster Studies, National Academy of Sciences–National Research Council, 1957), p. 127.

7. S. H. Prince, *Catastrophe and Social Change* (New York: Columbia University Press, 1920); R. I. Kutak, "Sociology of Crises: The Louisville Flood of 1937," *Social Forces*, 17:66–72 (1938); Charles E. Fritz, "Disaster," in *Contemporary Social Problems*, ed., Robert K. Merton and Robert A. Nisbet (New York: Harcourt Brace, 1961).

8. Martha Wolfenstein, *Disaster: A Psychological Essay* (Glencoe, Ill.: Free Press, 1957).

9. Allen H. Barton, *Communities in Disaster* (New York: Doubleday, 1969).

10. Fritz, op. cit.

11. William Freudenburg. See, for example, Freudenburg and Timothy R. Jones, "Attitudes and Stress in the Presence of Technological Risk: A Test of the Supreme Court Hypothesis," *Social Forces*, 69:1143–1168 (1991).

12. A good example is provided by Kroll-Smith and Couch, op. cit.

13. Jonathan Kozol, *Rachel and Her Children* (New York: Crown, 1988), p. 179.

14. Quoted in Lawrence L. Langer, *Holocaust Testimonies: The Ruins of Memory* (New Haven: Yale University Press, 1991), p. 59.

Acknowledgments

Writing acknowledgments for a book that covers as much ground as this one does verges on the impossible, but my debts are so great that I must at least make a beginning.

I mentioned a number of people in the chapter on Grassy Narrows who were of special help, but at the risk of repeating myself let me again thank Simon Fobister, Hiro Miyamatsu, Peter Usher, Christopher Vecsey, and particularly Anastasia Shkilnyk.

My work in Immokalee would have been impossible without the support and friendship of Robert Williams and Lynn Peterson or the assistance of Jackson Francois, Ann Rendahl, and Melinda Sewell. I would also like to acknowledge—and not for the first time—my debt to Arnold Porter and particularly to J. Bradway Butler, David Greenberg, Thomas Milch, and Richard Schifter. Christopher Erikson gave me several valuable suggestions.

I was introduced to East Swallow by William R. Gray, whom I came to respect without reserve, and I was assisted every step of the way by Kay Hutchinson, whom I came to rely on without reservation.

Esther Berezofsky and James H. Short, Jr., both contributed in many ways to the chapter on Three Mile Island.

The chapter on Yucca Mountain borrows from so many colleagues that I am touching only the surface if I thank William Freudenburg, Steven Frischman, John Gervers, Roger Kasperson, Howard Kunreuther, James Short, Paul Slovic, Joseph Strolin, and, in a place of his own, Roy Rappaport.

The essay on Hiroshima was sharpened by three friends, two of whom—Elias Clark and Leon Lipson—have serious reservations about my views of the matter, and a third—Jonathan Fanton—who was (once again) immensely helpful. McGeorge Bundy, whom I scarcely know, wrote a gracious yet sharply questioning letter when an earlier expression of those views appeared in print, and his challenge sent me on a far more thorough round of research than I had at first thought necessary.

The influence of Robert Jay Lifton is reflected throughout these pages in more ways than I may know. He and I shared a part of two of the research errands described here, and we have done a good deal of intellectual sharing over the years, largely as a result of meetings at Wellfleet now in their twenty-fifth year.

Henning Gutmann of W. W. Norton & Company has been a valued partner in the making of this book.

Above all, my thanks to Joanna Erikson. Her intelligence and grounded good sense have enriched everything I do.

Index